BEHIND
THE
BADGE

THE FUNNY SIDE
OF THE
"THIN BLUE LINE"

BEHIND THE BADGE

THE FUNNY SIDE OF THE OF THE "THIN BLUE LINE"

To Suzanne!
All Thank you for
with you've done
Appreciation!
Best Wishes!
Harry

Harry D. Penny Jr.

Cartoons by Claude Anderson

TS TRUTH SEEKER
Escondido, California

Reviews for . . .
BEHIND THE BADGE: The Funny Side of the "Thin Blue Line"

We've all heard that truth is stranger than fiction. Harry Penny's new book proves without a doubt that the truth is funnier than fiction! This book is a must read and nearly impossible to put down once you've begun. If you are a cop, this book will bring back mostly enjoyable memories. If you are not in law enforcement, you'll get an inside look at how officers maintain their sanity when dealing with incidents that sometimes defy the imagination. Factual, informative and humorous . . . a great combination and a great read.

  — *Jerry Boyd*
     Los Angeles County Sheriff's Department 1968–1975
     Chief of Police (Ret.), City of Martinez, CA
     Author of Five Steps to Officer Survival

It takes an extraordinary mind to see, and be able to convey, the humorous side of police life. Harry Penny has that type of mind and he has the great gift of story telling that has given us this masterpiece that will have you laughing from cover to cover.

  — *George Bancroft*
     Ph.D., Vice Chairman,
     PEERA, San Marcos , California

After 30 years in the business I thought I had heard them all, then Harry comes out with this book. This riot of a read owned my attention and made me laugh. These true stories capture the essence of how funny and crazy a cops' world is. This is the real deal—cop humor at its best!

  — *Clyde R. Kodadek, Lieutenant, (Ret.)*
     San Diego County Sheriff's Department

Behind the Badge: The Funny Side of the Thin Blue Line is a collection of memories and stories from the purest source: deputies and officers relating their own experiences and the moments that carried them through. It's an engaging glimpse into the humorous side of Southern California law enforcement "back in the day" and a unique snapshot of the way things were for those who worked the trenches. The contributors are not professional writers. They're law enforcement officers. These are the stories they tell themselves, related here just as comfortably as if they were unwinding after shift. The humor is sometimes slapstick, sometimes oblique, almost always self-effacing, and these stories are an enjoyable read.

Humor isn't a motivator when one thinks of a career in law enforcement. Honor, Duty, Responsibility, Commitment, Involvement, and a keen sense of morality and Right . . . these are the reasons law enforcement officers do what they do. It's at once as simple and as complicated as that. But those pure hearted motivators can be an overwhelming load over time without the gift of humor to ease the way.

"Cop humor" is sometimes seen as dark and insensitive when viewed out of context by the casual observer. Most often it comes from a burst of incongruity and "I can't believe I just saw that in the middle of this dung storm." This collection helps put it in context. For the initiated, these stories will bring warm smiles of recognition and the knowledge that we're following in honorable footsteps.

 —*Tim Long*
 San Diego Police Dept. (Ret.), 1986–2007

From a "civilian's" view, this book brings a warm and light side to law enforcement. Cops are just like everyone else. Could not put it down without wanting to pick it up and read more . . . great book!!

 —*Linda and Bill Hironimus, Maui, HI*

I received a copy of your book, and from cover to cover, could not put it down! Many thanks, and what a great job! My great nephew in his vernacular would say . . . "the book really ROCKS !"
My hearty congrats and with multiple kudos

 —*Lorraine Anderson*

www.harrypenny.com
First Edition — January 2008

Cover design based on an idea by Sharon Penny
Cover photo of author by Brad Mills
Cover by design Greg Smith
Rear cover photo of author by Ralph Dicks ralphdicks@aol.com
Interior design by Book Works, Inc.

Published by:
Truth Seeker Company
239 S. Juniper St.
Escondido, California 92025
truthseeker.com

ISBN: 0-939040-47-6

To my wife, Sharon, aka Rosie.
Your unconditional love and support
have enabled me to turn my visions
and dreams into reality.

CONTENTS

ACKNOWLEDGEMENTS

Throughout my law enforcement career I have heard, and often initiated, the radio call, "officer needs help." The call could be anything from transporting a prisoner to jail, to the dreaded call: OFFICER DOWN. Never, in my twenty-plus years of experience, has hesitation or question ever been a factor in answering that call.

When it came time to write this book, I knew personally that many other officers had experienced funny situations themselves, and I thought that it would be great if they could share their moments with others. I had the unique pleasure and experience of working with many of these officers, from riding as partners in a radio car, to working side-by-side at a desk. So I put out the call. My call was answered immediately. The first one, Brad Mills, whom I have known for almost forty-five years, is an ex-partner of mine who always manages to tell some of the funny stories that happened when we were working a radio car in south-central Los Angeles, and still tells the same ones to this day. Then came Floyd Feese, a retired detective from the San Diego County Sheriff's Department, who kept me on track when we shared a desk for over five years. Their encouragement for me to finish this book (probably to stop me from telling the same stories over and over) was invaluable.

Two individuals who provided me with more than just their stories are Claude Anderson (LASD Ret.) and Jack Miller (LASD Ret.). Claude gave me over 100 of his cartoons to pick from and permission to use my own captions. His book, *Radiocar Toons: The Training Officer,* is a collection of over 200 of his cartoons scheduled for release in February 2008. Jack is the webmaster for the website: www.fpk.homestead.com, honoring all of the deputies who worked at the legendary Firestone Park sheriff's station in south-central Los Angeles. Many of the pictures used in this book were given to me by Jack in addition to his stories.

For the past six years there has been an annual gathering of former and retired LASD personnel and their families in Laughlin, Nevada. This is due primarily to the tireless efforts of Sgt. "Moon" Mullen, LASD (Ret.) and his wife Robyn, who spend much of their "retired" time in organizing this event. Seeing old friends and partners after forty-plus years jogged my memory banks for many of my stories in this book. "Moon" is also the creator of the website for retired LASD at www.lasdretired.org. To Gar Austin, I say thank you for your invaluable advice on keeping it real.

A deep debt of gratitude goes to all of the authors who graciously sent me their stories and their permission to use them. Lupe Avalos (CHP Ret.), Roy Beyer (LASD Ret.), Larry Brademeyer (LASD Ret.), Kimball Brown (LASD Ret.), Dan Castrellon (LASD Ret.), John Davis (El Centro PD Ret.), Vic Kretsinger (LASD Ret.), Dan McCarty (Capt. LASD Ret.), Dennis "Skip" Ryzow (Sgt. LASD Ret.), Russ Sletmoen (LASD Ret.), Dennis Slocumb (LASD Ret.), Stephen L.D. Smith (LASD Ret.), Jerry Timms, (Gardena PD/L.A. School Police Ret.), John Vogel (Lt. LASD Ret.), Ron Weber (LASD Ret.), Harold White (Capt. LASD Ret.), Ron Wisberger (LASD Ret.), Jack Wise (LASD), Jack Withers (LASD Ret.). To all of you I say THANK YOU from the bottom of my heart.

To my friend and publisher, Bonnie Lange of Truth Seeker Company: You are a gracious lady who looked outside the box and took a big chance with an unknown, first-time author. Your guidance and wealth of knowledge enabled me to tell this story. Your putting my words into the hands of your editor, Bill Lindley (a master of the English language, and a terror with his red pen), made this book a reality. Thank you so very much.

To my family and friends who put up with all of my stories over the years: I love you very much.

With great respect and admiration to all of you who helped me make this dream come true, I say again, THANK YOU.

FOREWORD

M any years ago one of the wisest men I ever knew told me that whenever I started to reflect on my life and found myself saying, "If I had my life to live over I would have done . . ." or, "I wish I had tried . . . because I know I could have done that," then in this wise man's opinion, I would have not lived my life to the fullest.

That wise man lived his life that way and when he passed on at age ninety, he had no regrets. That man was my father. I never forgot those words. I had the opportunity to pursue three life-long dreams about what I wanted to do in my life, and I did so. Now, I find myself pursuing another dream: to write this book.

Numerous books, both fiction and non-fiction, have been written about cops. Throughout the years many of these stories have been transformed into screenplays for both movies and television—they portray the dangers of a hazardous, life-and-death profession. At the time of this writing there are several "Reality TV" shows depicting these hazards.

Behind the Badge: The Funny Side of the "Thin Blue Line" is, by far, not your average crime story/mystery novel. It is exactly the opposite. It is a non-fiction book consisting entirely of true, funny, yes, funny stories that have been written by the officers who lived them. I know. Many of the stories are mine.

In my twenty-plus years of law enforcement, I was honored to have been a Deputy Sheriff of the Los Angeles County Sheriff's Department, Los Angeles, California, for almost 10 years, between 1963 and 1972, and the stories happened exactly as I have written them. The other stories are by officers, many of whom I have worked with, side-by-side in a radio car, or have encountered during my

Los Angeles Times photo, circa 1969.

career, and they have graciously given me permission to put their stories into print.

Each of us has, at some point in our career, faced a life-threatening situation in which we could have been seriously injured or even killed. *There is no such thing as a "routine call."*

According to the U.S. Department of Justice[1], the latest figures as of 2004 show that there are 836,787 sworn law enforcement officers[2] in the United States. Each day, many of these officers encounter a life-threatening situation. Many times no one is hurt or injured. It is all in a day's work. There are, however, those tragic situations wherein the officer gives the ultimate sacrifice.

The *badge,* sometimes referred to as the *tin,* the *shield,* or whatever term it is given, is that piece of metal that law enforcement officers wear proudly on the left breast of their uniforms. Whether their uniform is dark blue, tan and green, or even in civilian clothes, the symbol is truly a "badge of honor." With it comes an understanding

---

[1] U.S. Department of Justice, Office of Justice Program, Bureau of Justice Statistics.

[2] Local Police, Sheriff, Primary State, Special Jurisdiction*, Constable/Marshal, Federal**

Notes

* Special Jurisdiction category includes both state-level and local-level aencies. Consolidated police-sheriffs are included under local police catetory. Agency counts exclude those operating on a part-time basis.

** Non-military federal officers authorized to carry firearms and make arrests.

and responsibility like no other non-military profession. The understanding that you, the one wearing the badge, may have to lay down your life in the performance of your duty. The responsibility to protect the citizens of your community.

Their daily interactions with the criminal element, the oftentimes gruesome scenes involving death, destruction, and numerous other horrible atrocities, are not exactly the ideal subject for discussion over the dinner table. (What did you do at work today?)

However, there is usually one funny thing that occurs, to either the individual officers, or one of their cohorts. Over the years I have relayed my funny "work" stories to my family and friends, in most cases more than once. I have often been told that I should write a book so I won't have to repeat them any more. So . . . I did. This book reveals just a few of these funny things that happen "behind the badge."

I hope you enjoy this book as much as I have enjoyed writing it. And for those of you who have never had the experience of talking to a cop, and there are many who are in that category, just a nice, sincere "thank you" the next time you see one would be a great way to start.

—HARRY D. PENNY, JR.

It is not the critic who counts; not the man who points out how the strong man stumbles, or where the doer of deeds could have done them better. The credit belongs to the man who is actually in the arena, whose face is marred by dust and sweat and blood; who strives valiantly; who errs, and comes short again and again, because there is no effort without error and shortcoming; but who does actually strive to do the deeds; who knows the great enthusiasms, the great devotions; who spends himself in a worthy cause; who at the best knows in the end the triumph of high achievement, and who at the worst, if he fails, at least fails while daring greatly, so that his place shall never be with those cold and timid souls who know neither victory nor defeat.

—THEODORE ROOSEVELT

Experience is an author's most valuable asset; experience is the thing that puts the muscle and the breath and the warm blood into the book he writes.

—MARK TWAIN

INTRODUCTION

All of the stories in this book are the works of the officers who experienced them and wrote them. No editorial changes, other than punctuation, have been made, and the stories are non-fiction.

Most of the stories in this book take place in southern California, Los Angeles County—during the 1960s and 1970s. Los Angeles County covers an area of 4,083 square miles. It was, and still is, the most populous county in the United States. In 1960 the population was 6,038,771 and in 1970 it rose to 7,041,9880.[1] The Los Angeles County Sheriff's Department—the largest Sheriff's Department in the world (5,707 personnel consisting of 3,978 sworn personnel and 1,729 civilian personnel)—had the responsibility for providing law enforcement services in an area of 3,048.58 square miles of unincorporated area and 161.19 square miles of 29 contract cities—incorporated cities which contract for police services with the Sheriff's Department for a total of 3,209.77 square miles in which 1,751,159 persons resided.[2]

Normal day-to-day patrol functions were performed by approximately 1,500 sheriff's deputies assigned to Patrol Division with fourteen sheriff's stations located throughout the county.

During this era such things as individual body armor, individual hand-held radios, yellow crime scene tape, computers—especially

---

[1] CensusScope www.censuscope.org
[2] Los Angeles County Sheriff's Department Biennial Report 1965–1967 to the Honorable Board of Supervisors

Station #	Sheriff's Station	Los Angeles County Address	Unincorporated Area Sq. Miles	Total Sq. Miles in Station Area	Station Population
1	Firestone	7901 S. Compton Ave., Los Angeles	40.19	41.25	213,008
2	East Los Angeles	5019 E. Third St., East Los Angeles	8.43	17.32	151,024
3	Lennox	4331 Lennox Blvd., Lennox	160.91	172.13	210,620
4	Norwalk	11801 E. Firestone Blvd., Norwalk	19.69	51.30	285,698
5	Temple	8838 E. Las Tunas Dr., Temple City	44.91	64.15	167,740
6	Newhall	24238 N. San Fernando Rd., Newhall	726.77	726.77	37,825
7	Altadena	780 E. Altadena Dr., Altadena	23.96	23.96	45,177
8	San Dimas	122 N. San Dimas Ave., San Dimas	220.69	232.08	86,558
9	W. Hollywood	122 N. San Vincente Blvd., Los Angeles	3.17	3.17	41,261
10	Malibu	21323 W. Pacific Coast Hwy., Malibu	187.56	188.94	23,581
11	Antelope Valley	1010 W. Ave. "J," Lancaster	1279.66	1302.07	73,348
12	Montrose	3809 Ocean View Blvd., Montrose	233.52	233.52	44,593
13	Lakewood	5130 N. Clark, Lakewood	3.38	34.42	210,359
14	City of Industry	150 N. Hudson, Industry	95.74	118.69	160,367
	Sheriff's Department Totals		3,048.58	3,209.77	1,751,159

in-car laptops, cell-phones, pocket calculators, and the other technological advances we see today were not available. Yet the officers had the same responsibilities, and faced and conquered the same challenges as they do today.

Many of these stories take place out of the Firestone Park station (FPK) customarily referred to as "Firestone." Firestone's area is

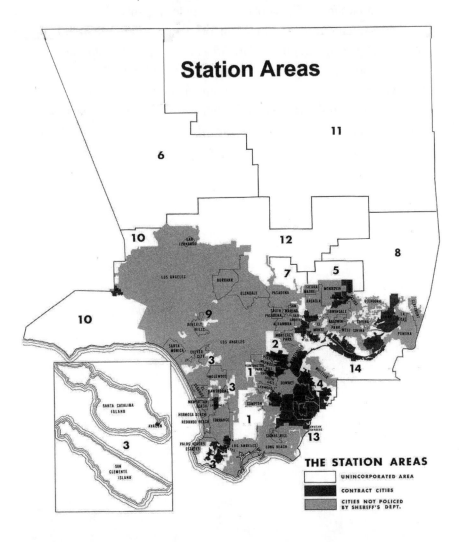

Taken from the Los Angeles County Sheriff's Department Biennial Report 1965–1967 to Los Angeles County Board of Supervisors.

depicted on the map with the #1. The other stories are indicated by the name of the station and the corresponding station number e.g., East Los Angeles (#2) etc. so that you, the reader, can get a glimpse of those areas in which the situations occurred.

In addition, there are stories from the Jail Division, Transportation Bureau/Technical Services Division, Homicide Division, Narcotics, and also stories from officers of other law enforcement agencies.

The white areas depict the unincorporated areas policed by the Sheriff's Department and the dark areas in the map denote the various incorporated cities that contract with the Sheriff's Department for law enforcement services. The numbers on the map indicate the Sheriff's fourteen separate patrol stations. The large grey area shows the incorporated cities, such as the city of Los Angeles, that have their own individual police departments.

MY FIRST ENCOUNTER AS A COP WITH MR. MURPHY'S LAW

— Harry Penny —

BUENA PARK POLICE DEPARTMENT
BUENA PARK, CA, CIRCA 1962

I had numerous occasions to meet Mr. Murphy when I was in the U.S. Navy. I figured that was normal, but that's another story. I never, in my wildest imagination, thought that he would follow me into law enforcement. (I never saw Sgt. Joe Friday, actor Jack Webb, on Dragnet have a situation involving Mr. Murphy.) Well, it didn't take long.

I had wanted to be a cop since I was seven years old. World War II had just ended. I was in the second grade, and the teacher asked each one of us to stand up and tell the rest of the class what we wanted to be. How many kids at age seven know what they want to be? The answers were varied and no two were alike. I was the only one who said, "I want to be a policeman." Seventeen years later I would achieve that goal. I started in law enforcement on September 14, 1962 (my twenty-fourth birthday) with the Buena Park Police Department.

I attended the Orange County Peace Officers Academy and during the five weeks of training I would work on weekends with the regular officers in the department. After graduation I was assigned to

Patrol Division. Three weeks of indoctrination with a T/O (training officer) and then . . . I was on my own.

In the north end of the city was a beautiful golf course/country club known as Los Coyotes Country Club. It was one of the gemstones of the city. Golfers from all over would come to play this course.

I was in my third month of being a cop and in late 1962 I was working the north end unit on the PM shift (3 PM to 11 PM) as I recall. I received a radio call to respond Code 3 (red lights and siren) to a highly evolved fire at—you guessed it—the Los Coyotes Country Club.

Upon arrival at the scene I was met by my sergeant and given my orders per the fire chief. I was posted at the barricades set up by the Fire Department and I was to allow no one other than fire personnel to go beyond the barricades. It had been determined that no persons or animals were in the structures and they were trying to get this fully evolved fire under control and extinguished. It was extremely dangerous and they didn't want anyone entering! If someone tried to enter and refused to cooperate, I was to arrest them. Sounded simple enough to me. Who, other than a fireman, would want to run into a highly burning building? Not me, that's for sure. Nope, I'll just stay here at the barricades and keep people back.

Within just a few minutes a crowd started to gather. I was the only police officer at the scene. I walked back and forth along the barricade and instructed them to keep back. So far, so good.

The crowd grew larger. By now I had gotten into a routine and everyone was cooperating. Even the press! (Unfortunately, I was unaware that *Mr. Murphy* had decided to pay me a visit.)

As I was walking back to my radio car, parked at the beginning of the barricade, I noticed a fairly large gentleman quickly emerging from the crowd and walking-half-running toward me. He was quite excited and frantically waving his arms and yelling, "My clubs! My clubs!" and pointing to the burning building. Just as he got within a few feet of me he said in a deep, thunderous voice, "I've got to get in there," and started walking toward the barricade.

I stopped him and told him that no one could go in there and to step away from the barricade. Again, in that deep voice, but in increasing volume he said, "You don't understand! I've got to get in there! I have a very expensive set of clubs in there!" I looked at him in amazement. Here he is worrying about a set of golf clubs and he is willing to risk his life to get them? I'd heard of avid golfers, but this was taking it to the extreme. *I don't think your mental driveway goes all the way to the street, Bozo.* Now it was time to use my most authoritative voice and tell him to step back away or else he would be placed under arrest. Then the unexpected happened: he moved the barricade and started to walk away from me and toward the burning structure.

Well now, you know that this ain't gonna happen on my watch! He had only taken two steps when I reached out and grabbed him by his coat tail. Did I mention that he was a rather tall and portly gentleman? Well, he was. I am 6'2" and 180 pounds, yet I looked rather frail compared to him. But I knew I was in better condition, or at least I hoped so. It took me a couple more steps to stop his forward progress. I think it was when I slapped my handcuffs on one of his wrists and said again in the most authoritative voice I could muster, "You're under arrest!" Yessiree! That got his attention.

He quickly turned around, and of course I still had one cuff on his wrist and the other cuff in my hand, so I was somewhat involved in his rapid turning movement. I was still in back of him and yet I had somehow managed to get the other cuff on his other wrist. It wasn't exactly like the textbook version they taught us in the academy, I thought to myself.

Now that I had his complete and undivided attention, I walked him back to my patrol car. (The one part I really paid attention to in my handcuffing techniques class was the part about when the suspect's hands are cuffed behind, grabbing the cuffs and raising the suspect's arms up in a position they were not originally designed to be, would get him to move.) I did just that and he moved without any hesitation. I patted him down for any weapons, retrieved his wallet from his jacket pocket, and then he got into the back seat of my radio car in a very obliging manner. I had figured that I had survived *Mr. Murphy*'s attempt to intervene. I was wrong.

I heard that deep, melodious, voice, now much quieter, more like a radio announcer, say, "Officer, do you know who I am?"

"Not yet, sir," I replied, "but I will as soon as I look at your identification." I then took his driver's license and upon seeing his name, I thought I recognized his voice. I called him by his name and said, "Sir, didn't you use to be on the radio in L.A. and have that midnight show . . . (I mentioned the theme song he used to close with every night) . . . ?"

"Yes," he replied, in a somewhat calmer manner.

I reached over and picked up my radio mike.

"Unit 23-11 to 23, (23 was our station call number) be advised I am 10–15 (prisoner in custody) with one white male at Los Coyotes Country Club.

"Station 23 to 23-11, 10-4. Be advised 23-Sam (the sergeant's call sign) is responding from the station. Go ahead with subject's identification." The station would automatically run the subject's name and check for any outstanding warrants.

I replied and was able to give my prisoner's name only, as before I could even spell it for them, I heard in the background, "HOLY SHIT! PENNY JUST ARRESTED THE MAYOR!" Then, immediately, "Station 23 to 23-11. Be advised 23-Lincoln and 23-Charlie are also responding to your 10-20." The lieutenant and the captain were also coming to my location. My heart jumped to my throat and then the next radio transmission made it almost jump out of my body. The chief was a retired LAPD lieutenant, and he had decided earlier to come and take a look at the situation and was just leaving his driveway when he heard my initial radio transmission. He radioed the station that he was also responding. *Well now, isn't this a great opportunity, Penny? You will have everyone from the mayor on down here. They will probably want to draw straws to see who is going to take your badge!*

I SEE YOU'VE MET THE MAYOR!

To make matters worse, the crowd had heard everything because I had my outside speaker on, apparently deciding that this was more interesting than the fire, the crowd now was gathered around my radio car. I told everybody to get back, but it was more like a valiant attempt to salvage mediocrity out of an impending disaster.

The sergeant, lieutenant, captain, and the chief all arrived within one minute of each other. I still had my suspect in cuffs and in the back seat of my radio car.

I had visions of my badge sprouting wings and flying away, but what ended up was amazing. I made the correct decision to get the mayor out of the car and un-cuff him while the sergeant was inform- ing the chief of the instructions I had been given. As they were all approaching me, the mayor walked toward them, and of course, I followed. No "How are you?" or "Mr. Mayor, this officer is new . . ." or anything like that. Nope! The mayor started it off. He told the chief that I had followed my instructions right to the letter, that he himself was in the wrong, and that it should be noted in my record that I did an outstanding job. He then turned around and thanked me.

A month later I was notified by the Los Angeles County Sheriff's Department that my background check had been completed and approval was given for me to become a deputy sheriff with the Los Angeles County Sheriff's Department (LASD).

I was making $490 a month with the BPPD and the starting pay with LASD was $510. That made quite a difference in those days, especially with a son who had just turned one year old. After a few agonizing days of deciding what to do, I finally made the decision to resign and accept my appointment with LASD. I put in my resignation and ultimately had to talk with the chief. He understood my reasoning and said he would probably do the same if he were in my shoes. He wished me the best and I became a deputy sheriff in late January, 1963. (So did *Mr. Murphy.* But that's another story.)

COURTROOM HUMOR

— Harry Penny —

Los Angeles County Sheriff's Department
Technical Services Div./Transportation Bureau, circa 1963

I was temporarily assigned to the Transportation Bureau of the Technical Services Division while waiting to start the next academy class.

My partner was the driver of one of the sheriff's buses that were used for transporting prisoners to and from the jail facilities to the various courts throughout Los Angeles County. These buses were like the ones used by various bus companies—designed to carry fifty passengers—but that was the only similarity. The Sheriff's Department had its own fleet. Each of these buses was painted black and white, had metal wire screens and bars on the outside of the passenger windows, a separate area for females, lettering on the sides that said SHERIFF LOS ANGELES COUNTY and the sheriff's badge insignia, and yes . . . even red lights and a siren.

On this particular day, a Monday, we had been assigned to the San Pedro Court House in San Pedro, a community within the city of Los Angeles. San Pedro is located on the western side of the Los Angeles harbor and houses the Port of Los Angeles. The Port of Los Angeles is one of the major California ports of entry into the United

Photo from Los Angeles Sheriff's Biennial Report 1965–1967 to the Los Angeles Board of Supervisors.

States. Others include San Francisco and San Diego. It is an extremely busy location, to say the least. Every day there are numerous ships sailing in and out to deliver their cargo to and from ports all over the world.

Of course, this being a waterfront area, the crews on those ships are going to do what sailors usually do when in a port: visit the local scene, which includes bars and restaurants, and other venues. One of these venues, one, in particular (referred to as "the oldest profession in the world") was prostitutes. The Los Angeles Harbor area had its share.

We arrived at the San Pedro Courthouse about 8:00 AM with our prisoners, two of whom were females. Most of the prisoners had been arrested over the weekend and this was their first court appearance. After we parked the bus in the designated area, the prisoners were unloaded and taken to the lock-up/holding cell area in the building. At the lock-up area were a member of LAPD, and several deputy Los Angeles County Marshals.

The Harbor Division of LAPD would bring their prisoners who had been arrested during the night and early morning and had not been transferred to the county jail yet. So one of their officers was assigned to be at the court to handle their paperwork. The deputy marshals were responsible for bailiff duties in the municipal courts.

Everything was going smoothly. Prisoners all accounted for and placed in the holding cells and now it was time for my morning "trifecta"—coffee, donut, and a cigarette. After this was completed it would be time for morning court.

Some judges would require that all of the prisoners who had cases before him be brought into the courtroom in groups of twelve or fewer and be placed in the jury box. Other judges might want only one prisoner at a time. In this particular instance, the judge wanted the two females, whom we had transported, brought into the courtroom separately, not with the male prisoners. I assisted the bailiff and escorted the two females into the courtroom via the door that led from the holding area, directed them where to sit in the jury box and then I sat in the chair by the door.

The courtroom was crowded. The area for spectators and audience —known as the gallery—behind the rail, or bar, was chaotic. Some of the prisoners' relatives were frantically trying to find a seat so they could see what was going to happen, others trying to talk with either the prosecutors or defense attorneys, and some just biding their time wanting to see what it was like in court.

The tables for the attorneys were up in the area called the "well," the area between the railing and the court clerk and judge's bench. Here were attorneys of all types: prosecutors from the Los Angeles City Attorney's office, public defenders from the County Public Defender's office and private practice attorneys. The combination of defendants, attorneys, and spectators, each thinking that if they spoke a little louder they would be more easily understood, resulted in a cacophony of human voices.

I overheard the two female prisoners talking between themselves. Both of them had been arrested for prostitution. One was telling the other that she had a long rap sheet and was probably going to get six months. The other one said she had only one prior and wondered what she would get. The other prisoner responded, saying she would probably get no more than thirty days. All of this chaos would come to an abrupt cessation the minute the door from the judge's chambers opened.

The judge entered the courtroom, stopped for a brief couple of seconds while looking at the crowd, then stepped up to the bench and took his seat. I had heard from the LAPD officer assigned to the court that this judge always had a frown on his face and did not tolerate improper attitudes in his court. (This is NOT Burger King. You don't get it YOUR way!)

The bailiff called the court to order. "All parties rise. The honorable Judge ————, presiding."

The judge took his seat and said, "Please be seated."

The court clerk called the first case and one of the female prisoners arose when her name was called. The charges were read. She had been arrested for prostitution, Section 647(b) of the California Penal Code.

When the judge asked her how she would plead she said "Guilty, yo' honor." She had a rap sheet of several pages and had been this route many times before.

At the end of the question-and-answer segment the judge looked at her, then looked again at the record in front of him, and said, "I sentence you to 180 days in the county jail," and with a bang of his gavel the case was over.

The next case was called and the second of the female prisoners stood up.

Same charges, same question-and-answer segment, and same plea—"Guilty, yo' honor"—but not in the humble fashion of her predecessor. This one, knowing that her rap sheet was not as bad as her friend's, had an attitude. She had figured she would get no more than thirty days. And that's what the judge gave her.

Before he could bang his gavel, she blurted out triumphantly, "Shit. Damn, yo' honor. Thank you. I can do that standing on my head!"

A few gasps were heard throughout the courtroom.

Without skipping a beat, the judge calmly adjusted his glasses then peered over the tops of them as he glowered at her and said, "Fine. I sentence you to another thirty days so you can get back on your feet" and banged his gavel.

The expressions of shock and amazement that were evident on the faces of those in the gallery were priceless. The majority of the attorneys were not shocked. Business as usual.

ACADEMY MEMORIES

— Harry Penny —

LOS ANGELES COUNTY SHERIFF'S DEPARTMENT
TRAINING ACADEMY, CLASS 97, FEBRUARY TO JULY 1963

Eight years after completing the Academy, I was working Patrol Division at West Hollywood (WHD) station. My partner and I were working the PM shift (3 PM to 11 PM) one Friday night in 1970 or 1971. At briefing we were told that SEB (Special Enforcement Bureau) would be working the area and in the field with us. That was good because on weekends it was not uncommon for 50,000 to 100,000 additional people to converge on the Sunset Strip and the additional patrol cars would be a great help. We were also told that there had been a recent string of car burglaries in the underground parking garages of the many apartment buildings that were in the West Hollywood area.

During our shift we were one of the units that had responded when a unit in the adjacent beat put out a call for assist. A couple of SEB units had also responded. After the call had cleared and we were getting ready to go back to our area, I recognized one of the SEB deputies, whom I had not seen since my academy training in 1963. He had been one of my TAC (Academy Training Instructors) officers. My memory banks automatically jumped into gear. (*Mr.*

32

Murphy seems to have followed me from the U.S. Navy into my career of law enforcement.)

It was February of 1963 when I reported to the Los Angeles County Sheriff's Training Academy at Biscaluz Center in East Los Angeles as a member of Class 97. I had awakened very early (o'dark :30) to be there beforehand. I had gone through the Orange County Peace Officers Academy the prior September when I had been accepted as a police officer with the Buena Park (CA) Police Department. (That's another story.)

It was 7:00 AM on a Monday morning when I got my first glimpse of our TAC officers. There were three of them and one sergeant. I say glimpse because everything came at us so fast. It was controlled chaos. The training would be what was known as "Stress Training." That was putting it mildly. It was definitely not like the academy I had completed just a few months before. I compared the Sheriff's Academy to the training I received as a navy hospital corpsman when I reported in to Camp Pendleton (CA) for advanced training at Field Medical Service School in 1957. There, our instructors were veteran hospital corpsmen and marines who had served in World War II and Korea. The navy instructors taught us the medical side and the marine instructors taught us about serving with the marines. They were all former drill instructors (DIs) at U.S. Marine Corps boot camp. They were definitely not "touchy-feely" back then.

So here I was, standing along with approximately ninety-nine other members of my class, called "cadets." The TAC officers looked as if they were poster models for the Los Angeles County Sheriff's Department: uniforms with vertical military creases so sharp they could cut meat; "high and tight" haircuts, just like marines (except for one who looked like the model for the label on the 'Mr. Clean' bottles, complete with muscles). Their shoes, leather gear, and badges were polished so brightly that when the sun would reflect off them it could blind you. Their voices rounded out the overall appearance. They definitely did not need the use of any amplification devices such as a microphone or a bull-horn. (I don't think any of them ever learned how to whisper.) They were intimidating, to say the least. In fact, as I recall, about seven cadets resigned right there on the spot. One cadet, who was standing right in front of me, was a former marine who said he . . . "had had enough of this shit in the corps and am not going to put up with twenty more weeks of it again."

Twenty weeks of this? Yikes! I thought to myself. But I was determined I was going to make it. Hell, I did my time with the marines! They could do anything but kill us and eat us. That was against the law!

Our uniform of the day for Monday through Thursday was short-sleeved khaki shirts, a black clip-on tie, gold tie bar, khaki trousers, black leather belt, black socks and black shoes (the kind like I wore in the navy). Our hats were the kind that the "Maytag repairman" wears. (We would not go to helmets for another couple of years.) Our official name tags were the kind you see people wearing at conventions, reunions, etc., that are encased in a small plastic tag holder that pins to your shirt.

Every morning we would report in and the first thing was inspection . . . just like the military. All three TAC officers would line up and the class "sergeant" would follow along behind them with a clipboard. His job was to write down any discrepancies ("gigs") that were noted by the inspecting party. The bad thing was that if a "gig" was missed by the first TAC officer, one of the other TAC officers would pick it out. I think they did that on purpose just to lull us into a false sense of security. I had no problems with passing inspection for the first few weeks. Until . . . *Mr. Murphy* showed up and tapped me on the shoulder.

After the first five weeks of classroom training we would get assigned to "ride-along" training. On Fridays, each of us would be assigned to ride patrol at one of the fourteen sub-stations throughout the county. We would report in, wearing our full dress (Class A) uniform, which was also the regular working uniform, and be assigned as a second or, in some cases, a third man in a radio car. We would go on patrol for the weekend(!), and then back to the academy the following Monday. So much for enjoying weekends off.

Los Angeles County Sheriff's Training Academy, Class 97, July 1963.
The author is on the far right of the top row.

On this particular Monday morning I was exhausted. I had just finished working my weekend assignment at Firestone station. On Sunday I had worked the PM shift (3 PM to 11 PM) which lasted a little longer due to the number of calls and activity my particular "partner" handled that night. I didn't get home until 2:30 AM Monday morning. I had to get up at 4:30 AM to get ready to go back to the academy.

After less than two hours sleep, I got up and started getting ready. Fortunately I had three pair of my navy black shoes. I kept two pair at all times shined to a luster. But I had to iron my khakis. So I got out the ironing board, and began. I always took extra care in putting military creases in my starched shirts. Little did I know that *Mr. Murphy* would be hiding in the iron.

One of my classmates, "JD," lived in the same area that I did. He was a former 1st Lt. USMC, and a Korean War Veteran, and he and I hit it off from the first day. We arranged it so that we would carpool to the academy. Fortunately for me, it was his turn to drive so I could at least relax on the way in. We left early enough to stop by the donut shop and get our morning "trifecta."

No, it's not what you may think—making morning bets on the horse races. Our "trifecta" was a large cup of steaming hot black coffee, a big humongous donut, and a cigarette. Now you may think this would be ill-advised, but we were clever. We would wear just regular jeans and a shirt while driving in, thereby having our uniforms, neatly ironed, and hanging on hangers in the rear window of the car. That way we would not tempt *Mr. Murphy* who says that, "A clean pressed uniform will always attract jelly-donut, catsup, or gravy stains at any time." Plus they would not get wrinkled from the thirty-minute drive. We would stop at a gas station that was close to the academy and then change into uniform, arriving sharp and looking good. Yes, military training did have its advantages.

Everything went according to plan. We made it on time for inspection and were standing in ranks.

The inspection party passed me and no "gigs" were noted. I was feeling confident until . . . they went around to the back. I could feel them right behind me. They stopped.

"CADET PENNY. WHAT IN THE HELL ARE THESE?" yelled the leading TAC officer, Deputy John Thurman, as he jabbed his finger into my back. I could tell he was in the vicinity of my military creases. *Uh Oh! I think Mr. Murphy has just announced his presence!*

"SIR. MILITARY CREASES . . . SIR!" I loudly responded.

"CADET PENNY. WHAT BRANCH OF THE MILITARY WERE YOU IN, IDIOT?" By this time his face was about two inches from my ear. Damn, he was loud.

"SIR. I WAS IN THE UNITED STATES NAVY . . . SIR!" I replied. I couldn't imagine what the hell he had found. I knew I had taken extra care in spraying a little starch on them right before I put the iron to them.

By now, the other two TAC officers had joined in. Two behind me and one came around and stood right in front of me. This was going to be one of the longest five-minute periods of my life. All

three of them yelling at the same time and each one saying something different. The main point was that they, in their military
careers, had never seen any military creases like mine. I had a fleeting thought that they were complimenting me since I had taken
extreme care. WRONG! Apparently in my morning stupor and grog-
giness I had failed to look at the position I had placed my shirt on
the board. *My military creases were razor-sharp and evenly spaced
. . . HORIZONTALLY!*

MR. MURPHY NEVER SAID THERE WAS A DIFFERENCE
BETWEEN A "MILITARY" AND A "CIVILIAN" IRON.

YOU'VE GOT
THE WRONG GUY

— Harry Penny —

LOS ANGELES COUNTY SHERIFF'S DEPARTMENT
HALL OF JUSTICE JAIL, CIRCA 1964

My first assignment, after completing the grueling twenty weeks of training at the Los Angeles County Sheriff's Academy in July 1963, was the Jail Division. I was assigned to the Hall of Justice Jail (HOJJ) on Temple and Grand in beautiful downtown Los Angeles. A fifteen-story building, one of the tallest buildings at that time, it housed the Sheriff's Office and various other divisions of the Sheriff's Department, various departments of the Superior Courts and other services, even the County Coroner's Office and the Morgue (in the basement). The jail occupied part of the ninth floor and the rest of the floors up to the fifteenth floor, the top of the building.

I was working the "Bath"—the ninth-floor section where the prisoners would be brought after going through the main booking process. The prisoners would be stripped down, showered, and then sprayed with a powder—to get rid of lice and hopefully to keep other "bugs" away. Their civilian clothing would be taken and stored, and they would be issued "jailhouse blues"—a light blue denim shirt and blue denim trousers each stenciled in white paint L.A. COUNTY JAIL. After completing this process they would then be taken to their respective cell block, which was more affectionately known as a "tank."

There were six deputies assigned to the bath, and one Senior Deputy as a supervisor. Every now and then, the Senior Deputy would be detailed to pick up a transportation vehicle and go to the new county jail that was being built, and almost completed, just a few miles away on Bauchet Street, and pick up a prisoner who had a court appearance at the Hall of Justice, or for other reasons.

On one particular day Senior Deputy Bill Flowers (a fictional name, as I have not received his permission to use his real name) received an assignment to go pick up a prisoner for a court appearance at the Hall of Justice. This started out to be a routine detail but what would transpire is a story that could not have been invented in any writer's imagination.

Senior Deputy Bill Flowers was a veteran cop in his mid-forties, standing about 5'9" and weighing 175 pounds, and a thick mane of salt-and-pepper wavy hair. His personality was infectious. After a number of years in patrol working the varied shifts—day shift, evening shift and the midnight /graveyard shift—and other details over a twenty-year span, he decided that a permanent day shift, Monday through Friday, with weekends and holidays off, was just the ticket. This was a fairly easy decision for him as he had just received a promotion to senior deputy. During this particular era there were no senior deputy positions in Patrol Division. That left Technical Services Division—Transportation Bureau—or Custody —Jail Division or Corrections Division—and maybe the Civil Division—as his only options. So he got assigned to Jail Division as a senior deputy.

After going to his locker and retrieving his gun, gun belt, handcuffs, baton, and his hat—department policy required uniformed deputies to be in full department uniform, including the hat, when on duty outside, and especially when driving official vehicles—Bill went down to the Transportation Bureau, on the main floor of the building, to check out a vehicle.

Headquarters for the Los Angeles County Sheriff's Department was in the Los Angeles Hall of Justice (above). The Jail Division is located on the upper floors with the columns.

The Transportation Bureau was a large operation in the Technical Services Division. The mission of the Transportation Bureau was the transportation of prisoners. This included transporting prisoners to and from the various courts throughout Los Angeles County and picking up prisoners from the Sheriff's substations throughout the county. There was a fleet of over fifty, forty-passenger busses, the same type as used by Greyhound and other bus companies, plus several station wagons, older patrol cars that were no longer being used by Patrol Division, and other assorted vehicles. Each of the vehicles was painted black with white doors, bars on the windows, red lights, a siren, and a radio with the big "whip" antenna. They all were lettered with SHERIFF LOS ANGELES COUNTY and had the sheriff's star on them. It was obvious to anyone who saw them that

the vehicle was some type of law enforcement vehicle. Duh!!! Well
. . . to almost anyone.

Bill checked out a 1961 Ford station wagon and started to pro-
ceed to his assignment. He was to drive to the new county jail, a
new, modern and larger jail, with construction almost fully completed, just a few miles away. It was only a short, ten minute drive
from the Hall of Justice, but it could take longer depending on traffic. This trip was going to take quite a bit longer.

Bill drove out of the Hall of Justice parking lot and headed south
on Spring Street. After a few blocks he stopped for a red light. The
light then changed to green and Bill proceeded through the intersection. All seemed to be going normal until a taxicab decided to
enter the same intersection. The only problem with this scenario
was that the cab had failed to stop for the red light and the taxicab
ran right into the rear fender of the Sheriff's Department station
wagon, causing both vehicles to come to a stop in the middle of
the intersection. A chain reaction immediately took form: drivers of
other vehicles skidding, tires screeching, and of course, honking
their horns. Not to mention several shouts of profanity. Not all L.A.
drivers are polite.

Bill was unhurt and got out of the car to see if the taxi driver was
all right. As I said, Bill was always in a good mood and not one to
get all riled up. Upon establishing that the taxi driver had not sustained any injuries, Bill returned to his vehicle and used his radio to
advise the Sheriff's dispatch center of the accident (non-injury) and
to request an LAPD traffic unit. Within a relatively few minutes the
sirens of an approaching police car and an ambulance echoed off
the tall buildings in downtown.

After radioing in, Bill began the task of directing traffic, which
as you can imagine, was developing into a large mess. He saw the
LAPD unit approaching and stopped traffic to allow for the police
car to get close to the scene. Right behind the responding LAPD unit
was an ambulance with red lights blazing and siren just hitting the
high peak. (You may recall that this was a non-injury accident.)

The responding LAPD officer got out of his car and, upon seeing the situation, went back and radioed in for assistance to handle the traffic that was begging to become an even larger mess. Sure enough, more sirens, which added to the confusion.

The LAPD officer approached Bill, who was still trying to direct traffic, and started asking questions. Fortunately, other LAPD units arrived on the scene and took over the traffic duties.

Bill and the LAPD officer went back to the crash scene and Bill began explaining what had transpired. The taxicab driver was leaning up against the side of his taxi, smoking a cigarette, as the two officers approached.

The LAPD officer asked both Bill and the taxi driver for their drivers' licenses and began his investigation. It became apparent to Bill, by the actions and questions of the LAPD officer, that the LAPD officer was a young individual who had just been on the job a short period of time.

During the investigation, the LAPD officer had radioed in to his headquarters and had run a check on both drivers' licenses. He advised Bill that his driver's license had become expired the previous day. Bill politely thanked him and told him that he would get it taken care of just as soon as he completed his assignment and asked for his license back as he had to return his vehicle back to the Hall of Justice and notify his superiors of what had transpired so that other arrangements could be made to pick up the prisoner. At this time an LAPD sergeant arrived on the scene and overheard the conversation. Bill explained the situation to the sergeant. Then the young officer explained the situation to the sergeant, who agreed with him.

To his surprise, Bill was informed that there was an arrest warrant out for him for unpaid traffic violations. To make matters worse, the officer said he was placing Bill under arrest for the outstanding warrant, which was being sent over to LAPD headquarters at Parker Center. Bill said that he would follow them in his Sheriff's vehicle, radio his dispatcher and request his watch commander to meet him at Parker Center and get things straightened out. He was told that he would not be allowed to drive his sheriff's vehicle and that it would be legally parked at the scene and that Bill would have to go with the officer in the LAPD unit. To compound this situation even more, Bill was told that he would have to surrender his service revolver to the sergeant before being transported to Parker Center. However, as a matter of professional courtesy, Bill would not be handcuffed and made to ride in the back seat.

Upon arrival at Parker Center, Bill asked that he be allowed to make a phone call to the Sheriff's Department as he had to advise them of what had transpired. He was told that he would be allowed one phone call.

Bill called, but his sergeant was out of the office. The call was taken by a jail deputy. When Bill started telling the deputy what had happened, the deputy started laughing and, thinking Bill was pulling a joke, hung up the phone. Bill explained the situation and started to make another call. He was told that he had completed his one phone call. After several minutes of argument and requesting to see a superior officer, Bill was allowed to make another phone call. This time he called the location where I was working and I took the call.

I, too, thought he was joking until I heard a tone in his voice that let me know he was serious. He told me what had happened and to notify the "brass" and get someone down to Parker Center ASAP. After hanging up the phone I contacted my watch commander and explained what had happened to Bill.

I would later learn, to quote Mr. Paul Harvey, "And now . . . the rest of the story."

The "brass" responded directly to Parker Center. Subsequent investigation revealed that indeed, an arrest warrant for the same name as Bill's had been issued. That was it! The young officer had been so excited that he had a warrant suspect that he did not bother to ask for a physical description. Only the name! The physical description was for a black male in his 20s, with black hair, brown eyes, standing 6'2" tall and weighed 200 pounds.

I think *Mr. Murphy* followed LAPD this time.

LAPD VS. FBI OR WHO'S GOT THE PRISONER?

— Harry Penny —

LOS ANGELES POLICE DEPARTMENT
NORTH HOLLYWOOD DIVISION, CIRCA 1963

I was going to college, taking night classes in police science—now known as criminal justice—while working day shift in the jail. The class was made up of a whole array of cops from various agencies—LAPD, L.A. Sheriff's, CHP, Burbank P.D., L.A. County Marshals. Each week after class a large group of us would go have a drink or two at a local "cop bar" in Van Nuys.

Our instructor was a grizzled veteran LAPD sergeant working Robbery/Homicide out of the North Hollywood Division. Big and burly was usually someone's first impression of him. He was about 6' tall 200+ pounds—not too much in the body fat percentage— and, well, not to say he was bald, let's just say he had a wide, very wide, part in his hair style. Or maybe you could imagine a guy with a fifteen-inch forehead. Most crooks, however, saw only his hands as he was placing them under arrest. However, he was quick-witted and had a great sense of humor. His smile, which crooks would sometimes see for a fleeting instant, was infectious.

One particular night we had left class and all met up at our establishment. Sarge was telling us one of his funny war stories and he had a bunch of them. He and his partner were working a murder case and the investigation later led them to a location that the suspect was known to frequent. This particular location was in San Bernardino (CA)—about seventy miles east on the I-10 San Bernardino freeway—just a tad out of their jurisdiction. Heck, it was even in another county. But that didn't matter . . . this was a murder investigation.

So, they tell their watch commander that they have a good lead on their suspect and maybe luck will be with them and they will be able to pick him up. After all, the information was fresh and the informant had been reliable so far. So off they go.

They get in an unmarked detective unit—I don't know why they call them unmarked—a light grey Plymouth four-door sedan, with black-wall tires, a California exempt license plate, and a small radio antenna on the rear, with two men in suits and ties, has a tendency to stand out in any situation and start a one-hour drive to San Bernardino. Fortunately the traffic was light at this time. Normally, distance is measured in miles, or "down the road a piece," or "as the crow flies."

However, southern California is different—distance is measured in time. Whenever someone asks directions the response is, "Usually it's about thirty to forty-five minutes from here or whatever amount of time it takes." When it comes to the traffic hours—which is all the time, except for that period of time between 2:00 AM and 4:00 AM, after the bars have closed and people are sleeping—the time is greatly increased.

They get to the location and sure enough it all falls into place and they arrest the suspect without any problem. They called into their office and made notification that the suspect was in custody. They put him in the back of the detective car and begin their trek back to North Hollywood. Sarge turns on the regular car radio. Might as well listen to something else besides police calls. It will take a little longer as traffic is starting to build up.

About thirty minutes later the radio announcer comes in with an important news break about the FBI. Sarge turns up the volume and hears that " . . . The FBI just announced that they have arrested a man in San Bernardino in connection with a murder . . ." The announcement went on to give the name and description of the subject and the location of the arrest—San Bernardino. (Makes one recall the old tag "film at eleven.")

Sarge started to go ballistic. The suspect mentioned in the broadcast was the same guy that he and his partner had in the back seat of their car. There weren't any FBI agents in the car. *Hmmmmmm.*

After Sarge and his partner finished cussing out whoever was trying to take credit for their arrest, Sarge got one of those devious grins on his face. The dynamics of this situation were about to change drastically.

As they neared another freeway that connected the San Bernardino freeway and went south to connect with the Santa Ana freeway, Sarge made a quick lane change across other lanes of traffic and got on the other freeway. They were now headed south.

They picked up the westbound Santa Ana freeway and headed toward downtown Los Angeles. However, that was not their immediate destination. No, Sarge had decided that maybe it was time to pay a visit to some of his buddies in another department. He drove to the city of Downey and went to the Downey police station.

After talking with the Downey PD watch commander and a couple of other friends of his, Sarge and his partner decided to book their suspect into the Downey jail for a few hours. Just to keep things straight, they booked the suspect using a phony name. Booking slip in hand, they went back to their car and proceeded to continue to North Hollywood. They knew what was happening there, from previous encounters with the FBI.

Sure enough. About thirty minutes after the news flash hit the airwaves—about 2:00 PM—FBI agents and TV news crews had descended, in full force, onto the parking lot of LAPD North Hollywood Division. Everything was set to film the momentous event and have it on the 5 o'clock news. Little did they imagine that they would be in for a long wait. Sarge and his partner stopped off and had some dinner—a full-course meal in fact, with dessert, and extra re-fills on their coffee!! They had had a strenuous day. They had left the station at ten o'clock in the morning and it was now nearing 6:30 PM.

They drove into the station parking lot, parked the car, and began walking into the station. They each had their ties loose, collars unbuttoned, and Sarge was carrying his briefcase. He and his partner seemed to be in deep conversation as they passed the horde, not bothering even to look up. Sarge opened the door and he and his partner entered the station. Sarge calmly walked over to the coffee machine and began pouring a cup of coffee. The watch commander approached him in a very hurried manner and wanted to know what was going on. It went something like this:

"What took you so long? Where in the hell is your prisoner?"

"What prisoner, Lieutenant?"

"What do you mean 'what prisoner'? The one you went and got in San Bernardino!"

"Oh, him."

"Yeah . . . him, dammit! Who the hell do you think I meant? Where the hell is he?"

Sarge was really enjoying this. Several other detectives had been quietly told by Sarge's partner as to what happened, and they eased their way into the coffee room, along with some FBI types, who were unaware.

"Well, Lieutenant . . . Charlie and I were just about to pull into the area where the suspect was supposed to be when we heard a news flash on the radio. Something about the FBI having just captured the suspect. Since the 'feebies' had him in custody we figured there was nothing for us to do so . . . we turned around and started to head on back. We figured we'd stop by headquarters and then grab a bite to eat. So we did. Why?"

According to the Sarge, he told us that he left the lieutenant sputtering, and walked back to his desk and started shuffling some papers. Almost immediately, the station captain approached the Sarge's desk. Sarge and the captain had known each other for many years.

The captain sat down on the chair by the desk and in a calm voice said, "OK. I know you're pissed at the stunt the feebies pulled and I don't blame you. We'll get it straightened out. Now, where did you stash him?"

In the end, Sarge and his partner went back to Downey PD, got their prisoner and returned to North Hollywood. The 11 o'clock news had revised the story. LAPD got the credit. *Film at eleven!*

NAMES CHANGE
. . . TRADITION
LIVES ON

— Harry Penny —

LOS ANGELES COUNTY SHERIFF'S DEPARTMENT
FIRESTONE STATION (FPK1)

California became a state on September 9, 1850 and the Los Angeles County Sheriff's Department was soon established. Operating out of downtown Los Angeles for almost seventy years, the department needed to establish its first sub-station in the 1920s, due to the growth in population.

Officially known as Firestone Park station (FPK), the new sub-station opened in the Florence/Firestone Park area of what is now known

Firestone Park station in 1956. Courtesy of Jack Miller, LASD (Ret), www.fpk,homestead.com

In Memoriam

...above and beyond the call...

Deputy Ronald E. Ludlow
March 9, 1939 - August 13, 1965

Firestone Deputy Roanld Ludlow was killed in the line of duty during the Watts riots, August 13, 1965. Image courtesy of Jack Miller, LASD (Ret.).

as south-central Los Angeles. The station would move three times in the area until 1955 when it moved into its new dedicated facility at 7901 South Compton Avenue, the third and final location until 1993.

In 1965, when I transferred to FPK, the station had an area of responsibility covering 41.25 square miles, with a racially and culturally diverse population of 213,00. Throughout the years, the men and women of FPK answered the call without hesitation, and faced the daily challenges with efficacy and aplomb. During its heyday the station would be home to 300 deputies and civilian personnel. FPK was reportedly the third busiest station in the nation, with New York PD's Harlem station being first and Chicago's southside being second.

FPK would be a central point in two major riots. The Watts Riots in August 1965 would tragically claim the life of one Firestone deputy, Deputy Ronald Ludlow, killed in the line of duty August 13, 1965.

Riots again erupted in Los Angeles in 1991 and FPK was again involved. The men and women of FPK answered the call in the same tradition as had been established by those before them.

Firestone station was a training station for thousands of deputies over the span of its sixty-five years, and lives on in the spirit and tradition in the hearts of those who were fortunate to have served there until 1993, when it was officially closed, and was removed from the department's rolls. Yet it still remains in the heart and soul of those who had the fortunate opportunity to serve there.

The area once patrolled by Firestone is now covered by three stations: Carson, Century, and Compton. NAMES CHANGE . . . TRADITION LIVES ON.

Firestone station was a training station for thousands of deputies over the span of its sixty-five years. Logo reprinted with the permission of clinklitho.com

During its heyday Firestone station was home to 300 personnel and was reportedly the third busiest station in the nation. Logo design by Harry D. Penny Jr.

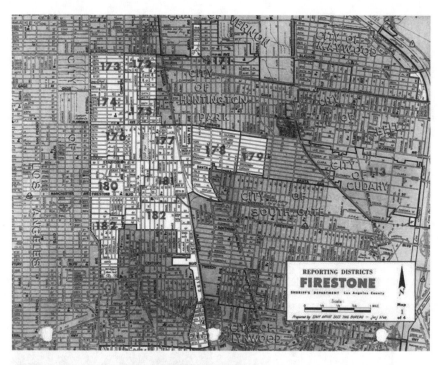

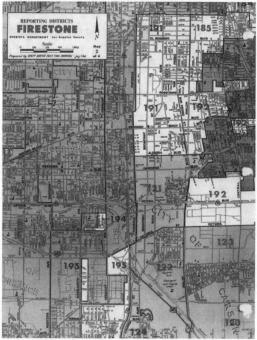

Reporting district maps for Firestone Sheriff's Department, Los Angeles County. These maps are the ones used by Firestone deputies in the late 1960s. The actual size of each map was 8 1/2 x 11 inches. Firestone areas are denoted by the blocks that have three numbers in them. Photos courtesy of Jack Miller, LASD (Ret.) and webmaster for www.FPK1@ home stead.com.

"CHOO-CHOO"

— Harry Penny —

LOS ANGELES COUNTY SHERIFF'S DEPARTMENT
FIRESTONE STATION (#1), CIRCA 1966

If you saw the movie *Top Gun* with Tom Cruise you probably noticed that all of the pilots and GIBS (guys in the back) had nicknames. Tom Cruise was "Maverick" and his GIB, the radar intercept officer (RIO), had the nickname of "Goose." Nicknames have been a common practice in Naval aviation for many years and continue to this day. Well . . . cops have their own versions of nicknames. This particular story is about a deputy, Vic Kretsinger, whom I had the distinct pleasure of working with, and whom I affectionately called "Choo-Choo."

I first met Vic in 1963 while working in the Jail Division at the Hall of Justice (HOJ) in downtown Los Angeles. Quite possibly you have heard someone make a growling sound using their vocal chords and such. Some can even make sounds like a barking dog, a meowing cat, cows mooing, birds chirping—you get the idea—and other animalistic sounds. Well, Vic not only had the ability to speak in various accents just as if they were his native language, but he had the unique ability to emulate various sounds: birds chirping, cows mooing, horses, goats . . . you name it and he could probably imitate it. But the one I found the most intriguing was when he made the sound of a

54

locomotive whistle. That's right . . . an honest-to-goodness locomotive whistle. You would think a train was actually nearby. This was a sight at the jail, especially down in booking, more commonly known as the Inmate Reception Center, and most effective when drunks were coming in by the droves. He would make the sound and the drunks would move to another side of the holding cell while looking for the train.

In 1965, when I transferred from Jail Division to Patrol Division, I got assigned to Firestone Park (FPK) station. One of the first deputies I encountered was Vic. After spending my time in training and becoming an honest-to-goodness Firestone Trained Deputy, I would have the chance to work a radio car with him. Hardly a week would go by without Vic picking up the microphone, switching it over to the PA system, and making his sound of the "Choo-Choo." It always made for laughs and chuckles.

One night, on PM watch, we were just doing "routine patrol"— as those of you know, there is no such thing as "routine patrol" in police work, and especially at FPK—and we had inadvertently crossed over into LAPD's area. I was driving and Vic was in one of those moods. There needed to be some levity brought into the car.

While stopped at an intersection, waiting for the red light to change to green and being a by-the-book regulation driver *"Nosiree, Sarge . . . I don't blow those long-assed lights in the city . . . I stop and wait for all of them to change. Honest."* I observed a textbook style of an inebriated individual. He was standing on the corner trying to keep the traffic light from falling over. Yes, this guy was the one they taught us about in the academy; he made Red Skelton's character, Freddy the Freeloader, look sober.

He was wearing a sport coat, complete with the patches on the elbows, what once had been a white shirt, as I could see by the one shirt tail that was hanging below the bottom of the sport coat, a pair of trousers that had never seen a crease since they had come off the rack, and to round out his "formal attire," he was barefooted.

As I said, this individual was holding onto the traffic light for dear life and even then, while using both hands, he was having a difficult time remaining upright. I was so intent on watching him

THERE NEEDED TO BE SOME LEVITY
BROUGHT INTO THE CAR.

that I sat through the green light. Lucky for me there was no other traffic in the immediate vicinity.

After sitting through the red light, the green light, and now waiting for another red light, I saw the drunk start to make his first of several valiant attempts to cross the street. Realizing that this was going to be an undertaking of epic proportions, I backed the car up and pulled over to the side of the street. This was going to be a valiant attempt to salvage mediocrity out of an impending disaster.

His first attempt was trying to put one of his feet down on the street, below the curb. He looked as if he was trying to pick out any land mines that might have been set. His foot would touch the ground then he would move it ever so slowly. If you ever saw any of the *Roadrunner* cartoons on Saturday mornings, you may remember Wile E. Coyote doing this maneuver. This took a couple of tries, as each time he would lose one of his hand-holds on the street-light, then quickly reach back and at the same time bring his foot back up on the sidewalk. Finally, he succeeded and proceeded to put his other foot down on the street. That process was the same as the first foot. After a couple of minutes he had both feet in the street and was holding on to the street light by just his fingertips and his momentum pulled him away from the streetlight. He bent over, touched the street with one hand and, reaching the conclusion that the street was not moving, he straightened up and started his own version of walking.

Vic and I were almost in a trance just watching this show when I saw a smile come on Vic's face. It was like the proverbial light bulb coming on saying, "Idea." Vic reached over and removed the mike from the dashboard, reached down and put the switch on PA," (public address) mode and turned the volume level to FULL BLAST.

"Chug-a chug-a-chug . . . Chooo-Chooo, Chug-a-chug-a-chug . . . Chooo-Chooo." The sounds emanated from Vic's throat and into the microphone. With the volume at full blast, the night air was filled with the sound of an approaching train. Had Vic not been sitting beside me, I would have looked for the train myself.

The drunk stopped suddenly in mid-step. His head snapped to the left then to the right, then back behind him. He turned around and made a dive for the curb and the safety of his street light. Once he had a good hand-hold, he began looking up and down the street for the train. Seeing that no train was going to come out of nowhere and run over him, he started his process of trying to cross the street again. This time he had the procedure down pretty good and it didn't take him as long. He was out in the middle of the street when again . . . Vic keyed the mike. "Chug-a chug-a-chug . . . Chooo-Chooo, Chug-a-chug-a-chug . . . Chooo-Chooo."

The drunk repeated his same actions: looking around for the train and then making his mad dash—in very slow motion—back to his streetlight.

This went on about four times before the drunk went over and lay down and curled up on the bus bench. It's a good thing he was in the city and especially not trying to drive a car. Can you imagine trying to give someone like this a field sobriety test?

When I was able to stop laughing, I put the patrol car into gear and Vic and I resumed "routine patrol."

WHERE'S THE TOP OF MY RADIO CAR?

— Harry Penny —

LOS ANGELES COUNTY SHERIFF'S DEPARTMENT
FIRESTONE STATION (#1), CIRCA 1967

This is one of those instances that you hear about happening to someone else. Yeah, right.

It was a Friday night at "The Stone"—a name that Firestone deputies affectionately gave to the station. Of course, this was one of those weekends when, after eight weeks of daily classroom training at the Los Angeles County Sheriff's Academy, the students, known as cadets, would be assigned to various patrol stations throughout the county to get some in-the-field hands-on experience in patrol. They would be assigned to work the PM shift (3 PM to 11 PM) or the EM shift (Early Morning 11 PM to 7 AM) on Friday and Saturday nights. This would be after a forty-plus hour week of sitting in class.

Each cadet would be assigned to ride as the second man in a two-man car. The watch sergeant would pick various cars and split the partners up with each regular Firestone deputy being assigned one of the cadets who would ride as the second man.

The regular deputy assigned as the second man would then check out another patrol car and also get a cadet to ride as second man, thereby affording the station the opportunity to field one or more extra cars, depending on the number of cadets who were assigned to that station. Although each regular deputy had gone through this when he was a cadet, it was not a choice assignment to get a cadet. No one really liked having to be split up, especially when you had a regular partner. But . . . this was not an option when the watch sergeant made the assignments at briefing.

As I pulled into the station to get ready to report for duty, I observed six brand-new cadets walking around the parking lot in a daze. They were trying to figure out how to enter the station from the rear. *Ah, yes . . . someone is going to be the unlucky one tonight. Not me . . . nahhhhh.*

This particular Friday night we were fielding twelve cars on the EM shift. Three of those cars were going to get split up; thereby we would have fifteen cars in the field.

In the locker room you could hear the normal chatter. Deputies each bitching and griping, par for the course. "Hey, I hope the Sarge doesn't pick me again this week." "Shit, I had it last week," etc., etc., etc.

I was doing my share. My partner, Brad Mills, and I had just finished a three-month stint as training officers, each with a new deputy who had just been assigned from the Jail Division, which is another story in itself, and we were eager just to get back to a normal tour. I was confident that Brad and I wouldn't get split up. We were assigned to car 18 in the Carson area. Carson was an unincorporated area just north of Long Beach. I was scheduled to drive that night. Coffee cup in one hand, cigarette in the other, I made my way from the locker room to the briefing room. Brad was following right behind me in the same manner; coffee cup and cigarette.

We read the briefing boards, made our notes in our notebooks, grabbed a "Hot Sheet"—LAPD would print out a page sheet with the license plates of the most recent stolen cars—which we would put on the sun visor with rubber bands. These were the latest thing during this era. We then went over and sat down at the long table. The table had enough chairs for the station deputies assigned to the shifts. The cadets were all standing at the back of the room at semi-attention. I, myself, understood what they were feeling as I had been in that position a few years earlier, but no way was I going to cut them any slack. Neither was anyone else.

The sergeant came in, took roll-call, gave briefing, and then proceeded to split up the various cars. He picked most of the north end cars and finally came down to deciding on the last one. We were sitting pretty. I knew he wouldn't split up the Willowbrook cars but still, we had a good shot at not getting picked. Until . . . Brad made some comment under his breath.

Without looking up from his clipboard the sergeant said, "Penny, you and Mills will be the final car." *Arrgggghhhhh!* Brad's comment didn't go unheard. "Mills, you will be 18-Adam."

After briefing and inspection, we left the briefing room and went and got our shotguns from the armory and proceeded out to the parking lot. It was normal procedure to show the cadet the proper way to check the shotgun, step-by-step, then have him do it. "Show and Tell." We had the Ithaca 12-gauge shotguns and one feature was that once you put one in the chamber it was ready to go . . . unless you put the safety on. If not . . . well, you can figure that one out. Also, if you kept your finger on the trigger you could just point-and-shoot rapidly by just pumping another round.

I followed procedure to the letter. I showed my cadet each step in loading and unloading, making sure that he understood completely. Then I handed him the shotgun and made him go through the procedure, explaining to me, what he would do for each step, and I checked the shotgun each time after he went through all the steps. Once I was satisfied that he could do it properly and safely, I would unload it and have him do it again and then put it in the shotgun rack. The shotgun rack was a metal clasp-type device that was attached to a strip of flat iron. There was a metal bracket, shaped to hold the butt of the shotgun, attached to the floorboard just to the left of where the passenger's feet would be on the floorboard. When the shotgun was placed in the brackets it would be in an upright position just a few inches away from the dashboard, between the driver and the passenger.

My cadet did it right the first time but just to make sure, I instructed him to repeat the entire procedure and the secure the shotgun in the rack. OK so far. I left him to do it and went over to where Brad's car was, about fifteen feet away. We were setting things up to make a meet once we got in the area.

Just as I lit my cigarette and got to Brad's car there was a loud *Ka-BOOM!* We all knew what that sound was and immediately ducked for cover, glancing around to see what idiot made his mistake. After determining that no more rounds were going to be forthcoming, nobody would be stupid enough to do that again, we all started coming out from cover. Of course, there was some laughter in the parking lot, with the exception of three individuals: The sergeant, the lieutenant, and . . . my cadet.

LET ME GUESS . . . YOU CLEARED
THE SHOTGUN INSIDE THE CAR!

I looked over to my radio car and there was my cadet . . . still half-way in the car, bent over in the same position as he was when he put the shotgun in the rack. His finger was still in the trigger guard, his eyes were tightly shut, and . . . one of the red lights from the top of my car was hanging down by the windshield and gently bobbing at the end of its wiring. The metal base plate, where the other red light, the siren and the amber light behind the siren were mounted, was sitting somewhat askew atop my car and there was a jagged hole in the top of the car, where the whole assembly had been. My trainee had accidentally jacked a round in the chamber!

Yes . . . it was going to be a long, very long, night. As a matter of fact, for a long period of time thereafter.

BLACK & WHITE TAXI COMPANY

— Harry Penny —

LOS ANGELES COUNTY SHERIFF'S DEPARTMENT
FIRESTONE STATION (#1), CIRCA 1966

The department policy was two-man patrol units on the PM and
EM (Early Morning) shifts. Day shift was normally a one-man
unit. However, after the Watts Riots in August of 1965 certain Firestone (FPK) units would be two-man units on day shift, especially in
the Willowbrook area, which borders Watts on three sides. On this
particular day my partner and I were a two-man car, 16-Days.

We had spent a goodly amount of time taking reports, which
was usually the case. In those days, if someone called into the station reporting any type of misdemeanor, and the complaint deputy
could not handle it over the phone, a patrol unit would be dispatched. This included John Q. Citizen reporting his son's bicycle
being stolen, or reporting a found bicycle, malicious mischief, vandalism or just about any misdemeanor and of course . . . felonies.
You get the idea, I'm sure.

We had just finished having some coffee at one of the many fire
stations in our area. We had a good rapport with the firemen as policy was whenever a fire engine was responding to a call, a Sheriff's
unit would automatically be dispatched. We would provide traffic

and crowd control; take reports if the damage was over a certain monetary amount; and in some cases, help them haul hoses if necessary. Many times there would only be three firemen on the fire truck and they would need help until others arrived.

This particular fire station was near the intersection of Redondo Beach Boulevard and Figueroa Street This particular intersection was a borderline of our area and that of LAPD's 77th division area.

We had just gone 10-8 (in-service) and were headed back out to the streets when a call came out over the radio. "Firestone 16 . . . man down at the intersection of . . ." The dispatcher continued, giving us the location, which was about six blocks from our present location. It was not a Code 3 call but still one of those calls where you were to respond as fast as prudently possible in case someone was hurt.

Enroute to the scene I observed an LAPD black-and-white leaving our area and heading west back into their area. This was not uncommon since our areas were adjacent. (Some of the LAPD officers liked to come into our area to grab a donut and not be caught by one of their supervisors.)

We arrived at the scene and observed a male individual lying underneath some bushes, and a whiskey bottle in his hand. Closer inspection—using the keen powers that all deputies at FPK possessed —plus a very strong alcoholic odor emanating from the immediate vicinity of his person, and a loud, audible snore, enabled me to determine that the individual was intoxicated. No distress noted. Nosireee! This guy was drunk! Great. Just what we needed: get tied up with an arrest, booking, and then another report. We were three reports behind and were only two hours from end of watch.

I had heard stories when I was in training about LAPD bringing drunks into our area rather than arresting them and booking them. Some of the deputies who had received the call had just taken them back and put them in LAPD's area. There was supposedly one occasion, I would later learn to be true, where they actually put the drunk in the back of a parked LAPD unit. Well, now . . . this seemed like

I SAID TO PUT HIM IN THE TRUNK. THIS CAR
DOESN'T GO FASTER THAN THE SPEED OF SMELL!

the perfect opportunity. That LAPD unit had been in our area. Oh,
yes . . . this opportunity was actually beckoning us to take advantage of the situation.

After quite some doing, we managed to get the subject somewhat conscious and awake and put him in the trunk of our radio car.
(He smelled so bad. But I was nice . . . I left the trunk open.)

A couple of blocks away was a restaurant where LAPD units
would go Code 7. We headed in that direction. At this point I was
silently wishing that our car could go faster than the speed of smell.
This individual not only reeked of booze, but his sanitary habits had
long been neglected.

As we passed by the restaurant I noticed an LAPD unit parked in
the back. Another pass-by revealed two LAPD officers seated at a
table and enjoying a meal. Yep, this was the time. We went around
the block and came into the parking lot from the rear driveway
which was out of view from the aforementioned LAPD officers.
LAPD and our department both had Plymouth vehicles and, in some

cases, the keys could be manipulated to open the doors of the same type of vehicle. I was hoping that this would be the case. As luck would have it, I didn't have to hope. They had apparently forgotten to lock one of the rear doors. Wasn't that thoughtful?

We put the subject into the back seat of the LAPD unit. I told him that we had ordered "Black and White Taxi Company" and for him to go ahead and lie down and get some rest. Then, when the "taxi" driver came back to the car, to just tell him where he wanted to go. He thanked us and assumed his horizontal position in the back seat.

We got back in our car and left the same way we entered the parking lot. No sense in advertising that we were out of our area.

We drove across the street and parked away from the corner, but where we could see the restaurant and the parking lot. My partner continued writing his reports while I Code 5'd (Cop talk for "staked out") the situation. About twenty minutes later the LAPD officers came out of the restaurant. One was lighting a cigarette and the other one was picking his teeth with a toothpick. They appeared to be a "rookie" and his old-timer training officer. They appeared to be in conversation as they approached their car. Neither of them even as much as glanced at the rear seat as they got into the car.

The car pulled out and was just approaching the intersection when the funniest sight appeared: the drunk arose from the back seat, reached forward and tapped the driver on the shoulder. The officers both turned their heads around so fast that it was a wonder they didn't each get whiplash. The car came to an abrupt stop in the middle of the intersection. The red lights came on, both the driver's door and the passenger's door opened simultaneously. The driver, the training officer, came out with his gun drawn while the rookie got hung up on his seat belt, and finally, got out and drew his gun.

Both officers had their guns pointed at the drunk in the back seat. As this was happening, cars were approaching the intersection and hitting their brakes to avoid the police car sitting askew in the middle of the intersection. My partner and I were laughing almost uncontrollably.

**THE TRAINING OFFICER CAME OUT WITH HIS GUN DRAWN
WHILE THE ROOKIE GOT HUNG UP ON HIS SEAT BELT.**

The older of the two officers took control of the situation. While his partner was handcuffing the suspect, the more senior officer started looking over in our direction. I turned on the red lights and tapped my horn. He apparently got my message as he gave us the finger and then put the drunk in the back seat of the car.

About fifteen minutes later I heard one of our north end units, possibly 12 or 12-A, get a "Man down . . . possible 647-f" (cop talk for drunk). Back at the station at end of watch I asked the deputies that got the call what happened. It was the same drunk. They put him in their car and conveniently put him in back in LAPD's area. It was quite possible that the suspect would sober up by the time LASD and LAPD finished playing ping-pong with him.

THE GREAT STICKER CAPER

— Harry Penny —

LOS ANGELES COUNTY SHERIFF'S DEPARTMENT
FIRESTONE STATION (#1), CIRCA 1966

My partner and I were working the EM shift (Early Morning), on patrol out of the Firestone Substation in south-central Los Angeles, the busiest station within the Los Angeles County Sheriff's Department.

There are times working the Early Morning (graveyard) Shift when things get slow: the bars have closed, the drunks have gone home, or found a place to rest their weary arms—from doing all that heavy lifting of liquid containers—and this gave us some time to actually snoop around and try and catch a burglar or two. So off we went, driving in alleys, looking for signs of pry marks on rear doors to businesses. (Yes, that was an actual way of using your flashlight for something other than bopping some bad guy on the noggin . . . only when he deserved it, of course.)

We were cruising one of the alleys in the vicinity of Rosecrans and Figueroa and as we passed between two buildings we could just barely make out the shape of a car. It was a fairly foggy night and the exhaust coming from the exhaust pipe on the car was visible. Hot Damn! We've got something going here. We definitely need to get a closer look and investigate this.

So . . . we pull up a few feet, park the radio car, sloooooowly get out of the car and quietly walk back to the area, keeping a sharp eye out for any movement, and a keen ear to hear any sounds. Ah, yes . . . these burglars won't even know we're here.

As we get to the edge of the building I can now see the outline of the car. *What the????* Two lights on the top, one on the left and one on the right, and a large round shiny object in the middle. *Hmmmm* . . . looks like two red lights and a siren to me. Definitely not an LASD patrol car, but it sure does resemble the outline of an LAPD unit. Their area ended a few blocks away—the LAPD 77th division bordered our area on the west side and ended at Central Avenue—and it was not uncommon to find them in our area at times.

Now we go into extreme silent mode. It is necessary due to it being foggy, no lights from any of the buildings, and not using our flashlights, we go tippy-toe-tippy-toe, as a matter of fact, a lot of tippy-toeing as they were about fifty feet away. Sound carries in fog and there is always something that could be in the alley: a rock, a broken bottle, tin can, and other things that could cause a person to stumble and make noise. Off we go, right up to the back of the car. It is Yep! LAPD. Windows rolled up and two officers inside. One in

Photo courtesy Jack Miller, LASD, (Ret.).

the front seat and one in the rear seat (they didn't have caged units in this era) and both of them were in a "resting-checking-our-eye-lids-for-light-leaks" position.

We wanted to make sure they were just sleeping. No sense in disturbing them. The light bulb in my head goes off and ideas start coming in bunches. I signal my partner and we quietly depart the vicinity, being very careful not to wake them from their beauty rest. The dynamics of this undertaking could suddenly change drastically if they were to be startled awake, which would definitely not bode well for us. They also carried guns.

We went back to our car, again in our quiet, stealth (sounds more professional than "tippy-toe") mode, and removed the bumper jack from the trunk, along with a couple of blocks of 4" x 6" wood. We then quietly headed back to the nappers. So far, so good, up to this point. I placed the bumper jack under the rear bumper of the LAPD car and slooooowly raised the car, one quiet click at a time, until we could place the two wooden blocks under the rear axle.

When we finished we silently departed, again, and returned to our car. Enroute, I got another idea: I get the newspaper (we need to keep abreast of current events, right?) and my pad of print stickers—4" x 6" heavy white paper with the type of glue like on postage stamps, that we used to lick and paste on items commonly found at crime scenes that needed fingerprinting, with big letters HOLD FOR SHERIFF. My plan is to cover their entire windshield with newspaper except for a small slit area big enough for them to see through. Don't want them driving completely obstructed. That's not safe. I'll paste the stickers in places to keep the paper from blowing off.

With newspaper and sticker pad in hand we make another silent approach to their patrol car. My partner and I each start quietly placing sheets of newspaper all over the front windshield, careful to leave just enough space for them to see through. That done, we again silently depart. This has taken us about thirty to forty-five minutes—it was a painstaking process for each click of the bumper jack—from the time we first saw them until now.

WE SLOOOOOOWLY RAISED THE CAR UNTIL WE COULD
PLACE THE TWO WOODEN BLOCKS UNDER THE REAR AXLE.

When we got back to the car another light bulb went off in my head. It would be another kicker to place another type of sticker on their rear bumper. The Sheriff's Department had a recruitment campaign for Deputy Sheriffs. Each station was given a bunch of light green bumper stickers with the words BE A DEPUTY SHERIFF, the sheriff's star, and the main phone number for recruiting purposes. The objective was to place them on our radio cars, and they also could be given away as public relations to businesses, etc., in the area. Being public relations-conscious as I was—yeah, right—I went back to their car and placed one right smack in the center of the rear bumper. That should get a rise out of someone back at their station.

My partner and I then drove back to the front of the buildings and stopped just before the entrance to the alleyway. Many of the deputies carried firecrackers in their individual "patrol box." I was one of them. You never could tell when they might come in handy. For what reason I never did know. I took three good-sized firecrackers and lit them and tossed them into the alley. As soon as they went off my partner turned on our siren and red lights.

Immediately, the headlights and red lights on the LAPD unit went on and the engine began to roar. Only one problem—the LAPD unit did not go anywhere with those blocks under the rear axle, which had raised the rear end of their car about one inch off the ground, and the newspaper plastering the front windshield. It took them a few seconds to realize they had been had. To add insult to injury, they had to scrape the stickers off the front window. They were definitely not in a happy mood.

We hastily departed the area. It was, however, somewhat difficult to drive while trying uncontrollably to contain our laughter. Back at the station, at the end of watch, we headed for our favorite cop bar for a little "choir practice" and related our story. It was the highlight of the night and everyone got a good laugh.

For the next several weeks we did not see any LAPD units parked in our area, but we were confident they had their ways of payback. They did, eventually, but that is another story.

IT WAS A DARK AND FOGGY NIGHT

— Harry Penny—

LOS ANGELES COUNTY SHERIFF'S DEPARTMENT
FIRESTONE STATION (#1), CIRCA 1966

Southern California is probably known best for the many pictures of palm tree-lined streets, warm sunny days, summertime all year, lots of beaches, bikinis, and all that travel brochure hype. Well, most of the time it is. However, during the "winter season"—yes, we do have some type of winter in Los Angeles—it gets downright cold. And quite often, very foggy. Foggy to the extent that visibility is sometimes only as far as the front of your car. This was one of those nights.

My partner and I were working the Early Morning (EM) watch, unit 17, in the south end of the district just north Long Beach. It was exceptionally foggy that night. Sometimes fog is good. Sounds carry in the fog. By parking your car and sitting quietly you can hear many things, such as someone breaking a glass window to commit a burglary, which has happened before.

Our patrol area was about five miles south of the station and we were taking our sweet time getting there slowly. I was driving this night and visibility was 100 feet at best. When we got to the intersection of Alondra Boulevard and Long Beach Boulevard the visibility had decreased to the point that we could just barely make out the large gas station on the corner. That was only because we knew what was there and could see the glow from the fluorescent lights over the pump islands. We decided to pull in there and park for a few minutes just to see if the fog would clear.

After parking the car, I got out and walked over to the station office, got two cups of coffee from the vending machine, and told the clerk that we would be over by the phone booth, which was about twenty yards from the building, along the edge of the lot.

Ah, yes . . . time to grab some coffee, smoke a cigarette, and just relax. Relaxing didn't last long, however. We saw the glow of a car's headlights enter the station lot and heard it go over the rubber tube that rang the "ding-ding" bell, and then the car stopped and the driver turned the engine off. The normal thing to do. We heard the sound of the car door opening and a voice said, "You pumps da gas whiles I goes and handle bidness."

The gas station attendant had started walking to the island when he heard the "ding-ding."

"Can I help you?" the attendant asked.

"Yeah, man . . . you gonna hep us all right. You can just walk wit' me back to the office and gives me yo cash while my padna get us some gas. OK?"

"Hey, man . . . " said the attendant. "What you doing with that gun? You don' need be pointing it at me. I take you back and gives you the money, jus don't do nothin' crazy."

Hearing this, my partner poked me in the ribs and we looked at each other in disbelief. We had to really control ourselves from breaking out into laughter. We slowly opened the car doors and got out as quietly as we could. We could hear the footsteps coming toward us. The attendant was bringing the crook right to us.

I motioned to my partner to indicate that I would go over to the car where the other suspect was. My partner waited by our car. I silently "tippy-toed" over to the island and walked up right behind the suspect. He had no idea I was there. I waited until I could hear what was going on back at our radio car.

"Hey man, this don't look like no office!" came a surprised voice. It was obvious that this crook's "upstairs carpeting" was definitely not wall-to-wall.

"Freeze, asshole!" came the low-throated gravel voice of my partner.

"Hey, Elroy . . . " said the gas-pumping suspect. "Wha' da fuck going on? Who say freeze?"

That was my cue. I un-politely stuck my gun in the back of his head and said "Freeze, asshole! Just like you heard that other voice say."

"What the . . . ?" said the gas-pumper as he started to turn around and then stopped in mid-motion as he heard me cock the hammer. To his surprise he momentarily forgot that he was pumping gas. *Another rocket scientist.* The nozzle came out of the opening and the gas then started to pour down his leg and onto his feet. When he realized this, he dropped the gas nozzle. The liquid running down his leg changed from gasoline to urine.

I put him down on the ground and cuffed him. Shaking him down was a little dicey since his pants were soaked with gasoline and urine.

After cuffing and shaking down both suspects, we recovered one .38 caliber revolver, one .25 caliber automatic, two nylon stockings, and a paper bag containing almost $300.

We finished getting the information from the gas station attendant and started to leave for the station and saw him laughing.

Needless to say, during the ride back to the station, nobody was smoking a cigarette. Back at the station, we told the story. At first, the watch commander and the watch sergeant didn't believe us. But that all changed when the suspects began talking. We left the entire station crew laughing as well.

Ah, yes . . . as some story line openings go . . . ."It was a dark and foggy night."

THE SERENDIPITY SUSPECT OR WHY YOU WRITE YOUR LONG ENTRIES IN PENCIL

— Harry Penny —

LOS ANGELES COUNTY SHERIFF'S DEPARTMENT
FIRESTONE STATION (#1), CIRCA 1966

My favorite shift was the EM (Early Morning 11 PM to 7 AM). But on this particular shift assignment I was working a day car, Firestone 18, in the south end just above Long Beach. My partner was on vacation and so the sergeant figured I should do a little time in "purgatory." Actually, it was the day watch acting watch sergeant who put me on days this month. (He had no sense of humor when it came to his brand new car, but that is another story which I will tell later).

I wasn't particularly fond of the day watch at all: burglary reports up the wazoo, petty theft reports, stolen/recovered bicycle reports, malicious mischief reports and on and on and on. Yes in those days we took reports on just about everything imaginable unless we could "kiss it off" with just a log entry—which was not as often as we would like. You could spend the whole day just going from one report call to another. Yep . . . "purgatory" was a good name for day watch at Firestone.

On this particular day it seemed that every burglar in the south end had been working overtime the night before. I rolled out of the station with five detail calls from the desk. These are those non-urgent calls that would come in to the complaint deputy near the end of the previous shift and would be held over for the oncoming watch to be assigned after roll call and briefing. Usually when we were checking out our shotguns and getting our keys for our vehicles, a call from the in-house station public address system would come out.

Just as I picked up my keys for the car, the voice came out loud and clear. "Firestone 18, see the desk for five calls." This was going to be a stubby-pencil-cramp-in-the-fingers day for me. All of them were 459-R (burglary reports) and there would be more reports before the day was through.

After putting my shotgun in the rack, loading my gear into the car, I got in and started to make my way down to my beat. (For those of you not familiar with southern California, here is a quick lesson in geography: Distance is measured in time rather than in miles.) For me, this was about twenty-five minutes from the station to my first call. I would pass two Winchell's donuts shops enroute and I could smell the cinnamon buns and hot coffee as I went past. But being conscientious and squared away as I was, I plodded on through the traffic without any attempt to quickly pull in, grab one of each and go. I did see two of the other units there and knew that each of them was thinking of me while they were laughing. *What the hell . . . I can grab a donut and coffee for my long trip down to the area.*

A quick u-turn and into the driveway was all it took. Yep . . . a hot steaming cup of coffee and not one, but two donuts and a cinnamon roll (I have always been able to eat a lot and not gain weight) and I was on my way, again. A little slower this time. I didn't want to spill my coffee.

The morning flew by. The next thing I knew I had taken five burglary reports, one malicious mischief report, and one stolen vehicle report.

It was department policy to take all of the information in your personal field pocket notebook and then complete your report when you had time. This would minimize the amount of time you were out of service. Then after getting all of the information, obtaining a file number, giving the informant/victim the pertinent follow-up information, you could theoretically (key word—theoretically) go park near any intersection and write your report. This was an attempt to have John Q. Public, who happened to be driving maybe a little fast or thinking about beating the light, take a different attitude by seeing a black-and-white on the corner. I opted to do mine at the A&W root beer drive-in at the corner of Avalon Boulevard and Carson Street. Well, at least I was near an intersection. (I had finished my donuts and three cups of coffee two hours earlier and I was getting hungry.)

In those days, grabbing something to eat was just that. Grabbing. Unlike LAPD who would be granted Code 7, we were constantly monitoring the radio. We worked straight eight-hour shifts and so there was no specific designation for Code 7. At best, if we were to go into a restaurant, we would radio in, "Firestone 18, Code 6 (out for investigation) at Station 23," for example. There were station designation numbers for various phone booths, restaurants, and other places where there were phone booths, all over the area—especially Winchell's donuts, and any drive-in restaurant in the area—and even into LAPD's area, which we bordered. The list was on the desk with the station number and phone number. We did not have walkie-talkies or hand-held radios during this era. Our radio was in the car. Our choices were very limited: we either were listening to the radio, or we were by a phone.

I pulled into the drive-in section of the A&W. Oh, yes . . . those were the days of drive-in restaurants where the waitresses were affectionately known as "carhops." There were some of them, like Stan's Drive-In up in the Hollywood area, where the carhops would be on roller skates.

I had acquired a few additional reports by this time, so it seemed all right to me. Just perfect for one of those great hamburgers, fries, and the famous A&W root beer in that well-known frosty mug. Let the stubby-pencil drill begin. Since I was going to be listening to my radio, I saw no need to radio in "Code 7." I would show it in my log as traffic observation, or something.

After having my well-balanced-all-the-food-groups lunch, I paid the check, yes, I said I paid for my food—including a tip for my carhop—and drove out. I started heading toward the northern end of my beat and decided to stop in at Fire Station 95 and have a quick cup of coffee. Coffee always did help my digestion.

Well, time got away from me. I looked at my watch and it was time to head back to the station, gas up my patrol car, turn in my reports, and call it a day. Hopefully.

I was working my way up to the station and decided that I should put something in my log to show I was doing something important. As if having coffee with the firemen and "getting information" wasn't important. One of the best log entries in those days was to run a 10-29 (check for wants) on a vehicle. Stolen cars were abundant. I didn't want to get into anything specific, so I decided to just run a car that I saw in a driveway. No way would it be a stolen, but it sure looked good on the log.

I saw a late model Cadillac in the driveway of a house with a nicely trimmed front lawn. Yep . . . I'll run this one. So I did. I jotted down the license number on my scratch pad and picked up the radio mike as I continued to drive on. I knew it would take a few minutes at least as this was the era of teletype—no computers, in either the station or especially in the cars. The dispatcher in the communications room in the Hall of Justice, would write down the license number, give it to another person who would insert it into a vacuum tube that went up to records where someone would enter the information on the teletype and send it to Sacramento. If all was going well, you could get your results in sometimes as little as ten minutes. If you were doing a "rolling 29"—actually following a suspicious vehicle—that would be a different story. Usually. Mine was just a regular 10-29. I kept on driving.

I had driven about a mile away when there were two beeps on the radio. That was an indication that something important was going to be coming out. I next heard the gravelly voice of the radio room sergeant. "Attention Firestone units. Any unit in the vicinity of Firestone 18 . . . identify." *Uh-oh. This has all the possibilities of me being in deep kim-chi. Mr. Murphy must be in the area)* . . . "Firestone 18 . . . what is your 10-20?" asked the radio room sergeant.

Hmmm. Could it have something to do with that Caddy I just ran? Where was it? Oh, yes . . . it was about a mile back. Yikes! I picked up the microphone and gave dispatch the approximate location where I had seen the Caddy.

The next radio transmission was an adrenaline-pumper supreme. The radio room sergeant came back on the air and gave the license number and description of the vehicle and added, "Subject vehicle was involved in a possible 187 PC," . . . and he continued with where the murder had occurred, date and time and then . . . "Firestone 18 . . . do you have suspects with your vehicle?" I recalled no one in the vicinity of the Caddy when I went by and advised him so. I hadn't seen anybody on the street or in any of the yards.

He went on to give the description of the suspect and that the suspect was considered armed and dangerous.

Oh, Shit!!! I did a quick calculation as to the exact location and put my radio car in a hard power u-turn. I was hell-bent for leather by now. I just hoped the vehicle was still there. I did some driving that would have made Mario Andretti envious. I made it back to the corner of the street where the Caddy was parked and it was still there. Whew! Talk about the "pucker factor." *What the . . . .? Oh, shit, here comes a guy carrying a long, very long, paper-wrapped object.*

"Firestone 18. Be advised that I now have a suspect approaching the suspect vehicle." I went on to give the description of the subject and that he was putting something in the car.

"Attention Firestone units . . . " the radio barked . . . "Units rolling to assist Firestone 18 . . . roll Code 3. Possible 187, suspect is approaching the vehicle. Units responding and ETA?"

The suspect had not noticed me or my radio car parked about fifty feet from him. I unracked the shotgun, took a stance behind the hood of my car, aimed very carefully and yelled "Freeze, A*$&^%#>!*e." He straightened up, looked at me, then looked back in his car—where I would soon discover his shotgun was in the paper wrapping—looked back at me again, and then put his hands in the air. At the same time I heard the sweet sound of sirens approaching. Other units had arrived and the suspect was taken into custody without incident. Of course, this would happen at end of watch resulting in paperwork: Arrest report, impounded vehicle report, booking the suspect . . . and of course . . . re-writing my log entry.

I learned one important factor: not all things are what they appear to be. Fortunately I used pencil on my log which made it easy to change my entry from "Suspicious Vehicle, no wants" to "Felony Arrest, see Report # . . ."

Mr. Murphy sometimes lets the good guys win.

OH NO! NOT MY NEW CAR!

— Harry Penny —

LOS ANGELES COUNTY SHERIFF'S DEPARTMENT
FIRESTONE STATION (#1), CIRCA 1966

It was a nice day in south-central Los Angeles. My partner, Brad Mills, and I were working the PM shift (3 PM to 11 PM) and had just reported in for briefing. We went over to the assignment board and noted that we would be working the south end in car 18 and then took a seat at the briefing table. The acting watch sergeant (A/Sgt.) was a seasoned deputy who would fill in when the sergeant was on a day off. He was a demon with a red pencil when reviewing reports. I often kidded him that he could pick "fly specks out of pepper." Each time he handed me back one of my reports it looked like a blotter at a blood donor location. He took roll call, passed on the latest briefing information, and gave us special attention regarding a recent series of auto thefts in the area.

We left the briefing room and got our gear, the LAPD Hot Sheet, a shotgun, some new flashlight batteries, and keys to our radio car, and went out to the parking lot. On the way we saw the A/Sgt. standing next to a brand new car. With him were the watch commander and the patrol sergeant. The A/Sgt. was telling them that he had just picked it up. He had parked it on an angle covering two parking spaces to make sure that one of the other station personnel didn't accidentally bump into it. Our radio car was almost next to his new car. He gave Brad and me the "eagle eye" when we approached.

I was "booking" that night, which meant that I had to shake down the radio car—checking for any damage, removing the rear seat to make sure that no contraband was left in it from any suspects (they would stuff things between the seat so that they wouldn't be caught with anything when they were being booked) and then checking to make sure all of our equipment was in good working order. After completing this, I took the shotgun from my partner, checked it again (we would always do a double check just to make sure there wasn't a round in the chamber—I had already been through that experience) and then secured it in the shotgun rack. As I was doing this, the A/Sgt. said, jokingly, "Don't forget, Penny, you still owe me a shotgun shell from that last incident." This made for a few chuckles from the guys who were in the vicinity.

Brad and I then left and proceeded down to our area. On the way down we heard one of the Willowbrook units get a "hot call" and since we were about two blocks away I radioed our location and indicated we would handle the assist.

We arrived at the call at the same time the handling unit did. It was a brawl between four guys and involved broken beer bottles, a knife, and other implements that can put serious entries into a victim's medical record. Two other units had rolled by and stopped to assist when they saw what was going on.

It resulted in all four of them being "hooked and booked." We transported two of the suspects back to the station and booked them. The actual report would be completed by the handling unit. That done, we went back out to our car and started to leave. But as we passed the A/Sgt.'s new car, I got an idea.

Brad had just gotten a fresh cup of coffee and was in the process of taking a sip when I told him what I had come up with. I just barely made it out of the way before Brad started spitting out his coffee as he began laughing.

We had to figure out a way to get the A/Sgt.'s keys to the new car so we could unlock the door. I left that up to Brad. (If you ever saw the movie *Operation Petticoat* you might recall Tony Curtis in his role of being able to obtain just about anything by employing methods that no one else could come up with. Brad was the department's version of Tony Curtis, and forty years later, still is to this day.)

A few minutes later Brad returned with the keys to the car. We were in business. We quickly unlocked the driver's door and then Brad hustled back into the station to replace the keys.

We looked around and at that particular moment there was no one in the area. We pushed the car out from its parking spot and then continued pushing it all the way up to the back doors of the station. It was only about seventy-five feet or so, but it seemed like seventy-five miles. Luckily no other units had pulled into the station and no one had come out of the station either. It was like we had all the time in the world to complete our task.

The back doors leading into the station opened inward only so that anyone leaving the station had to pull the doors toward them to exit. This was just another small safety feature just in case a prisoner tried to run out of the station.

Once this was done, we went to the door that led into the detectives' area and went inside and used one of the phones. Brad called the main radio room (Station A), which was located downtown in the Hall of Justice, and spoke with the sergeant. We knew him, and Brad told him what we were doing. He thought it was funny and went along with our plan. I went back outside and grabbed the radio mike from our car.

"Firestone 18 . . . 10-29 (check for wants) on California plate . . . " and I gave the plate number of the A/Sgt.'s car.

Brad went over to where he could see the A/Sgt. in his office and signaled me, letting me know that the A/Sgt. was busy at his desk going over the arrest reports that the other unit had brought in and he was very attentive with his red pencil. I hoped that he would be so involved that he would not pick up on my request for the

10-29 on his own plate as there was a radio speaker right behind the desk. Luck was with me.

About five minutes later the radio dispatcher came back, as pre-arranged with the radio room sergeant.

"Firestone 18 . . . what is your 10-20 (location?)" came the voice of the radio room sergeant. I gave some intersection down in our area.

"Firestone 18 . . . No wants on your vehicle. Stand by for R/O (registered owner) information." A slight pause then "Firestone 18 . . . the registration comes back to a . . . " and he gave the description of the A/Sgt.'s new car and his name and the station address.

"Firestone 18 . . . 10-4" I replied. I then continued on to request a tow truck, stating that the car had been stripped and abandoned, and gave the location.

By this time other deputies, including the watch commander and the patrol sergeant, had come out and I explained to them what we were doing. Fortunately, they thought it was kind of funny too. Luck was really on my side that night.

Almost immediately, as I put the mike back in the car, the rear doors to the station flew open and the A/Sgt. came out at breakneck speed screaming, "Oh no! Not my new car!" for about five steps and then came to an abrupt stop as he literally ran right into the front of his car.

Once he had calmed down, he started laughing almost hysterically. He knew he had been had.

"Firestone 18 is 10-8," I radioed in and we went back to work.

He and I got along very well and in 2005, we saw each other at a reunion. He gave me his enormous bear hug as he said, with a grin . . . "You still owe me that shotgun round."

WHERE'S YOUR CAR?

— Harry Penny —

LOS ANGELES COUNTY SHERIFF'S DEPARTMENT
FIRESTONE STATION (#1), CIRCA 1966

My partner and I were working the PM shift (3 PM to 11 PM). Our radio call sign was 15-David. Our beat was in the Willowbrook district. My partner was driving that night and I was the "book-man," the guy who had to do all the writing. In those days all reports were printed in longhand, in pencil, and in the narrative format. *Computers? What's that? Dashboard writing light? Huh?* Nope . . . at night when we had to do any writing, we either had to cradle our flashlight under our arm and then try to write or turn the spotlight on, aim it up toward the inside of the window, and use the reflection of the light hitting the window. It may have looked odd, but it worked.

The call originated from our station. It came in to the "complaint deputy" at the front desk. The complaint deputy was assigned to answer the phones and take all of the information from the person calling. He wrote it down and gave it to the dispatch deputy, who then picked up a red phone at his desk. The phone was connected directly to the radio room located in the Hall of Justice in downtown Los Angeles. No dialing was needed. It would be picked up by the dispatcher who was responsible for handling a certain area of stations, in this case Firestone, East Los Angeles, Lennox, and Lakewood. The complaint deputy also had a radio speaker at the desk, as did the watch sergeant and watch commander, and would monitor the radio transmissions. He would give the dispatcher the exact words and the dispatcher would repeat the transmission, word-for-word.

We were about an hour into the shift when the call came out over the radio: "Attention Firestone units. Firestone 15-David handle, 15, assist. 211, shots fired . . . 901-S." We had a robbery in progress and an ambulance rolling. The dispatcher continued giving the name of a liquor store and the address and the name of the ambulance company. This was not an unusual call for Firestone units. Hardly a shift went by without at least one of these calls coming in.

We were only a few blocks away. I reached over and grabbed the radio microphone from its hook on the dashboard and acknowledged the call, giving the dispatcher a one-minute response time, "15-David, 10-4, ETA 1."

Our radios had only two frequencies: frequency two was where we could only transmit to, and receive from, the dispatcher at the communications control room. We could not talk car-to-car unless we changed to frequency one. The station, however, was able to monitor all of the calls.

Unit 15 radioed immediately that they were tied up on another call. At that time another Firestone unit, 16, radioed in that they would assist and gave an ETA of eight minutes.

"15-David—handle Code 3, Firestone 16 is rolling Code 3 also, ETA 8," came the voice from the radio dispatcher.

My partner hit the red lights and siren and punched the gas. A block away he killed the siren and we made the standard "silent-approach." I keyed the mike and said "15-David, 10-97" (arrived on scene) and threw the mike on the dash for easier access later.

We were very familiar with the area and knew the liquor store was the second building from the corner. A "standard" approach was to pull up and park the car close to, but not in front of the building, which in this case we parked right on the corner.

I unlocked the shotgun rack, grabbed the shotgun and racked one into the chamber as I got out of the car. My partner started running back along the street to the alley behind the buildings so he could get to the rear and we could contain the building. He would be able to see two sides of the building and I would be able to see the other two sides. We would not be able to be in contact with each other as those microphones you see on police officers today did not exist during this era. I ran over to the street side of the building and put my back against the wall, keeping my eye on the front of the liquor store. No sooner than my back hit the wall, I saw the liquor store clerk come out of the front door holding his arm, which was bleeding. He had been shot. He saw me and said, "He's gone," and tried to point down the street. I went over to the patrol car and grabbed the mike. "Firestone 15-David, Code 4, suspect GOA (gone on arrival) . . . 211 info will follow."

The victim and I then went back into the liquor store. I went to the back door and saw my partner and told him the suspect was gone. A quick search of the adjacent area was negative. The time that had elapsed for this was less than thirty seconds

I obtained the suspect's physical description and type of weapon used and went back out to the patrol car to put out the broadcast information. We did not have individual portable radios in those years. The only radio we had was in our patrol unit.

It was wired into the ignition in such a way that the ignition had to be on for the radio to work. The broadcast would go to central dispatch. I picked up the microphone and requested an emergency clearance so I could give out the initial information which would be relayed from central dispatch to all units.

"Firestone 15-David, 10-33 for 211 information." Since the victim did not see which way the suspect had gone, I said the suspect had fled possibly on foot in an unknown direction. Further information would follow as it was obtained.

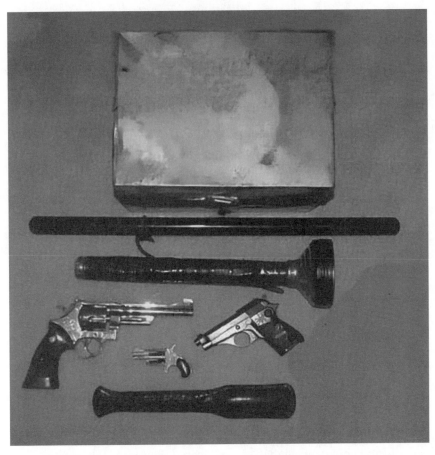

What the well equipped FPK deputy carried in the early 60s—patrol can, flashlight, service revolver, nightstick, backup gun, and "Gonzalez Sap." Photo courtesy of Jack Miller, LASD (Ret).

"10-4, 15-David. Attention all units, special attention to Firestone units. 15-David advises a 211, 245 just occurred . . . " The dispatcher continued repeating the information I had just given.

Just as I was getting out of the patrol car, another deputy approached me and said, "Hey, Harry! Where did you guys park? We heard you go 10-97 but didn't see your car."

"What are you talking about? We parked right here" I said as I pointed to the car.

"That's not your car. We just parked there and were looking for you."

I started to argue and then I looked in the back seat. We didn't have caged units and we would put our coats, helmets and our patrol cans in the back seat. Each of us had our own way of marking our patrol cans. Mine was definitely not in the back seat.

Uh-oh. Aw, shit! The bastard stole my car! (You may recall when I said that our radios were wired into the ignition which meant that the keys were left in the ignition and the motor running). Not a good thing at this time.

Using my keen powers of detection, I now figured out why we could not locate the suspect. *Duh!* I would later learn that he had waited until I had gone in the store with the owner then came out of his hiding place, a convenient dumpster next to the building, saw a nice shiny black and white car with pretty red lights on top and the motor running. Beats running away on foot. You guessed it. The crook stole my car.

I reached back for the microphone. "Firestone 15-David, 10-33 for additional 211, 245 information." "Go ahead 15-David."

"15-David . . . be advised that suspect may possibly be driving a 503 (stolen vehicle) described as a 1965 Ford, four-door sedan, black with white doors, with Los Angeles County Sheriff decals on the side doors and emergency lights on top. License number to follow."

When the radio dispatcher keyed her microphone to put out the additional information I could hear raucous laughter in the background along with other radio cars commenting to dispatch such as "How can we tell? There are a lot of those vehicles in the area" . . . and again lots of chuckles. Finally the radio room sergeant came on and said, "Simple stupid, the driver won't be wearing a uniform."

A few minutes passed but it seemed like hours. Not only had I obtained all of the information for my report, the ambulance had come and treated the store owner, but the addition of having my radio car stolen caused the patrol sergeant and the patrol lieutenant to respond. This was turning into quite an unusual situation even for Firestone.

During this time, one of our other units had observed the suspect driving my patrol car and a pursuit started. They just had to put that over the air. They only chased him a few blocks when he suddenly pulled into a driveway and jumped out of the car and ran into a house.

Unfortunately for me the suspect didn't turn the motor off or put it in park. That meant the car was still in gear and continuing to roll . . . right into the rickety, old, wooden one-car garage, through said garage, out the back wall of said garage and came to a sudden stop against a tree that was about five feet behind the garage. The red-lights and siren, which had been mounted on a bracket on top of the car, had been higher than the garage door were now hanging over the side door being held only by the wires. (When a moving object strikes an immovable object, something is going to give.) The nice shiny black paint was now marred with various coats of white paint from the garage, brown paint from the inside of the garage, several other colors from paint cans in the garage that had not been sealed tightly, and a fresh indentation in the shiny bumper which had managed to stop the tree from smashing into the grill and the hood.

They arrested the suspect, who was only fifteen, and recovered the gun, the money, and oh, yes . . . my car.

Yep! It was a very long shift that night. And a topic of conversation for many more days (years, to be more realistic) to come.

"DIAL-A-PRAYER"

— Harry Penny —

LOS ANGELES COUNTY SHERIFF'S DEPARTMENT
FIRESTONE STATION (#1), CIRCA 1966

Firestone station had a reputation for being the fastest station within the Patrol Division of the Los Angeles County Sheriff's Department. It was said that Firestone was actually the third busiest police/sheriff's station in the United States when measured by the number of calls per officer. Not all deputies who came to Firestone actually made the cut. Most of them did and those in this category were a different breed of patrol deputies. Firestone station was located at 7901 South Compton Avenue at Nadeau Street in south-central Los Angeles. One of the patrol areas, Willowbrook, almost encircled the LAPD area called Watts. Those of you who remember the Watts Riots in August of 1965 will recall that Firestone was very thoroughly involved.

I had the fortunate opportunity to work with almost every deputy there at one time or another. Several deputies were veterans of Korea and Vietnam. In Naval aviation the pilots and crew-members each have a particular nickname they use as their call sign. Many of the Firestone deputies also had nicknames. One in particular, whose real name I won't use because I haven't received his permission, was not only a good cop but very muscular—I think when he was born his muscles had muscles—and very innovative. I called him Dial-a-prayer.

We were working the PM shift (3 PM to 11 PM) in the Willowbrook area and our call sign was Firestone 15-David.

The riots had been over for a few months but, needless to say, things were still very tense. We had three other units, 15, 15-Adam and 15-Boy. 15 and 15-Adam were the actual beat cars. 15-Boy and 15-David were assigned as back-up units. They were known as the "PR" cars. Our station captain, Captain Dargan, implemented the cars with the explicit instructions that they would each be made of a three-man team: one white, one black, and one Latino. Both of my partners were college graduates, very articulate, and downright great cops. I was extremely proud to have been chosen to work with them. We were working a four-and-two schedule (four days on and two days off). So for two days I would work with one deputy and then two days the other deputy, and then they would work together on the two days I was off. We would not be assigned any calls per se such as any calls requiring reports. Our main function was just to talk to the citizens, merchants, and be available to roll as a backup.

It was policy, at that time, to roll two units on every call. Once the situation was assessed then the second unit would either remain, or, if all was Code 4, they would go back and patrol in the vicinity, never being too far away . . . just in case.

We assisted 15-Adam with a "family 415" (family disturbance now known in the politically correct arena as domestic violence). It was over very shortly. He thumped on her, she retaliated with a cast iron skillet to his head. No way to kiss this one off. "Hook 'em and book 'em" time. We took him, they took her. Oh this was going to be another doozy of a night.

After booking him into the station we were getting ready to leave when the watch sergeant called us into his office. He had something for us. One of the other units had spotted a well-known pimp, I'll call him John Paul Jones, driving in the Willowbrook/Athens Park area. Sarge gave us a felony warrant for his arrest. It seemed that he had decided to get a little rough with one of his new "ladies" that he had taken into his stable and her boyfriend didn't like it one bit. You can imagine how that went over. Not a good idea. It is best not to bring a knife to a gun fight. So we had this felony attempt 187 (penal code for murder) warrant.

Dial-a-prayer and I decided to hit the favorite haunts as John Paul Jones' car was very easy to spot; a '64 Caddy El Dorado convertible, candy-apple red with a white top and twin spotlights on the corners of the windshield. No such luck. His car was nowhere to be seen. So . . . time to cruise the neighborhood.

After about an hour of cruising the residential streets and alleys it was getting time to get some coffee. I was driving and so I headed for the local Winchell's donut shop. Where else? That was when Dial-a-prayer spotted John Paul Jones' car. Oh, yes . . . this was our lucky day. Mr. John Paul Jones was standing next to the car talking to a member of the female gender.

"Just pull up as if we were going to pass him but do it slow," said Dial-a-prayer.

Just as we were passing Mr. Jones and his car, Dial-a-prayer yells out the window in a voice loud enough for both Mr. Jones and his companion to hear, "Hey, Sam! . . . Hey Man! . . . How goes it? Stop the car, partner. I just saw a friend of mine."

I barely had the car stopped when Dial-a-prayer throws open the door and starts walking toward the couple. *Oh, shit! Now what?*

Dial-a–prayer yelled back to me, "Hey, pard . . . all's OK. Jus' talkin' to a friend of mine." He put his hand in the air with four fingers raised indicating it was Code 4. So I pulled the car over to the curb, legally parked it, and then got out just as if nothing was going on. I could hear the conversation as I approached them.

"Who you talkin' to, pig?" said Mr. Jones.

"Hey, Sam . . . don't get an attitude, man. Just 'cause we ain't seen each other for a long time don't mean I forget all them good times. You don't look like you have changed any, man." Dial-a-prayer then leaned against the shiny Cadillac which almost caused Mr. Jones to have a heart attack.

"Whachoo talking about? . . . Hey, get off my ride, man . . . don't you be putting no marks on my short and my name ain't Sam."

"Ah, c'mon, Sam . . . don't give me that shit. Just because I have this here uniform on don't mean that I ain't the same guy I was in school." Dial-a-prayer was a very articulate-speaking individual, but in this situation I knew his college English professor would cringe if he heard Dial-a-prayer speaking that way. He went into the talk that was prevalent throughout the south L.A. area.

"I done tol' you man, my name ain't Sam!" said John Paul Jones, in a somewhat agitated manner.

"Is you sure you ain't Sammy Iverson?"

"You damn straight I ain't no Sam . . . or . . . , Iver whateverson. My name is John Paul Jones!" His attitude was turning uglier each time he spoke.

By this time I had seen Dial-a-prayer reach into his pocket, pull out a coin—which was always a dime—and put it in his left ear. *Uh-oh! I knew what was coming next.*

It is extremely important whenever getting ready to place anyone under arrest to try and avoid injury to either the officer/s or the subject. We both saw Jones start clenching his fists and assuming a combative stance. Not a good thing.

"Hey, Pig! . . . wha' dat dime shit in yo' ear?" said John Paul Jones as he pointed to Dial-a-prayer's ear.

"Oh, this? Well, it's for you," he said as he took it out of his ear and held it up so John Paul Jones could see it. Then he dropped it on the ground. John Paul Jones, not being the brightest bulb in the lamp, bent down to pick it up and said, "Whachoo you mean fo' me?"

"We got a warrant for John Paul Jones and since you say you're him it's for you to call yo' momma, call yo' attorney . . . or you can Dial-a-prayer, asshole," and with that Dial-a-prayer unloaded his right fist from the ground floor and hit John Paul Jones with such force that it lifted him off his feet and he fell back on to his nice shiny car . . . unconscious. Dial-a-prayer calmly reached over, handcuffed Mr. John Paul Jones and then slung him over his shoulders as if he were a side of beef. This was some sight to see as Dial-a-prayer carried him over to our radio car and deposited him in the back seat.

We were three blocks away when John Paul Jones came back into the world of consciousness.

The watch sergeant had to constrain his facial expressions when John Paul Jones was trying to explain how he "was given a dime to call his mama and then got hit with a club or somethin."

We booked him and went 10-8.

HEY, CROOK! OR "PR" IS NOT MY STRONG SUIT

— Harry Penny —

LOS ANGELES COUNTY SHERIFF'S DEPARTMENT
FIRESTONE STATION (#1), CIRCA 1966

I was working a fill-in/vacation relief one night and got assigned to work 15 PMs with another deputy who was quite often referred to as "Firestone's Mayor of Willowbrook." He was a "very seasoned" deputy and well respected by not only the station personnel but also many of the citizens in our patrol area. (Well, maybe it was a little more like the citizens were somewhat intimidated by him.) I had ridden with him before when I was a cadet in the academy and was assigned as a ride-along during one of my weekend assignments.

About 10:15 PM we were driving north on Alameda. My partner was driving and I was booking and had finished all of my reports. We were just taking our time and looking for something to put in as a log entry while waiting to head back to the station and end of watch. I saw a car parked over by one of the auto wrecking yards on the west side of Alameda. I pointed it out to my partner who turned on the spotlight and pointed it at the car. The wind-wing—back in those days cars and trucks had a small separate window in front of the driver's and passenger's windows; they were real convenient to allow ventilation without having to roll the full window down—had been broken and there was a gaping hole where the glass had been. He turned the spotlight and pointed it to the ground below the door and the broken glass glittered on the ground.

He made a u-turn and we pulled up behind the car. It had been raining earlier in the evening and the ground was muddy. We got out of the car and noticed muddy footprints on both sides of the car. A visual check revealed that the radio had been forcibly removed from the dashboard—wires hanging down and frayed ends were a good indicator. I ran a 10-28/29 on the plate and it came back showing the R/O—registered owner—lived in the northern end of the San Fernando valley about thirty-five miles north of us. There were no wants on the plate. That didn't mean that it hadn't been stolen, it probably just hadn't been reported yet.

We got back in the car and headed back toward the station. About six blocks later we see this young fellow doing the "Willowbrook shuffle"—a particular style of walking—on the east side of the street. We both noticed that his tennis shoes were very muddy and the sidewalk was dry and had no evidence of mud.

My partner tapped the horn and yelled out, "Hey, CROOK!"

The young man did the usual: looks at us then looks around in all directions and then back at us as if to say, "You mean me?"

"Stay right there, stupid!" yells my partner, as he pulls another U-ey and stops the car just inches away from the young man. We both get out of the car. I am 6'2", 185 pounds and my partner is bigger and heavier than me. He is towering over this clown who was probably all of about 5'6" and 130 pounds.

"Where're you going?" asks Doug.

"Where am I going?"

"Yeah, where are YOU going?"

"Oh, jus' goin' home. I jus' lef' my girl's house and goin' home."

"Where's the radio?" (So much for probable cause.)

"I din't take no radio from that car!" says the kid in a shaky voice.

Doug turned and looked at me and said, "I am the judge and you are the jury. I say he is guilty. Don't you agree?"

In my attempt to control my laughter I answered with my standard-issued-Firestone-get-their-attention voice, "Yes sir, Judge. He is guilty."

My partner turned back to him and said, "You heard the jury and I think you deserve the death penalty."

The little crook's eyes got as big as saucers. He couldn't believe this was happening to him.

My partner looked down at him and said in an unusually soft voice, "Turn around and lay across the hood, crook!" while at the same time he unsnapped his holster.

The crook was starting to shake and sob. My partner motioned for me to go get a firecracker from my patrol can which I did. All this time my partner was telling the crook how it was against the laws of nature to lie to the police.

I came back with the firecracker and my partner nodded for me to light it which I did.

The firecracker exploded! The crook jumped almost across the hood of the radio car and screamed, *"Gets me a amblance. Them other mo' fo's is in them bushes."* At this time two other young men came out, dropped the radio, and other items and did a rapid "ankle-express" in opposite directions.

When the crook realized he was alive he looked at us and my partner and I were laughing so hard he took off running like a scalded cat.

I quickly scratched out a report of "found property." We gave the information regarding the car to the oncoming crew.

Firestone 15 is 10-7.

WHAT'S OUR 10-20, TRAINEE?

— Harry Penny —

LOS ANGELES COUNTY SHERIFF'S DEPARTMENT
FIRESTONE STATION (#1), CIRCA 1966

A training officer (T/O) in Patrol Division was a position that most of the deputies at Firestone sought after, even though there was no extra pay. We had all been trainees ourselves at one time and had then served as regular patrol deputies for about a year or so. Firestone station had the reputation as being the busiest and fastest station of all of the fourteen substations in Los Angeles County. The assignments were made by the station captain upon recommendation from the sergeants and lieutenants. I was fortunate enough to be selected as a training officer.

I would be assigned to the EM shift (Early Morning) working in civilian terms the graveyard shift (11 PM to 7 AM). This is usually the slowest shift at several stations, but Firestone was not one of them. If it were to be slow it would be between the hours of 4:30 AM and 6:00 AM and that depended on the day of the week.

Weekends were the busiest on the EM shift. It was a good shift to break in a trainee. The bars closed at 2:00 AM and you can imagine what situations would arise: anything from a plain drunk to fights, assaults, drunk driving, responding to the numerous silent burglar alarms, robberies, and on occasion, even murder. There was no such thing as a "routine" call.

I got to the station early before briefing and met with the watch sergeant. I was told that I would be working various beats so that my trainee would get the advantage of learning all of the areas in the 41.25 square miles. That is a feat in itself. Our northern boundary was roughly 58th Street and Central Avenue and down to Lomita Boulevard (roughly 250th Street). A major western portion of our area was bordered on the city of Los Angeles, which is covered by LAPD. A prime example was Central Avenue. On the west side it was LAPD territory and directly across the street it was LASD territory. Sound confusing? You're not alone. There were other cities such as Hawthorne, Gardena, Wilmington, Harbor City, Long Beach, and Compton, to name a few. Somewhere in our district we would border one of those cities.

One of the required items, which all deputies carried, in addition to the maps prepared by the department that outlined our individual reporting areas, was a *Thomas Guide* map. That was a life saver. With an area the size of ours, we had four different 8 1/2 by 11 inch map sections. It was faster, easier, and the best way to refer to the *Thomas Guide* to find a particular location.

After talking with the watch sergeant I went to the locker room, changed into uniform and got ready for briefing. I was ready to meet my new trainee. We would be partnered up for the next three months.

Roll call was held and the patrol sergeant glanced at me twice. He was amazed that I was not rushing in at the last minute, out of breath, and just making it on time. Then he realized that only applied to me when I was assigned to day watch—not exactly my favorite shift. I don't do mornings very well.

My trainee had been previously assigned to Corrections Division at Wayside Honor Rancho for the past two years. His only experience in Patrol Division was when he attended the academy. During academy training, after the fifth week, the cadets would be sent out to the various patrol stations for the weekend and ride along as either the second or third man in a radio car. My trainee had never been to Firestone station. This was going to be culture shock and an eye-opening experience for him. I would see to that.

So here he was. Brand new uniform, shoes highly polished, and his leather gear, which was still somewhat new, that "squeaked." He didn't wear it while working corrections. He had his brand new metal "patrol can"—a metal file box that is designed to keep papers and documents in, you know the kind, I'm sure. These file boxes are found in any stationery store—complete with dividers. Oh yes, he was ready. He had arrived at the station, even earlier than me, and had been given some advice by other deputies as to what things he should put in the box: blank daily log sheets, blank report forms, and the myriad of other forms we would use, scratch paper, extra pencils, a small pencil sharpener, extra flashlight batteries, extra ammunition, and of course, his trusty new *Thomas Guide*. (I would-n't tell him about carrying firecrackers until much later.)

He looked like he was trying to be a poster model for the Sheriff's Department.

After briefing we checked out the keys to our patrol car, went to the armory and got a shotgun, and proceeded out to the parking lot. I was somewhat apprehensive about giving him the shotgun as I had had one sphincter-pucker-factor experience a few months earlier. My cadet trainee had blown the roof and the red lights off the top of my radio car when he was attempting to put the shotgun in the holder in the car. (That's another story in itself.)

My new trainee and I would have a very serious talk this time.

Just as we approached the door to go out and get our radio car, the station PA system blared out, "19 . . . check the desk for calls."

Ugh! This was not starting out good. This meant that we already had at least one call that had come in during shift change and needed to be handled as soon as we went 10-8. So much for showing him how to get to our area which was about seven miles away.

I told my trainee to go out in the parking lot and find our radio-car. That was an easy task as they all had specific numbers on the right rear of the trunk. (I did not give him the shotgun. I didn't give him the keys either. I wasn't taking any chances.) I went back to the desk and got the detail slips.

For our daily log purposes we had three classifications: (1) Call (calls which were received via radio while on patrol, (2) Detail (calls that would come into the station that had been received and were awaiting to be given to the units at briefing by the sergeant or by the desk personnel, and (3) Observations (OBS) which were situations that we observed and took some type of action during our patrol shift.

I don't recall the exact nature of the detail but it was one of those that had to be handled right away, such as a burglary report. In many cases, a call such as this would come in to the station right at shift change. The complaint deputy—the deputy assigned to the desk that took the phone calls and also any complaints from citizens who came into the station to make a report or such activity—would get the information and if it was determined that a unit did not need to respond immediately, would advise the caller that a unit would be sent from the station. As an example: if the situation had occurred earlier and the suspect or suspects were long gone, etc., but a report needed to be taken as soon as possible.

I recall that this particular detail was something like the victim had just returned home from work and found that his house had been burglarized sometime while he was at work.

I went out to the parking lot and saw my trainee standing almost at attention by our radio car. You may recall that I didn't give him the shotgun or the keys.

The first thing I did was unlock the car and tell him to lift out the back seat. Why, you ask? Suspects have been known to place guns, knives, syringes, baggies of dope, and various other items in the back seat of a radio car when they were being transported to the station. (Sometimes other cops—yours truly was no exception—would put a drunk in the back seat of another radio car instead of having to do the reports and booking.) Even though their hands were handcuffed behind them and they were secured to the seat by the use of the seat belt, they would find a way to wiggle around to get rid of these contraband items. It was standard operating procedure (SOP) for the deputies to check the rear seat area once they had the suspect at the station. If the deputy neglected this procedure it could be very embarrassing, to say the least. Or the worst-case scenario would be for another suspect to find a weapon in the rear seat and use it to injure or maybe even kill another deputy.

Once this was done and my partner had placed his gear in the rear seat, we went 10-8 and proceeded to contact our burglary victim, survey the scene, and take the report.

A little while later, after having made my first coffee and donut stop (very important, especially on this shift) I decided it was time to see just how aware my trainee was.

I was slowly driving through a residential area when I suddenly stopped the car in the middle of the block and said to my trainee, "OK, here's the scenario. We have just been shot at by someone and I have been hit. You need to get on the radio and get us back-up and an ambulance. What's our 10-20? Where are we?"

A look of surprise and horror came on his face. He had no idea. That was typical. I was just as confused when my training officer did the same thing to me when I was in training.

"Well, I guess the thing for you to do is get out of the car and find out where we are," I said.

He opened the door, got out, and went back to the street we had passed, shined his flashlight on the sign and noted the name of the street. I waited until he started back from the intersection then I put the car in drive and took off for the next block. I saw him in the rear view mirror as he began to run to try and catch up with me. I stopped in the next block and waited.

He got in the car, out of breath and told me the name of the street he had gotten from the street sign. "Nope," I said. "We are past that street." Just then we got a radio call and left the area.

After handling the radio call, I decided it was time for more "10-20" training. I stopped in the middle of a block and asked him where we were. Again, same response. Out the door and back to the street sign he went. Off again I went to the next block. This went on for about three or four more times. Each time he got more frustrated.

Now he began looking at each street sign we passed. He was okay as long as we were going slow but when I sped up and got on the Harbor freeway . . . well you can imagine what happened when I determined that there was no traffic close to us and pulled over to the side and stopped. I was in between two turnoffs. No signs in the vicinity.

Finally it was time to put an end to this aggravation. After all, this was his first night.

I told him that when he got out of the car in the residential area, instead of going to the street sign that was behind us, he should look ahead and go to the street we were approaching. In each of these instances I had purposely pulled up to within fifty feet of the next intersection. Bingo! The light came on.

WELCOME TO FIRESTONE OR DID THE PARADE LEAVE WITHOUT ME?

— Claude Anderson, LASD (Ret.) —

LOS ANGELES COUNTY SHERIFF'S DEPARTMENT
FIRESTONE STATION (#1), CIRCA 1958

I always looked back at my first few days at Firestone and even to this day (over forty years ago!) I have to laugh. I was working Main Office Transportation, driving the bus on the evening "south loop" (4 PM to midnight). I volunteered to be transferred to Firestone because I heard it was the "station to work if you wanted to do police work." I think I applied one day and two days later I was transferred!

Normally when one takes on a new assignment there are new surroundings, new faces, and new things to learn, and . . . anxiety! But one knows that the new supervisors will always greet you with a grin and a handshake and welcome you aboard. ARE YOU SERIOUS? AT FIRESTONE?

The date is December 8, 1958. I reported for the evening shift and was taken in to see the watch commander. He was known as "Iron Fist." He was a stocky men with a face like . . . forget that! He says . . . "What the hell do you want?"

Shaken a bit, I tell him, "I've just been transferred."

"What have you done?" he says.

I tell him, "I worked transportation, wayside, and Mira Lo . . . " when he interrupts and says "No! No! Not that crap! What kind of a 'beef' are you riding?"

When I told him I volunteered and never had any disciplinary problems, he went through the roof. I had never seen veins in a neck stick out so far.

"You're a liar!" he screamed. "Nobody works Firestone unless they are riding a beef." (Later I found out this is not true.) Then he tells me that Firestone is the third busiest station in the country as far as calls per car and crimes of violence—only the precinct in Harlem, New York and the precinct on the southside of Chicago were numbers one and two ahead of Firestone. Then he tells me, "You're the sorriest looking deputy I ever saw" and that I'm "not going to last a month!"

He asked me what my job was before some "idiot" gave me a badge. I told him I was an air policeman in the Air Force. He tells me to get ready to "re-enlist."

"What's that?" he says, pointing to the handcuff case on my Sam Browne belt. When I stumble out the words "hancu . . . " he goes on to say, "In my day it was considered 'sissified' to carry cuffs . . . you just knocked them in the head and drug 'em in!" He then calls in my training officer (T/O) . . . and I'm off for who knows where.

My T/O gives me the rest of the introduction and welcome . . . six words: "EYES OPEN, EARS OPEN, MOUTH SHUT!!!!" (Again, no "Welcome to Firestone!") "We're car 11 tonight," and he hands me the car keys and tells me to carry all his gear out to the car: shotgun, flashlights, clipboards, and a large metal box filled with report forms, and his lunch.

Ten minutes later I report back that I can't find the car in the parking lot! My T/O becomes violent! The lot is full of Black-and-White '57 Fords and I can't find one with this number! (He groans about being given another rocket scientist to train.) He points out a '56 Ford, gray in color in one corner of the lot with an orange-colored siren on the roof. (How was I to know?) The sheriff's star is pasted on the rear window. It's known as the "gray ghost" and the only car like it left at Firestone as the department went to black-and-whites in 1957.

My T/O is not happy as "real deputies drive black-and-whites." He tolerates me like you tolerate a cockroach in your kitchen. A trainee at Firestone is lower than, using the lieutenant's exact quote, "lower than seven layers of whale s**t in the deepest part of the ocean."

The rest of the shift I remember only the consistent groans and mumbling from my T/O. When I got home that night, the wife asked how I liked my new assignment. I answer, "I'm not really sure . . . wondering if the French Foreign Legion is still taking applicants."

Night two . . . car 11 (north end, evenings, 3 PM to 11 PM) . . . it should be noted that the duties of a trainee are to run after anyone who runs from us, climb any structure, jump any fence, change the flat tire for any woman driver who is alone, personally handle any situation with odors or toxic spills, get the coffee and donuts for everyone, and never attempt to speak to the general public. (A trainee never knows what he's talking about anyway.) "If a citizen asks you anything you are to nod towards the training officer."

That second night we received an assist call regarding "burglars now" at a food market on Florence Avenue Upon arrival, you know who climbs up on the roof! After walking around I trip over a guy-wire holding up a TV antenna. I fall forward at the edge of the building, hitting the edge diagonally across my body and I drop eight feet into the dumpster. (I would have been killed if I had hit my head on the steel edge of the dumpster.) The dumpster was filled with spoiled vegetables, sour mayonnaise, some type of orange salad dressing, lettuce, rotten tomatoes, and overripe bananas.

"Here's one now," yells some deputy and suddenly I'm being beaten around the head and shoulders by about five enraged deputies, swinging batons.

Someone (God bless him) found my cap on the ground and caused the others to see who they were swinging at. "It's Billy's (my

T/O) trainee!" the guy yells and suddenly I was left alone with my training officer glaring at me!

When I hit the edge of the roof, my badge was caught and the star actually folded in half like a clam. All the blue enamel filling was gone and I'm sure the California bear in the center looked scared.

Two burglars were caught by "real deputies" inside the building while my T/O, amid catcalls from the other deputies, took "Mr. Salad Dressing" back to the station.

Does he take me in the back door? No way! I'm led through the Detective Bureau, the Juvenile Bureau, past the secretaries, the main desk area, the watch sergeant's office and the watch commander . . . at least fifty people get to view my sorry condition.

Finally in the locker room, I looked in the full-length mirror and I scared myself. I was a complete mess! It looked like I was the target of about one hundred seagulls with diarrhea.

A hot shower and a clean uniform did wonders. I still had to report to the watch commander, however, for a replacement badge. The lieutenant whom I had encountered on my first night was off that night and another lieutenant ripped me over, a standard procedure, handed me a replacement badge, and sent mine into the shop.

It should be noted that at no time did anyone ever ask if I was hurt. And . . . I was! I had lumps on one side of my head, and I thought one collar bone was broken—it wasn't, just bruised—and one knee and ankle were not aligned too well. I think landing on a case of rotten eggs in the dumpster did that. But a trainee never shows pain—another rule passed on to me.

For the rest of the evening my T/O told me how embarrassed he was in front of his peers, how I embarrassed the station, the sheriff, the department, etc., etc. (Yeah and millions of Chinese too.)

When I got home that night, the wife took one look and said, "What happened to you? You look like you fell off a building!"

On my third night car 11 (3 PM to 11 PM), car 11-A calls for assistance regarding a family fight. We roll, along with cars 12, 12-A, 13, and 15, that had all just left the station. At the location, a neat frame home, a huge man is throwing deputies around in the living room like a dog shaking water off his back.

The man is 6'8", 400+ pounds, with a shaved head and a face only a mother could love. He is a drunk and a professional wrestler. No deputy dared pull a gun or attempt to hit him with a baton as he would have shoved it right up their nose! My T/O looks at me and says, "Go in there and throw yourself on the fire!"

Well, if the good Lord ever decided to give me a break, this was it! I knew this wrestler personally, unbeknownst to any of the deputies. I walked up to him and saw the recognition. I whispered his name and said "Follow me!" He gave a sigh and, like a little puppy dog, followed me out of the house and into the back seat of the radio car. He's apologizing like mad, saying how sorry he is, and that he never wants to hurt anybody, and apologized for getting drunk, etc.

None of the other deputies could believe this . . . him following me without me even placing an arm on him. Suddenly the "Mr. Salad Dressing" name was forgotten! (Eight deputies were frozen in time with their mouths open.) My T/O is one stunned deputy.

I told him that we were ready to go to the station as I slipped into the back seat with my prisoner. I could see my T/O adjust the rearview mirror so he could watch us, and his eyes were as big as saucers. Two other units fell into line behind us as an escort.

My T/O couldn't hear what we were talking about, as I was whispering. I told my prisoner that he was being arrested on a simple drunk charge and that I would personally call his son, also a professional wrestler, to come down and bail him out. "One favor," I say, "don't let anyone know we're friends. Just do as I say and everything will be okay."

We pull into the back of the building and we get out and I escort this giant inside. Now I'm 6'1" and 230 pounds and beside this man I look like a small undernourished boy!

I'm the only one booking the suspect—car 11-A said we could handle the call. I catch the rest of the station personnel peeking around corners. When I finished, I called the jailer and we placed the suspect in the drunk tank. As we leave I tell him that if he pulls any of the bars apart, or rips the door off, he's going to be charged.

"Yes Sir," he says. "Thank you for your kindness!"

The jailer almost faints thinking of this guy tearing the doors off.

Thank you for your kindness!!! Words unheard of around Firestone. Had the lieutenant I met my first day been on duty, he would have had a heart attack.

Outside, the deputies are waiting with a thousand questions. I just smiled and said I was just doing as my T/O told me. Of course, my T/O sucked this up like a sponge in a desert rainstorm. Other T/Os wanted to change trainees with him, but he said, "I don't know about this guy, but he's mine!"

Suddenly I gained a few layers of whale poop in that ocean and was allowed to enter the coffee room. I'm still "pond scum" but things are looking better. As we walk out of the station, the watch sergeant has to get in the last word, of course, yelling at my T/O for letting me bring a prisoner into the station unhandcuffed. My T/O tells him that cuffs aren't made that big. His wrists were as big as the sergeant's thighs and we did not have time to wait until a "cargo net" could be brought in from the shipyards in Long Beach. That took care of that!

My T/O and I worked together for four months and really bonded as a team. He was a great patrol deputy and I learned very much. I also learned that the sergeants and lieutenants were really "good guys just acting tough" to keep you on your toes and keep your guard up and not getting you killed.

I fooled that first lieutenant. I lasted more than a month. I spent twelve years at Firestone with seven of those years as a training officer. I finally retired after twenty-five years of service.

THE HANDCUFF SONG

— Claude Anderson, LASD (Ret.) —

LOS ANGELES COUNTY SHERIFF'S DEPARTMENT
FIRESTONE STATION (#1), CIRCA 1961

In 1961 while assigned to Patrol Division at Firestone station, I wrote a little song. I love music and love to play the piano. My partners and I had a lot of fun with the song through the years.

Imagine it's a quiet graveyard shift and the watch sergeant is almost ready to nod off. Suddenly the back door of the station flies open and the "Yahoo"[1] deputies come through singing and dragging a bewildered drunk driver in for booking. At the end of the song, both deputies do a little tap dance shuffle. Most sergeants (completely lacking in musical talent) just yelled for us to book'em and get out. But the rest of the station was awake!

We performed this once in the field while making an arrest with half the neighborhood looking on. But my partner, David Galceran, broke out with the song. Everybody thought it was unusual as they had never witnessed "singing deputies." Lots of smiles and giggles. One woman called it police brutality! (Another critic.)

Sung to the tune of *I'm Looking Over a Four-Leaf Clover,* here are the lyrics.

THE HAND CUFF SONG [2]

I've got some handcuffs,
Some brand new handcuffs,
That I haven't used before.
They're all chrome plated,
With a double lock too . . .
Oh how I wish . . .
To click them on you.
No need explaining,
The reason for detaining,
Just why I'm arresting you . . .
I've got some handcuffs,
Some brand new handcuffs . . .
That I haven't used before.

[1] Yahoo . . . (nothing to do with the internet service!) In *Travels to Several Remote Nations of the World,* writer Jonathan Swift describes Yahoos as the most unpleasant creatures on earth with a natural disposition for dirt. They live on the island of Houyhnhnms in the south Atlantic. Their leader is always the ugliest and most deformed.

[2] *The Handcuff Song,* copyright 1961 by C.J. Anderson #1922.

THE FAMOUS "BAT SIGNAL" FLASHES OVER WILLOWBROOK

— Claude Anderson, LASD (Ret.) —

LOS ANGELES COUNTY SHERIFF'S DEPARTMENT
FIRESTONE STATION (#1), CIRCA 1965

One of my favorite partners of all time was a Deputy named Victor Kretsinger. When he was assigned to me as a trainee, the lieutenant told me that I was going to be in for an experience as Victor brings new meaning to the word HYPER, and that psychological help would be provided by the county if I needed it.

Victor had the ability to come up with any dialect you can imagine. He could pass himself off as a Berlin police officer with years patrolling the autobahn or tell of his exploits as a Puerto Rico highway patrolman. Neither I nor the patrol sergeants would know what he would come up with next. He had the uncanny ability to spot burglaries, either in progress or just before the attempt was made. One month we led the entire station in "Felony Observations" thanks to him alone. I told the brass I was the only training officer who had a trainee as a training officer.

During the time when "Batman and Robin" first hit the TV, Victor decided that we would become "Batman and Robin." Victor could imitate, perfectly, that high-pitched whining, whimpering, sucking-up-to, voice of Robin. Naturally, I tried to imitate the flat, boring, understated monotone of Batman . . . complete with "Yogi Berra" type of sayings such as . . . "when you steal, you're taking things that don't belong to you" or "when you drive intoxicated, you're not sober," or "a criminal is a sick person and sickness makes me ill." (Enough of this!)

Victor had a rubber plastic-type device he would slip over the right spotlight on the radio car. When the light was turned on . . . WOW! The Bat Signal was produced on walls, buildings, and drunk drivers.

One evening while working car 15, it was still light and I was driving slowly down an alley when Vic saw some movement near a fence. We couldn't make it out but it looked like some type of animal perhaps caught in the fence.

We found two little boys lying on their stomachs with their little butts in the air trying to pull a bicycle under the fence. They might just as well have tried to pull a sixteen-wheeler through as the hole was only about a foot wide.

They turn around and see us and the first boy says the famous words, "Uh oh!" When asked what they were doing the second boy tries out excuse #1: "What bike? I'm just walking home from school."

Naturally a good deputy has to examine alibis and this one had two flaws—who mentioned anything about a bike and today was a Saturday!

Boy number one tries excuse #2: He "found" this bike and was going to take it home and try to find the owner. This excuse also seemed flimsy as the bike seemed to be already "home."

Then Victor comes out with that infamous Robin voice and says, "Golly gee whiz, Batman . . . it looks like we captured the bicycle miscreants. Looks like a long stay in the calaboose."

My stupid part of the act: "No, Robin. Our duty is not to punish. That's up to the judge in Gotham City. Our job is simple apprehension as . . . Evil is a bad thing."

These two little guys, (brothers seven and eight years old) now get very excited, asking if we were really Batman and Robin. Victor

HEY TRAINEE . . . ROBIN YOU AIN'T!

explained that when we are not in costume we patrol this area without our masks. Now both boys can't talk fast enough—nobody lies
to Batman and Robin. They tell us their names and point out a location where stolen bikes, radios, TVs etc., are stashed in a garage.
Vic's notebook gets a workout.

We drove our "almost bicycle thieves" to the local ice cream
parlor where we bought each of them a three-scoop cone, then . . .
home to grandmother.

When we pulled up at grandmother's house, she was sitting on
the front porch. Vic got out to talk to her first and I keep the two little guys in the car. She asked Vic, "What did those two little fools do
now?"

Vic told her the whole story and she had tears in her eyes from
laughing. She was a fine lady trying to raise two boys while their
mother worked odd hours as a waitress. Grandma went along with
the entire story and could believe the size of those ice cream cones
the boys had. She made sure they thanked "Batman and Robin" and
they promised to be good citizens of "Gotham City."

After we pulled away it was our turn to laugh. Perhaps we
helped a little? It's certainly not stuff you see on TV, but it's police

work nobody notices, and the satisfaction is ours alone. The next day, we learned that our juvenile detectives loaded up a pickup truck with recovered items.

The next night Vic and I passed a group of teenage girls and they all waved saying, "Hi, Batman and Robin." Now how did the word get out so fast? Must have seen Vic's "Bat Signal."

For the next few months I understand our units in that area never took another stolen bike report!

SEMPER PARATUS OR FIRESTONE WE HAVE LIFT OFF

— Claude Anderson, LASD (Ret.) —

LOS ANGELES COUNTY SHERIFF'S DEPARTMENT
FIRESTONE STATION (#1), CIRCA 1969

It seems that most of us were blessed with a certain sense of humor that saw us through the stressful situation that working Firestone threw at us. I was at a point that I pulled duties as vacation relief for the three court deputies and then took over as utility deputy for a six-month period.

I had the honor to work side-by-side with a great corrections officer named Oscar. Oscar had retired as a chief petty officer from the U.S. Coast Guard and had become a corrections officer. He was assigned to Firestone station.

Oscar assisted me in keeping the radio cars in working order and in supervising the twelve "trusties"—prisoners who were serving time and were not deemed to be an escape risk. These prisoners would be assigned to work at the various stations while serving their sentence. They washed the vehicles, changed the tires, and kept the cars gassed up.

Oscar always had a grin from ear to ear and was always there to assist anybody, from trainee to the undersheriff. I don't remember him ever being late for work or even taking a day off. Oscar was one dedicated officer.

Oscar, however, could not accept stupid orders or being ordered to do things he knew were wrong. He would not say anything, just get red in the face and appear like the steam whistle on his Coast Guard cutter . . . ready to blow!

One day he and I were going crazy trying to field enough units for the evening shift as several day crews had had some engine trouble and the units were kaput. That afternoon I was called to pick up a brand new unit (1969 Plymouth) at the shop downtown. When I arrived back at the station with the car, I was met by the watch commander who took the car keys from me and said that nobody was going to drive the car but him. He was getting ready to go out in the field and check on the troops. Far be it from me to say anything . . . I couldn't care less. But this set Oscar off to no end.

Our 10-Sam (designation for the field patrol sergeant) was given our "wreck of the week" to drive. We often did this, not that we had anything against the Sam units, but they don't usually go Code 3, and speeding is rare.

Oscar told the sergeant, "Don't go over forty, don't even think about turning off the engine, and one lollipop red light"— the term we used for the red light assembly on the top of the radio cars—"is out on the roof and a trusty is trying to find a replacement bulb."

The more Oscar thought about this new radio car sitting there the madder he got. Finally he said, "This does it!" He went to the trunk of his car and came back with a bright yellow cylinder. Picture this . . . a cylinder six inches long, one and a half inches in diameter, with a six-inch bare wire coming out of each end. The object was adorned with "chinese characters" and covered with a light coating of wax. Oscar raised the hood of the new radio car and attached the bare wires to two spark plugs. (I never interfere in what looks like some type of scientific experiment.)

Just as Oscar finished and closed the hood, another sergeant, our administration officer, came out to find out why the vehicles for the evening shift were all shot and asked, "Why isn't this new unit in service?"

We told him it was under the lieutenant's orders. We sweated this out as we could not let him move the unit. (We didn't want the surprise to be on him.) Fortunately he had no keys.

Finally the lieutenant came out and got in the car. We were watching from the garage office. When he turned the key, I was expecting a terrific explosion . . . something like the volcano "Krakatoa" when it erupted in the Java Sea in 1883. Not so. Have you ever chased a burglar running on a rooftop and he slipped and fell off? That's what it sounded like—a low "whrump." Then came the smoke so thick and pure white that if we had a space station in those days you could view it from outer space. It covered the entire parking lot and visibility was ZERO. Also, there was a high-pitched whistle that lasted for about thirty seconds.

At the first sound, the lieutenant did a tuck-and-roll somersault, flying out of the driver's side and hitting the parking lot running . . . right into the station! The detectives from the back room came out and immediately knew what happened.

HOW THIS BECAME A SAM—UNIT IS
ON A NEED—TO—KNOW BASIS ONLY.

The administration officer came out and Oscar told him it was a "manifold problem" and he would have a trusty fix it. The admin officer said nothing, just turned and walked back inside the station. The smoke cleared in about ten minutes and in looking under the hood, no evidence of the cylinder could be found. The lieutenant had left the keys in the car and Oscar drove it over to the gas pumps, then called 10-Sam to 10-19 (radio code for return to station). Oscar told him to test-drive this new vehicle just in case the "manifold problem" was not fixed! (Ha!)

We never heard a word from the lieutenant, and the admin officer kept a closed mouth about the incident. This unit became a "Sam unit" until we began getting more new cars.

As far as the lieutenant's tuck-and-roll somersault . . . in Olympic scoring I would have given him a nine.

I saluted our Coast Guard Chief—who once again had that wide grin. SEMPER PARATUS forever!

THE TOOTH FAIRY?

— Jack Miller, LASD (Ret.) —

LOS ANGELES COUNTY SHERIFF'S DEPARTMENT
FIRESTONE STATION (#1), CIRCA 1963

One night in late 1963, my partner and I were working the PM watch in car 11-Adam when we rolled to assist car 12 on a 415 —disturbance call—in the north end area around 95th and Croesus.

The disturbing party was a large female—Amazon would best describe her size. As we attempted to cuff her, she was knocked to the ground. I grabbed her arms and stepped over her to get a better position on her when she lunged up and bit the crotch of my uniform pants. Luckily she missed the vital organs which were in close proximity or I'd be singing falsetto today.

At any rate, my partner grabbed the 187 Gonzales—a particular style of leather sap not found in police uniform stores for a myriad of reasons—and applied it vigorously to the bridge of the suspect's nose.

She let go and we got her restrained sufficiently to place her in the back seat of the radio car where she proceeded to kick the crap out of the seat.

We transported her to the station where she was finally taken out of our hands. I then checked my trousers and found that she had bitten a hole in the crotch and, in the process, she had lost a tooth (false I think) in the bottom of the zipper.

I didn't keep the tooth.

I CAN'T WAIT TO SEE
HOW YOU WRITE THIS UP!

A NEW VERSION OF UP-A-TREE

— Jack Miller, LASD (Ret.) —

LOS ANGELES COUNTY SHERIFF'S DEPARTMENT
FIRESTONE STATION (#1), CIRCA 1962–1963

It was either late 1962 or early 1963 and my regular partner was off IOD—injured on duty—and I had a reserve deputy working with me. He enjoyed working with me and said I kept him awake, whatever the hell that meant. We were working car 11-Adam, PM watch. It was colder than a brass toilet in the Klondike. The deputy working the adjacent beat car, car 11, also had a trainee as a partner.

Car 11 received a call over the radio, of a "suspicious circumstances—unknown moaning" and gave the address. On a call like this we would go over to the edge of our beat closest to the location of the call to be ready to roll if backup was needed. However, due to the nature of the call, we couldn't resist responding to assist. We were closer than car 11 and we got there before they arrived.

When we arrived, we got out of the car and we could hear this god-awful sound coming from the outside and rear of the house. It sounded like a dying animal or one in extreme pain. With guns drawn, a round jacked into the chamber of the shotgun, and our six-cells (big flashlights) lit, we proceeded to investigate.

What we saw silhouetted in our flashlight beams was this beat-up black male about thirty years old or so, naked from the waist down, sitting on a tree stump, with his scrotum nailed to the stump, and a knife in his hand.

It seemed that he was caught screwing someone else's woman, and that person took grave exception to this activity. As the story went, three unknown black males accosted him, beat the crap out of him, stripped him, and nailed his scrotum to the stump. One of the suspects gave him the knife and told him if he wanted loose he'd have to cut his balls off. (That's a visual in itself.) According to the victim, he was also told that if he identified any of them they would return and cut the rest of his private parts off.

Since this was 11's call, we let them handle it, which was just as well as my partner and I couldn't stop laughing long enough to do anything.

The Fire Department was called, as well as an ambulance. After some deliberation the firemen, to a chorus of loud screams from the

YOU SHOULDN'T HAVE THREATENED TO ARREST
HIM BECAUSE HE HAD A SWITCHBLADE.

victim, sawed the tree trunk off. He and the tree trunk had to be lifted into the ambulance, also to a chorus—an octave higher as I recall—of screams, and was transported to the hospital. (I can just imagine the looks on the emergency room personnel when the ambulance arrived at the hospital.)

My partner and I were still laughing when we got back to the station.

THE CONFUSION

— Jack Miller, LASD (Ret.) —

LOS ANGELES COUNTY SHERIFF'S DEPARTMENT
FIRESTONE STATION (#1), CIRCA 1961–1962

It was either '61 or '62 on a Friday night Early Morning shift (11 PM to 7 AM) on the desk. I had been working as complaint deputy on the PM shift (3 PM to 11 PM) and then doubled back onto the Early Morning shift with Henry (Buddy) Barrett as dispatcher. The phones had been lit up all night; it was either a full moon or the county welfare checks had come out or both.

During a lull in the action, Barrett picked up a call around 2:00 or 3:00 am from an unknown female who inquired if he knew the phone number to the local witch doctor. Now Buddy, not being one to let an opportunity like this get away from him, motioned me to push the button on my phone so I could listen. He asked what the problem was. The female explained that she and her neighbor had been fighting all day and she had put the "confusion" on her, and she needed to have the witch doctor break the hex. Buddy tells her not to worry, that the Sheriff's Office (it was an office then, not a department) had the manual with the recipe on how to break the confusion hex. He asked her to hang on the line while he found the right page. By this time I was laughing and it was hard to keep it quiet.

127

Photo courtesy of Jack Miller LASD (Ret.).

Buddy came back to the line and began to recite the recipe. "One chicken with neck just wrung complete with legs feathers and guts boiled with a combination of mice tails and snails (the more the better) in either red mountain or T-bird depending on whether the hexor and/or the hexee was light-skinned or dark-skinned."

By this time I was out of control I was laughing so hard. Buddy goes on and on until he finally starts to lose it and has to break it off and tells her that was it and it should work. She thanked him and asked his name and then the poop-head tells her "Deputy Miller." I could have killed him.

Two or three nights later I'm back out in the field working the north end in one of the Adam cars, 11-A or 12-A. We had an occasion to roll back to the station, either 10-15 (prisoner in custody) or on a chow run, whatever. In any event the same Buddy Barrett tells me that a package was dropped off at the desk for me. He then hands me a dirty paper sack with a voodoo doll in it. I'll leave it to your imagination where the pin was stuck. I can only guess that the recipe for the anti-hex didn't work and this was her way of getting even. These were the days before name badges so I wasn't worried, I just blended into the sea of tan and green. Some time later I did get even with Barrett, but that's another story.

WHERE ELSE WOULD IT BE?

— Dennis Slocumb, LASD (Ret.) —

LOS ANGELES COUNTY SHERIFF'S DEPARTMENT
FIRESTONE STATION (#1), CIRCA LATE 1960S

I was working the desk as Complaint Deputy on the EM shift (11 PM to 7 AM). Not many people come into the station during those hours so it is relatively quiet—quieter than being out in the field. However there are times when the unusual happens.

One particular night the doors opened and in walked a lady who looked like she had gone through a mine-field just to get here. Her clothing was disheveled and in quite a disarray, her hair was messed up and she looked like she had been assaulted. She approached the desk and in a rather loud voice said, "I've been raped!"

I asked her when this occurred and she said, "Just a few minutes ago." I was scribbling notes and getting more information and I asked her, "Where?"

Without any hesitation, she reached down to the bottom of her dress, pulled it up, way up, thereby revealing that she had no underwear on and thus her genital area was highly exposed. At the same time, she took her other hand and pointed to her genital area and said, "Right here! Where else do you think?"

WHERE'D YOU STEAL THE CAR, KID?

— Brad Mills, LASD (Ret.) —

LOS ANGELES COUNTY SHERIFF'S DEPARTMENT
FIRESTONE STATION (#1), CIRCA 1966

It was a couple of months after Harry Penny's academy dummy blew the emergency lights and siren off the top of Harry's radio car. (*See* "Where's The Top of My Radio Car?") As an aside, I recall mumbling under my breath when it looked as if the Sarge wouldn't break us up, something like, "Oh shit, the dumb sumbitch is going to get me in trouble again." The sergeant may have heard this comment but probably didn't know if I was talking about him or Harry.

Harry and I survived our academy ride-a-longs that night and were once again riding a car together—15 PMs on a Saturday night. At the conclusion of briefing, the PA rang out with those words we all just loved to hear, "15 PMs, check the desk." Since Harry was booking, I got the shotgun and put our gear in the car while he checked with the dispatcher.

Harry came out to the car a few minutes later with five "details." I fired up the car, went 10-8 and headed for our district. En route to the district, we received two radio calls. Now, Harry has SEVEN things to handle. After handling the first three details, Harry has THREE reports to write. He's working on the first report as we are rolling south on Willowbrook Avenue.

It's just turning dusk, we're between 124th Street and El Segundo Boulevard and Harry is writing away. Traffic is moderate and normal for the area. Notice I said "normal," but apparently not to Harry, whom I've never known to be "normal." All of a sudden, Harry looks up from his report and says, "I want to stop that car."

I responded, "Harry, what the hell for? You're two reports behind and we still have two more calls to go."

Harry said, "I don't care, I want to stop that car." Since Harry was booking and in charge of the car, I dutifully followed his order and lit the car up thinking, "I'll get even with Harry tomorrow night when I'm booking."

When we had him stopped, we did our crisscross and Harry walked up to the driver's window. Harry, being the smart ass he is, said to the driver, "Where'd you steal the car, kid?" To which the driver, a dumb-ass teenager, replied, "over there," pointing to the heart of Willowbrook. After Harry recovered his composure and told me what the kid had said, Harry obtained more information on just where "over there" was.

We asked another unit, probably 15-A, to check it out for us. They responded that they had a car theft victim who had just discovered his car gone when they contacted him and they would take a report. With that Harry hooked up the kid for grand theft auto (GTA). So . . . because of Harry's smart-ass remark, or maybe damn good police work, we had a suspect in custody and an impounded vehicle. However, because Harry was still behind answering details, calls and writing reports, I took pity on him and wrote the CHP 180, the arrest report and booked the little scrote.

To this day (2002), I still don't know why Harry wanted to stop that car. (Neither does he.)

And . . . I've never let him forget how I bailed him out. No, I never got Harry back! Harry and I are still working together after thirty-six years, as court security officers at the Federal Courthouse, San Diego, California. (So I've still got a chance to get him back)

I KILLED SERGEANT TURRENTINE'S HUBCAP

— Brad Mills, LASD (Ret.) —

LOS ANGELES COUNTY SHERIFF'S DEPARTMENT
FIRESTONE STATION (#1), CIRCA 1968–1969

It was around 11:00 or 11:30 AM on a sunny, clear weekday in Watts. I was working a one-man car, 11-A Days, the station car. For a day shift, it was relatively quiet. Then . . . the radio came to life. "11-Adam, 415, possible 647-F (disturbance, possible drunk) at the liquor store, Alameda and Nadeau - one one A." I picked up the radio mike and replied, "11-Adam, 10-4, one one A."

The liquor store at that location was also a large discount gasoline station. Knowing that the location had been the victim of numerous armed robberies (211) as well as drunks always causing a disturbance, I didn't take any chances and rolled as if it might also be an armed robbery in progress. No reflection on my fellow desk officers, but sometimes the "informant" had their head up their ass and didn't give the desk all the pertinent information.

When I arrived at the location, I checked out the area and contacted the informant. I was relieved that there was not a 211 in progress. As pointed out by the informant, it was simply our local drunk, Legless Joe, messed up as usual. He had been indulging in numerous "short dogs" (half pints of "dago red," "T-bird," "gallo," etc.) and was totally drunk, which was his usual "MO." Actually he was a harmless, non-violent drunk.

Just so you know, Legless Joe had no legs. His legs had been amputated just below his hips, for whatever reason. He was mobile by "sitting" on a padded four-wheel furniture dolly and using his gloved hands to propel himself along the sidewalk. He occasionally strayed into the street and traffic when he was "shitfaced," and often fell off his furniture dolly, landing in the traffic lanes which required the area car to respond to a 647-F or "assist citizen" call. Any deputy who worked the north end knew Legless Joe and where he lived – on Nadeau, about four or five blocks west of Alameda.

I contacted Legless Joe and ascertained that he was not injured, just drunk. He stunk of wine, urine, gunk and grime, and was so grungy that even his own mother wouldn't have loved him. I told him it was time to go home. I asked him if there was anyone home at his house so I could take him home, "So I won't have to arrest you for being drunk." He slurringly replied, "Beats the shit outta me."

Since I knew where Legless Joe lived, I loaded him into the front seat of my radio car and seatbelted him in, so I could take him home. (We didn't have cage cars or shoulder belts then, so in a one-man car you had to put the suspect/subject in the front seat with you using only a lap seatbelt.) I put his furniture dolly into the back seat of my radio car and headed for his house. When we got there, no one was home. I knocked and knocked and knocked on the door. No one answered.

"Oh Shit," I thought to myself, "I'm gonna have to book this shit-head after all. The Jailer's gonna kill me." (I'd been the station jailer and the last thing I had wanted to see come in the back door was some stinking, sloppy drunk to be booked. Especially on the day shift when I knew that TSD (prisoner transportation) wouldn't be there until nearly the end of the PM shift to pick up the daily station bookings. I loaded him back into the front seat of my radio car and seatbelted him in so I could to take Legless Joe to the station for booking. I radioed, "11-A, 10-15, one one A." "10-4, 11-A, 10-15, one one A" the radio room responded.

I put a leather glove on my right hand, grabbed a handful of Joe's shirt and pushed him against the right door of the radio car. I wanted him as far away from me as possible because of the stench and the grunge. I drove west on Nadeau from Legless Joe's house and headed for the station. As I neared Babe's Café on the south side of Nadeau, out of the corner of my eye, I saw Firestone Adult D.B., Detective Sergeant Harvey Turrentine standing on the south sidewalk in front of Babe's Café watching me drive by. I thought, "He's checking on my welfare since I have a prisoner in the car."

As I got abreast of Sgt. Turrentine, I glanced to my left at Sgt. Turrentine. Just then Legless Joe turned to his left, looked at me and let go with a burst of puke that saturated me from my right ear, right side and all the way down to and through my weapon. I was wearing a short-sleeve shirt and the puke got down my shirt collar, into my armpit, between my gun belt, my pants belt and my shirt. Remember, I had my right arm extended holding Joe against the right door of the radio car. (Talk about being pissed.)

Simultaneously I heard, "WHACK, WHACK!" I had no idea what the "WHACK, WHACK" was. I continued on to the station, about three blocks away, and parked my radio car at the back door to the station. I unloaded Legless Joe and hauled him into the booking cage. The jailer was irate. I tried to explain to him that I had tried to take Joe home but that no one was home to care for him. I wasn't forgiven but the jailer understood.

About that time Sgt. Turrentine slammed open the back doors of the station and confronted me at the booking cage. He screamed at me, "YOU ASSHOLE, YOU KILLED MY HUBCAP!" Of course I had no idea of what he was talking about. I'm standing at the booking cage with drunken puke running down the side of my face, off my elbow, dripping off my gun, the right side of my shirt saturated with puke and Sgt. Turrentine is yelling at me that I killed his hubcap.

Then . . . I pissed him off even more because all I could do was laugh. His face turned bright red and the veins in his neck stood out so far I got out of the way in case they would burst. I had no idea of why he was so pissed and he had no idea of why I was laughing.

The watch sergeant (WS) came out of his office, adjacent to the booking cage, and placated Sgt. Turrentine. Then the WS called me into his office to explain.

Once I had explained to the WS what had happened, he told me about Sgt. Turrentine's frustration. Sgt. Turrentine was in the process of restoring a 1957 Chevy. He was driving the '57 Chevy to the station that day and one of the hubcaps came loose, fell off the rim and landed in the street. The hubcap, I later learned, that I had flattened and destroyed, the hubcap he was waiting in front of Babe's Café to recover, once I had passed.

Armed with that information, I went to one of the local contract tow companies and obtained four pristine hubcaps for a '57 Chevy. I took the hubcaps to the station and put them in a prominent place on Sgt. Turrentine's desk in the station Detective Bureau. I never heard anything more about the incident until April 2005, but I'll remember it vividly forever.

Harvey and I saw each other at the LASD Roundup/Reunion at Laughlin, Nevada in April 2005. I reminded him of the incident and we had a good laugh over it. I *think* Harvey has forgiven me.

THE CASE OF THE PHANTOM PHARTER

— Brad Mills, LASD (Ret.) —

LOS ANGELES COUNTY SHERIFF'S DEPARTMENT
FIRESTONE STATION (#1), CIRCA 1968

Almost every weekend we had academy cadets assigned to LASD Firestone station patrol as ride-alongs to gain experience. At briefing, the patrol sergeant broke up regular partners and assigned a ride-along to each partner.

At the time of the Phantom Pharter incident, Deputy Megeath (not his real name) and I were assigned 11 EM, a north end car, graveyard shift (11 PM to 7 AM). The patrol sergeant broke up Megeath and me and assigned academy ride-alongs to each of us. The patrol sergeant made Megeath and his cadet 11, and me and my cadet 11-A. (Me comes before Mi.) At that time, 11 and 11-A were known as the "station" cars, meaning they worked the patrol area around the station.

The watch sergeant and dispatcher each had a radio speaker mounted on the wall next to their ear so they could monitor the radio room assigning calls to the various cars and the cars acknowledging the calls. During the early morning hours the volume of the speakers was loud because of the noisy activity in the lobby and the desk area was lower and quieter.

It was around 3:30 to 4:30 AM, on a weekend, when, "BRRRRA AAAPPPP" first came thundering out of the radio loudspeakers in the sergeant's office and at the dispatcher's desk. The watch sergeant came running out of his office yelling, "What the hell was that?" The dispatcher responded, "Beats the shit out of me!" Things settled down and nothing else associated with "BRRRRAAAAPPPP" happened that night.

It seems that this phenomenon only happened during the early morning hours of a weekend, never on a week day. "BRRRRAAAAPPPP" continued to happen every weekend for about a month and a half between 3:30 to 4:40 AM, but only when we had academy "ride alongs." It began to drive the watch sergeant nuts! Then the watch sergeant finally figured out what was causing the "BRRRRAAAAPPPP." The watch sergeant began questioning every deputy who turned in a report for approval. "Are you the one who's farting into the radio microphone?" Every deputy questioned answered with a straight face, "Not me, Sarge." The watch sergeant let it be known that, "I'm goin' to get that sumbitch if it's the last thing I do! When I do, he's gonna be cleaning out the drunk tank for a month."

Then one morning, "BRRRRAAAAPPPPppppffffffffffttttttttt" came over the speakers. The Phantom Pharter struck again! Was this a loose one?

It happened on a quiet early morning shift which was unusual for Firestone. The watch sergeant was caught up on his report reading and approvals and left his office to get a cup of coffee from the coffee room. (Trainees and academy ride-alongs were not allowed in the coffee room as it was the size of a small closet.) The watch sergeant saw an academy ride-along standing in the hall outside the door to the coffee room and asked him what he was doing there.

Response:	I'm waiting for my partner, Sir.
Sergeant:	Who's your partner?
Ride-along:	Deputy Megeath, Sir.
Sergeant:	Where's Deputy Megeath?
Ride-along:	He's in the locker room, Sir.
Sergeant:	What's he doing in the locker room?
Ride-along:	He's changing his uniform, Sir.
Sergeant:	Why is he changing his uniform?

Ride-along:	He had an accident, Sir.
Sergeant:	What kind of accident?"
Ride-along:	In his pants, Sir.
Sergeant:	In his pants?
Ride-along:	Yes Sir, in his pants.

You've got to give that cadet ride-along credit. He didn't offer any information. The watch sergeant had to interrogate the ride-along every step of the way.

The watch sergeant immediately ran into the locker room and caught Megeath with one leg in and one leg out of his uniform pants. The watch sergeant observed a large "nicotine" stain on Megeath's jockey shorts. The watch sergeant hollered, "AHA! I got ya now!"

After further investigation by the watch sergeant, it was determined that Deputy Megeath, as the radio car TO and driver, when he felt the need, would raise his right cheek, key the radio microphone and pass gas. Only this time he had an accident. And . . . got caught!

The case of the Phantom Pharter had been solved!

TRAINEE, FIRESTONE STATION ALREADY
HAS A PHANTOM PHARTER!

AMBER LIGHTS AND MOUTH

— Brad Mills, LASD (Ret.) —

LOS ANGELES COUNTY SHERIFF'S DEPARTMENT
FIRESTONE STATION (#1), CIRCA 1968–1969

I came to work one Monday morning and at briefing, discovered that I was assigned to work car 13-Days, (7 AM to 3 PM), a one-man car, the only car assigned to Cudahy. I wondered which sergeant or watch deputy I had pissed off this time.

Cudahy was a contract city about one square mile in area and, at the time of this incident, populated by about 14,000 Okies. We had a standing joke about Cudahy . . . "How do you know there's a rich Okie living in Cudahy? . . . He's got TWO cars jacked up in the front yard."

Cudahy was approximately two and a half to three miles east of FPK's north end. Even though it was small in area, there was always something going on, 24 hours a day, 7 days a week. 13's closest backup cars were 11, 11-A, 12, and 12-A (when we had the Adam cars.) Their arrival time, if they weren't busy, could be five minutes or more. They had to travel across Florence Avenue, a major east/west thoroughfare that was two lanes each way and most times clogged with heavy traffic. If a Cudahy car needed immediate assistance, the Cudahy deputy's pucker strings could get tight waiting for a backup car to arrive.

139

I got my shotgun from the armory and checked with the dispatcher. No calls or details for 13-Days. I took my gear out to the parking lot, loaded up my radio car, went 10-8 (in service) and headed for beautiful downtown Cudahy. Maybe, since I had not received any calls or details out of briefing, it was going to be a quiet day in Cudahy. This was not to be.

Soon after arriving in my patrol area, I received a radio call at approximately 7:30 AM, about a family disturbance with a possible drunk involved. "415-F, possible 647-F." I acknowledged the call and headed for the location, arriving in about a minute and a half. I went 10-97 and so far so good. No outward appearances of anything astray.

I contacted the informant, a woman who stood at about 4'2". She pointed out her husband, an Okie who stood at about 7'6" at least 300 pounds and was built like a lumberjack. (At that time I was 5'9 1/2" and weighed about 133 pounds.) I remember thinking, "I hope this sucker is peaceful because if I have to fight him, I'm going to be the one that goes to the hospital."

She told me that he had just come home after staying out all night drinking and that he couldn't go to work because he was still drunk. She was pissed because he wouldn't earn any money by missing a day's work. Even though she was small in stature, I wouldn't have wanted to tangle with her. He seemed to not give a shit about what her opinion was, which pissed her off even more.

She told me she wanted me to arrest her husband for being drunk. (She didn't say anything about making a citizen's arrest, which was a relief to me. My handcuffs would not have fit around his wrists.) I calmed her down and asked her to go inside her house so I could talk to her husband. Luckily, she complied with my request.

I asked her husband to come over to my radio car with me so I could talk to him. To my surprise, he did. I asked him for his driver's license which he *reluctantly* handed to me. His reluctance set off an alarm bell in my head. I asked him to place his hands on the roof of my radio car. I told him I was going to do a customary, cursory, pat-down search of his person to check for weapons. "Is that

OK, Sir?" I asked. He agreed. I wanted to maintain control of the situation and didn't want him to think he was in control. While he was not overly aggressive, his mere size gave me cause for concern. Luckily, he was clean. No knives, guns, axes, or bazookas hidden in his clothing.

I asked him if there was someplace he could go for a while, other than a bar, to give his wife time to calm down. He informed me vulgarly, in no uncertain terms, that he wasn't going to go anywhere other than inside his house and go to bed. This was unacceptable to me. I could just envision a radio call coming out later, "13, return to the location of your 415-F and HANDLE TO CONCLUSION." No Firestone deputy ever wanted to receive a "return to, handle to conclusion" call. And If we did receive a "return to, handle to conclusion" call, it usually ended with the suspect(s) at least going to the hospital before being booked at the station or maybe being booked into the jail ward at Los Angeles County General Hospital.

Due to the subject's refusal to leave the area for a while and his reluctance to give me his driver's license, I figured, "He's dirty." My first course of action was to run him for wants or warrants. I had to control the situation. I obtained a 10-34 (routine clearance) from the radio room to run one subject.

"10-4, 13, go ahead." I transmitted the required information and the radio room replied "10-4, 13, stand by."

The Lumberjack and I stood beside my radio car waiting for his clean bill of health from records. Funny, but all of a sudden all radio traffic ceased. After about fifteen to twenty minutes, I picked up the radio mike and said "13, any return on my subject?" No response. "OK," I thought, "the radio room is busy."

Just then Claude Anderson—Bless his Soul—who was working 11-Mary, a three-wheeler parking enforcement unit in FPK's north end, comes ROARING up to my location on a kick-start, Harley three-wheeler. He's almost out of breath and there's smoke coming out of the poor Harleys engine. "ARE YOU ALL RIGHT?" Claude yelled at me. I replied, "Yeh Claude, it's Code 4." Claude then radioed, "It's Code 4 at 13's location."

Claude told me that apparently my radio had taken a dump right after I had given the subject's information and the radio room had acknowledged my transmission. Although the subject did not have any wants or warrants, when the radio room tried to contact me to advise me of this, they could not contact me. The radio room didn't know what happened. Was I lying as a tangled mess in a gutter somewhere?

As a result, the radio room put out a call, "Any Firestone north end unit, to assist 13, unable to contact him by radio after he ran a subject." The radio room had the location of my 415-F call so that's the address they put out over the air. THANK GOD FOR THE RTOs THAT LOOKED OUT FOR OUR ASSES IN THE FIELD.

After I thanked Clyde for the backup, I asked him why his three-wheeler was smoking so much. He replied, "When the call came

CLAUDE, RIDING UNPROTECTED, WITH ONLY A HELMET,
HAD COME TO THE AID OF A FIRESTONE DEPUTY.

out to assist you, no one else was clear except me. I acknowledged the call and rolled across Florence Avenue, *Amber Lights and Mouth,* yelling at cars and pedestrians, "Get The Fuck Outta My Way." (The three-wheelers didn't have red lights or sirens. They only had amber, "safety," lights mounted on the front wheel forks).

Claude, at great personal peril, riding unprotected, with only a helmet on an open vehicle, had once again come to the aid of a Firestone Deputy. THANK YOU, CLAUDE!

Oh yes, the Lumberjack. Apparently when he saw Claude roll up and maybe based on his previous experience(s) with Firestone deputies he apparently decided he was going to be a "good boy" and not mess with Firestone cops. Mrs. Lumberjack "relented," let him in the house and he went to bed.

I (we) did not get a "return to, handle to conclusion" call.

LET'S GET THE SNEAKY SERGEANT OR THE MARBLES STORY

— Brad Mills, LASD (Ret.) —

LOS ANGELES COUNTY SHERIFF'S DEPARTMENT
FIRESTONE STATION (#1), CIRCA 1969

We had a PM patrol sergeant who took great delight in sneaking up on radio car crews to try and catch them at some nefarious activity. Of course we'd never do anything to call attention to ourselves or bring discredit on the department. We'd never leave our area to go get some BBQ over in the city, or play footsie with some chick while on duty, or hide out, or make too many bar checks at topless bars in Carson . . . we just wouldn't do that. We were fine, upstanding, young deputies cut in the Elliot Ness mold. But . . . the sergeant apparently didn't think so. Maybe he remembered the days when he was a young deputy and some of the stuff he undoubtedly pulled.

This particular sergeant, after it was dark, would cruise the area with his lights off. He'd use the emergency brake to stop so his brake lights wouldn't flash. He kept the volume on his radio turned down so low he could barely hear the radio room dispatching radio calls. We figured this kept him from showing up on many of our calls. He took the light bulb out of the dome light. Are you getting the picture?

Just when you'd least expect it he'd show up and start getting on our cases about, "Where's your tie?" "How come your sleeves are

144

rolled up?" (We wore long-sleeve WOOL shirts even in the summer.) "How come you're parked on the wrong side of the street?" "Where's your helmet?" "Who's the handling unit?" He was driving us nuts!

One night he was off duty for two days. This gave us an opportunity to get together and form a game plan. That is, when we weren't running from call to call. We agreed that we all would give some thought about how we could solve our mutual problem.

We met the next night to plan our strategy—some might call it a conspiracy. Being originally from Wisconsin, I told the guys about a prank my dad and his buddies pulled on each other.

They would get a piece of Limburger cheese (a rank smelling cheese) and place it on the car engine block. Eventually the cheese would melt and the stink would permeate the interior of the car. I told them that even in southern California, this would work. We decided not to do this as it would be unfair to the other sergeants that would have to use the car during subsequent shifts. Back to the drawing board.

We had another opportunity a week later. At this planning meeting, one of the guys brought in a bag of marbles that he said his kid contributed to our cause. We agreed that the plan of action would be for a couple of us to distract the sergeant inside the station while the rest of us "modified" the sergeant's car.

The next night after briefing, one of the crews distracted the sergeant with some question that would take some research and time on the sergeant's part to answer. I believe it was an obscure question about the nuances of forgery. The rest of us, with the knowledge of the dispatcher and watch deputy (they had been victims too), "modified" the sergeant's car. We took all four hubcaps off the sergeant's car and put six to eight loose marbles in each one. Before we put the hubcaps back on the car, we taped another six to eight marbles inside each hubcap.

My partner and I were working 11PM on a summer night with the windows open in the station car, so we were "detailed" by the guys to stake out the sergeant when he left the station parking lot to go on patrol. We hid out in the adjacent welfare office parking lot and waited for sarge to leave. He rolled out of the station lot at approximately fifteen miles-per-hour. He got about twenty feet out of the lot when we heard KLACK, KLACK, KLACK, etc. All of a sudden the sergeant's car comes to an abrupt halt. Not legally parked, I might add.

We watched the sergeant get out of the car, walk all around it looking very puzzled. He opened the trunk, opened the hood, opened all four doors, and peered intently into each opening. Apparently he did not detect any defect as he closed everything up, re-entered the radio car, put it into gear, and started to drive away. KLACK, KLACK, KLACK, again. He had traveled maybe twenty feet. He repeated the above described actions again and again. Time #3, #4, #5.

Finally he got smart. He opened the trunk, took out the tire iron, and popped off the left front hubcap. Out fell the loose marbles. He put the hubcap back on the rim, missing the taped marbles. Then, as he started to drive, with a satisfied look on his face, KLACK, KLACK, KLACK again. Now when he stopped, he used the tire iron to remove the remaining three hubcaps and dump the loose marbles. He learned quickly. However, again he missed the taped marbles in each hubcap. With an obvious sigh of relief he began driving east on Nadeau at about thirty-five to forty miles-per-hour, anxious to get back in the action, with us following him WITH OUR LIGHTS OFF. Again we heard KLACK, KLACK, KLACK.

I must note that by this time, my partner and I were doubled over with laughter. We couldn't have acknowledged a radio call if our life depended on it. I could barely manage to drive our radio car. The other "victimized" units, 11-A, 12 and 12-A had covered for us while we handled our "detail."

The sergeant pulled his radio car to the curb. He took the tire iron out of the trunk and took off all four hubcaps. This time he looked inside the hubcaps and spotted the taped marbles. Ten minutes later he had removed all the taped marbles from all the hubcaps, put hubcaps back on the rims and driven away. WITH HIS LIGHTS ON!

We had no further "problems" with this sergeant.

DISPATCHING

— Victor Kretsinger, LASD (Ret.) —

LOS ANGELES COUNTY SHERIFF'S DEPARTMENT
FIRESTONE STATION (#1), CIRCA 1970

All of us have stories about funny things that happened to us and others at Firestone station. We also have some stories about some "goofs" on the radio, such as the "Red Wig Caper"—which is another story in itself. Then there was Burris Sutton's short test count.

Working car 11, Sutton received a radio call from the radio room requesting a "short test count." That was a no-brainer. Just pick up the mike and count from one to five. Piece of cake, right? Well, not exactly. His response was nowhere near the norm as he said, "One, two, three, four, five, six, seven . . . All good deputies go to heaven." This was immediately followed by the radio room sergeant who said, "Firestone 11, 10-21 (call the station) the admin sergeant."

One BUSY evening I was dispatching and I put out a call concerning a shooting at one of the local establishments in the Watts/Willowbrook area and that Schaefer's ambulance was notified. It went like this:

"Firestone 15 handle, 15-Adam assist, 245 shots fired, 901-S, Schaefer's at the Diggity-Dog, 1200 Imperial."

15 acknowledged the call and went 10-97 (arrived at scene) within one minute.

About thirty seconds after going 10-97, 15 was back on the air saying, "15, what's the ETA of my ambulance?"

Well, we've all been there. Crews ask a question that if they thought a few seconds, they wouldn't have asked the question in the first place.

Remember "Situation Awareness," and factoring in time, plus dispatching over one hundred calls during your eight-hour shift, you're kind of short-fused.

So with baited breath, I waited for Station B to call for an ETA. When the phone rang, I picked it up and spoke freely to them: "##$(*& ()!!%(&," after all, Station B normally cleaned up our act and kept us out of trouble.

Station B put out a DIRECT quote. "15, your desk advises, put your fingers in the bullet holes. The ambulance will be there momentarily."

When I heard my quote, and picked myself up off the floor, I reached for the long form memo. I knew my body was "going directly to jail, not passing go, and not collecting $200," and waited for the dreaded call: "Kretsinger, report to the watch commander's office."

GOD was on my side that night. The hammer never fell. NO ONE ever talked to me about this little goof.

Talk about skating.

WOLFMAN JACK

— Stephen L.D. Smith, LASD (Ret.) —

LOS ANGELES COUNTY SHERIFF'S DEPARTMENT
FIRESTONE STATION (#1), CIRCA 1969

I was transferred to Firestone station from Special Enforcement Bureau (SEB) in December of 1969. I had called the station to see what my assignment would be. I was told I was working a three-man car on PMs, (4/10 schedule). I knew only a few people at Firestone and was definitely the new guy. I had over three years experience in patrol, including most of eleven months at SEB. I had, however, worked this geographic area while with the Marshal's office, was conversant in "ebonics" and knew how to tell when a constituent was lying.

The afternoon I came to work, after dressing in the locker room I went to the briefing room and checked the in-service schedule posted on the wall. There I discovered I was now assigned to a car with a partner by the name of Varno (not his real name). I had no idea who he was or what his background had been. When I met him he was a very young athletic man with an extremely sharp uniform appearance. He seemed smart and very articulate in his speech. I would later discover that he was fluent in several languages.

After we got out of briefing and in the field, he wanted to talk. I asked him if he knew why I wasn't working the three-man car they assigned me to. He said he heard I was being transferred from SEB and figured there was a good chance that I knew what I was doing. He said he was just released from training and felt inadequate and had not learned enough. He indicated that he had gone into the scheduling lieutenant's office and asked if he could be assigned to work with me. This was because he was sincerely hoping to become the very best cop he could possibly be. He thought I might have enough knowledge and experience to help teach him some of the many things that he wanted to learn. Varno and I got along very well and he had an incredible sense of humor.

The first couple of weeks that we worked together were really great; he was very bright and absorbed information like a sponge. We bantered back and forth and kept the atmosphere very light at all times. He would ask me questions about things that he had not experienced or learned. In most cases I was able to find some example to teach him a lesson in that area forthwith.

One day we were driving south on Wilmington around 117th Street when he asked me if I would show him what a "hype" looked like. I slammed on the brakes and skidded the radio car to an immediate halt. Varno looked around wildly and said, "Why did you stop here?"

I giggled, looking out the driver's-side window and pointed to a black man standing at the east curb on the sidewalk. "There's one right now," I answered, indicating a "hype."

I knew full well from working SEB that a local heroin dealer sold drugs on that corner whenever he happened to show up, and there he was. We then turned around and talked with the young man. I had him essentially undress for Varno so he could see his tracks. We also checked all the alternative spots where addicts shoot up like between the toes and under his tongue. He was wearing three long-sleeved flannel shirts, a jacket, and two pairs of pants. Both his jacket pockets were full of salt-water taffy, which he was eating on a continual basis as we talked. I had Varno search him, looking for paraphernalia; there was none on his person.

When I was in high school I was really into 1950s rock and roll. I spent much of my time over those years listening to that music on the radio. Of course Wolfman Jack was a popular disk jockey then. I served in the U.S. Marine Corps and learned how to use my command voice. I got in the habit of talking like the Wolfman Jack frequently and did so while working in patrol, sometimes on the public address system. I guess I did this a couple of times around Varno and one day he looked at me with a big grin on his face and said, "You ain't got a hair on your fanny if you don't go around talking like the Wolfman all day." My immediate response was, "They don't call me Magilla Gorilla for nothing. I got hair all over my body, not just on my fanny."

The very next call we got was a neighbor's dispute over some money. We responded to the location and looked up the driveway. There were six little clapboard cabins, three on each side of a common driveway. Each cabin had a raised porch, most of which appeared to be over two feet high. Standing on the middle porch at the left side of the driveway was a little black man who appeared to be in his eighties. He was no more than five feet tall and couldn't have weighed any more than a hundred pounds. He had an obviously hunched back and his neck came straight out of the top of his shoulders, parallel with the ground. His head was in front of his body instead of on top of it.

I recalled what Gary said to me about hair on my fanny and hooked my thumbs into my Sam Browne. I looked straight into this old man's eyes and said in my very best rendition of Wolfman Jack, "Hi. Who called, what's going on here?" The old man answered in a perfect mimic of my best rendition of Wolfman, saying, "I called. Why you talking like that?" I continued saying, "I always talk like this; I had something happen to my voice box and I've talked like this since I was very young." The old man and I went inside his cabin and I looked around and couldn't see Varno.

I excused myself and walked out to the radio car looking for him. When I reached the driver's side of the car there was Varno with his torso through the window parallel with the floor of the car. He was laughing so hard he couldn't seem to straighten up. Finally he withdrew himself from the interior of the car and accompanied me back inside the cabin. I continued my investigation speaking every word in my very best rendition of Wolfman.

At this point the other person involved in this disturbance arrived and entered the cabin. He was a younger male neighbor from across the driveway and had what I usually referred to as a high-pitched whiney tenor in his voice. He started by saying, "He say I come over and take his money off the dresser while he sleep." I then responded in a likewise high-pitched whiney tenor asking, "You mean he say you come over and take his money off the dresser while he sleep?" The old man instantly whirled around and asked me in his perfect rendition of Wolfman, "Why you talking like that now?" I responded in the same whiney voice, "Sometimes my voice just seems to slip and I sounds like this fo a few minutes." I then returned to my best rendition of Wolfman Jack and continued questioning the victim.

By that time I had completed the interview and we left the location. We both laughed the rest of the week about that contact. It was hard to believe, but that old man talked like Wolfman every breath of his life.

A few days later I came up from the locker room walking toward the briefing room. I saw a small deputy I didn't even know come around the corner looking up at me. He then hooked his thumbs into his Sam Browne, saying in his best rendition of Wolfman, "Hi, who called . . . what's going on here?" I cracked up, thinking to myself, *Boy, things get around pretty fast at this place.*

I know that there were many dark, as well as some moonlit nights throughout Firestone's area. During these nights the friendly, gravelly voice of the Wolfman Jack was undoubtedly heard by some of his fans in the local neighborhoods. I'm also convinced that from time to time Wolfman did a little howling at the moon over the PA his of 1968 Plymouth Fury.

GOOD EVENING MADAM, WHERE DO YOU RESIDE?

— Stephen L.D. Smith, LASD (Ret.) —

LOS ANGELES COUNTY SHERIFF'S DEPARTMENT
FIRESTONE STATION (#1), CIRCA 1969–1970

I was working the north end one evening with a new trainee who had two Baccalaureate degrees in music education from UCLA and I kinda, sorta, nicknamed him, "The Student Prince." We got a call next to the liquor store located on the south side of Firestone Boulevard, a few blocks east of Compton Avenue. As I recall, between my senior moments, the nature of the dispatch was a possible person down. We arrived at the location, which was a dirt parking lot right next to the liquor store.

All of the local sages were sitting around on milk crates and the hoods of various vehicles imbibing in either the grape or the grain with joyful glee. There was a great deal of bantering going on between them. We saw an old 1959 Plymouth hardtop parked there with both front windows wide open. We observed a woman lying across the front seat with her head on the passenger side arm rest and her feet tucked under her toward the driver's side of the car. She appeared to be unconscious. From the odor of an alcoholic beverage emitting from her breath and person, there was more than a good chance she might even be 647-f. Her sweater had been pulled

THERE ARE EASIER WAYS TO GET
A NAME AND ADDRESS.

up and her bra was now crumpled up beneath the shoulder line of
the garment. He pants were unzipped, with her belly exposed, and
had obviously been pulled down before an attempt was made to
restore them to their rightful position on her body.

I had a nagging suspicion that perhaps this lady had been the
unfortunate victim of a forcible rape. I asked my trainee to go over
and see where she lived. He walked up to the passenger side of the
car and looked into the window with disdain. He then gingerly
reached into the car and gently shook this sleeping beauty. He then
quietly said in his clearest voice, "Good evening, Madam. Where
do you reside?" The sages tried to muffle their laughter so as not to
embarrass my trainee. I then asked him to attempt once more to find
out where she lived with just a little bit more gusto. He once more
reached into the car and shook the lady with a little more force this
time. He then stated rather loudly, "Good evening, Madam. Where
do you reside?" One more time. There was still no response from the
woman in the car, but the locals busted up, laughing loudly.

I then told my trainee to watch me and said to him, "In order to find information in the ghetto, you have to relate to the folks up front." I then opened the driver's side door and reached inside the vehicle with my open right hand. Simultaneously I swung my open right hand down toward her bare belly and stated, "Say, mama, where you stays?" as I slapped the bare skin of her exposed belly. She sat straight up in the seat with her eyes wide open and said, "1234 East 88th Street." I then asked her name, which she gave me, after which I asked her if she needed any help getting home. She refused any assistance from us, saying that she would take care of it by herself. And so it was the very first in a long chain of rescues performed by the student prince for a damsel in distress.

COME OUT WITH YOUR HANDS UP!

— Stephen L.D. Smith, LASD (Ret.) —

LOS ANGELES COUNTY SHERIFF'S DEPARTMENT
FIRESTONE STATION (#1), CIRCA 1999

I was working the north end one evening with Deputy R. who was my current trainee. He was fairly new and hadn't experienced very much as yet. We got a burglar alarm call at a body shop located with one side on Firestone Boulevard, the other on Manchester Place just off Alameda. During my time at Firestone this alarm went off frequently. I had never observed any live human being inside the fenced yard or the central paint and equipment building. As far as I knew, the primary source of the alarm was a set of motion detection beams across the yard at various locations. I had observed a number of cats and numerous birds in the yard, but none of them were worthy of booking. Most of them were not subjected to a trip to the gray bar. This because most were not adequately qualified to intelligently answer the questions asked from the admonition card carried in our notebooks to waive their right to an attorney before answering any of our questions.

Because my trainee was relatively new, I stopped in front and dropped him off to cover any attempt by suspects to leave the scene over the front gate, just as we were taught at the academy. I then

156

drove around to the back of the yard located on Manchester Place. I parked the unit across the street with the front end facing south toward the yard. Then, just for the purpose of being theatrical, I turned on the PA system with the volume turned all the way up. I took a deep breath and stated in my most officious loud voice, "This is Inspector Erskine of the FBI, we know you're in there, surrender yourselves and come out at once with your hands up."

Almost simultaneously another Firestone unit approached, driving westbound on Manchester Place toward my location. They had apparently heard my demand for the suspects to surrender. Suddenly there came this loud broadcast from their PA system with a believable German accent. "You vill give up at vonce or you vill be shot!" and this was repeated once again.

Almost immediately, after the second broadcast, there was a call for all units to respond, a 918-V (mentally ill, possibly violent suspect), armed, with shots fired, somewhere way up in the north end. The other unit roared by me and took off west on Firestone Boulevard. I immediately pulled away from the curb and turned to drive to the front of the body shop.

It was just getting dusk, and as I pulled up in front I saw my trainee crouched down with his flashlight turned on, extended to his side at arm's length, in his left hand. As I stopped I observed that he had his revolver in his right hand extended forward toward the yard, aiming through the fence. To my absolute total surprise there were two young black men walking in a file in step with their hands held as high as possible. I had absolutely no idea these two guys were inside that place. They approached the fence and I told them to climb over the gate. When they did, I put each one on the ground and handcuffed them. I then placed them in the rear seat of our unit and arranged my booking gear so it was between them on the seat with the microcassette recorder on record. My trainee asked me, "How in God's name are we going to write this one up?" I told him that it would reflect just exactly as it happened. Deputy Smith dropped deputy Deputy R. off to cover the front of the business.

ON PROWLER CALLS, WHY DO TRAINEES
ALWAYS FORGET TO LOOK UP?

Deputy Smith then drove to the rear of the location in an attempt to determine if there was anyone inside at the location.

After a period of search and observation Deputy Smith sensed the presence of the suspects inside the location. He then made a verbal demand for them to surrender themselves and they complied. The suspects were arrested, then transported to and booked at Firestone station.

It was incredible to listen to what these two guys had to say to each other about what they were doing in there on the tape. This was just your standard culmination of a training exercise in the most ordinary positive way. The sort of thing that happens day in and day out at good old Firestone.

THE "RITE REVEREND CC"

— Stephen L.D. Smith, LASD (Ret.) —

LOS ANGELES COUNTY SHERIFF'S DEPARTMENT
FIRESTONE STATION (#1), CIRCA 1973

In 1971 I left Firestone to go to the Bailiff Bureau at the Brunswick Building. After eight months of law school I quit the department and went into the masonry business. I worked for a friend of mine for a while then went into business for myself. I was away from home more than when I was working at the "Stone." In an attempt to avoid a divorce I decided to go back to the Sheriff's Department. I got hired off the street on April 9, 1973, four days before my thirty-fifth birthday, which was the cutoff. When the sergeant in the Personnel Bureau called Firestone to ask the station captain if he would take me, the captain asked what was my name and when he was told S.L.D. Smith he asked to have me report for PMs that very day. I went to the academy and drew my uniforms, then went to the station to go to work.

A short time after I returned I came to work and found I had been assigned to work as watch deputy. I had been hired off the street as a Deputy 1, Step 1. While at the desk that night for EM shift I started going through the watch deputy routine and noticed that the dispatcher was watching me. I didn't know many of the deputies because I had been gone for two years.

159

The dispatcher was a deputy with a nickname of CC. He came over to my desk and asked me, "How come you as a Deputy 1. Step 1 are in a supervisory position over me, a Deputy 3, Step 4?" I was as honest as I could be and told him that I came in that evening and saw I was scheduled to work the watch deputy slot. I added that I was up there struggling through this work which I knew nothing at all about. The next evening CC greeted me and said he heard from some folks that I had been at Firestone before. CC and I became really close friends and remain so today.

One night CC and I were working the Willowbrook together, both with trainees. He got a 927-D call—the radio code for a dead body—and I rolled over to the location with him to see if I could be of assistance. When we went into the modest little house, the occupants were having a small party. The person they called about was named Sylvester and he was over seventy. Sylvester was seated in a Mission-style chair with wide flat arms. His right hand was around a cocktail glass with a fairly large puddle of water around its base. His eyes were closed and he looked as though he may have been asleep.

Sylvester's girlfriend, Aretha, who was about the same age, was quite concerned about him. She was very much afraid that something had happened to him. She said they were only two weeks short of the seven years required living together to become married under common law.

We examined Sylvester and found him to have no pulse or sign of respiration. When we attempted to manipulate his hands and arms it became apparent that he was in a state of rigor mortis. Further examination revealed his having post-mortem lividly, horizontally along the lower half of his thighs and down his lower legs and feet.

I know in my heart that Conrad felt very sympathetic toward Aretha. The next thing I knew he sent his trainee out to their car to get his bible out of his booking gear. This was one of those golden moments when you see just what kind of fabric a man's character is made of. The "Rite Reverend CC" was fixin' to perform directly from his heart for the benefit of one of his constituents. The trainee returned

MY TRAINEE HAS JUST LEARNED THE ART OF COMPASSION
FROM THE "RITE REVEREND CC." SOON HE WILL REALIZE
THAT COMPASSION IS AN IMPORTANT PART OF BEING A COP.

with the bible and the following scenario unfolded in front of everyone there.

CC explained that Sylvester had died and comforted his girlfriend who was crying and yelling hysterically. CC then proposed to
Aretha that he could marry her and Sylvester. She seemed to calm
down significantly and listened intently to what CC asked her to do.

He explained how in this particular type of ceremony any non-
response by one of the participants would be considered an affirmative answer. He gave her specific directions as to just how to
complete each step of the process. He then asked each of the
betrothed the normal list of questions included within the marriage
ceremony. Of course Sylvester was given credit for all affirmative
answers. The "Rite Reverend CC" then continued with the ceremony
after reading some applicable scriptures. When he reached the completion of the ceremony he asked Aretha to participate in his giving

of the oath. She placed her left hand on his badge and raised her right hand as Conrad solemnly administered the oath, "With the power vested in me by the NAACP I now pronounce you man and wife."

The lady was ecstatic not only because she believed she was now legally married to her deceased fiancée but also because she would now inherit the corpus of his fortune which may have been as much as $70 in cash. She would also become the legal owner of his 1964 Chevrolet station wagon. CC then proposed that he perform a divorce between them so she would not have to stand the expense of burying him. He explained the required steps to her and once again she had her left hand on his badge and her right hand in the air as he again administered the oath. Subsequent to these ceremonies CC prepared two separate officious certificates on the always useful and invaluable SHR 49 forms (one of the many forms used by the department). This was to memorialize these extremely serious acts that CC had performed. I honestly think CC helped that lady feel much better about Sylvester's death.

I was sure that I was back at home where I belonged, working with folks who knew just how to reveal the subtle reality of their sense of humor no matter how solemn the occasion.

HOW TO GIVE TRAFFIC DIRECTIONS AT THE ROSE PARADE

— Kimball Brown, LASD (Ret.) —

Los Angeles County Sheriff's Department
Training Academy, circa 1960s

While I was in the academy, learning how to become a Los Angeles deputy sheriff, I got first-hand knowledge how the department assisted the Pasadena Police Department during the

THERE'S NOTHING LIKE HAVIING YOUR TRAINEE TO GIVE DIRECTIONS AT THE ROSE PARADE ESPECIALLY SINCE HE HAS NO IDEA WHERE HE IS!

annual Rose Parade. Supposedly, the word "volunteer" was in there somewhere, but in the academy it wasn't used much. Drafted was more like it.

We were loaded up on the Sheriff's buses and taken to the area. I was dropped off at some lonely spot where I hadn't a clue as to where I was and didn't know anything about the geography. I told the sergeant that I couldn't give anyone directions if I didn't know where I was myself.

The sergeant said, "If anyone asks you directions, say 'Go two blocks down and make a left . . . you can't miss it.' Make sure to add 'You can't miss it' because they'll figure they misunderstood you and won't come back to ask again."

Well, it worked like a charm and I've used it ever since. Don't forget, "You can't miss it." And, if some cop gives you those directions, just nod and smile, and ask a taxi driver.

WHAT IS MALIBU STATION? WHERE IS IT? I'VE BEEN TRANSFERRED!

— Harry Penny —

LOS ANGELES COUNTY SHERIFF'S DEPARTMENT, MALIBU STATION (#10), CIRCA LATE 1967

I never knew that the Sheriff's Department was the agency that patrolled the area until I became a deputy sheriff.

I had grown up in the San Fernando valley and was living in Van Nuys. Before I was old enough to drive, my parents would take Sunday drives down to Malibu, as a friend of my father's owned the Malibu Inn restaurant. Later when I got my driver's license, I would spend a lot of time at beach parties while I was in high school.

I was transferred from Firestone station to Malibu in late 1967, at my own request.

I left my house early this particular Monday morning with all my gear, especially my trusty *Thomas Guide* map. I didn't have any problem getting over to Malibu. I even had the address. I was used to Firestone and I had been at other various stations and they all were easy to find. Malibu wasn't. I drove by it not once, not twice, but three times! (I wasn't going to call the station and ask how to get there.)

Not a black-and-white in sight! So, not to look too stupid, I drove on past and then parked so I could take my binoculars out of my patrol can and zoom in on the address. That's when I saw the sign. *Smart police work, Harry!* I reported in.

Malibu station's area covered almost 189 square miles. A lot of it was mountainous with many canyons. Do you recall the movie, and later, the long-running television series M*A*S*H*? It was filmed in those mountains between the coast and the valley. They are known as the Santa Monica mountains.

Malibu's area is bordered on the south by the Pacific Ocean. (Yes, on the south.) Malibu beach is one of the south-facing beaches on the west coast. Pacific Coast Highway (PCH) is Highway 1 and it runs east and west. The eastern border of Malibu station's area is the city of Los Angeles, with the northern and western borders being Ventura County.

There were only two main thoroughfares through the mountains: Topanga Canyon and Malibu Canyon. During my time at Malibu,

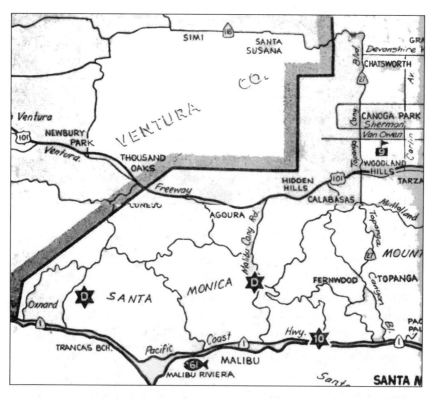

A section of the Los Angeles County Sheriff's Department Pocket Guide, circa 1968, depicting the Malibu station area. The star with the number 10 is the location of Malibu station.

These pictures are of the gas pumps, locker room, and parking lot of the Malibu station. At the end of the parking lot was the station and courthouse.

I never knew the exact mileage between the northern and southern boundaries (I estimated it was about forty miles), nor the eastern and western Boundaries on the valley side (which I estimated at roughly twenty-five miles.) The stretch of Highway 1 was approximately twenty-eight miles. In our daily travels, distance was measured in time rather than miles. On weekends, during the summer, it could take an hour or more to go from Topanga Canyon and PCH, over the mountains, across the valley and up to the northern end of the area. The same along the coast.

The entire area had a population of only 23,581 in 1967. (*Mr. Murphy* was only a part-time resident, as you will see in the following stories.)

THE
WHITE HOUSE
IN THE CANYON

— Harry Penny —

LOS ANGELES COUNTY SHERIFF'S DEPARTMENT
MALIBU STATION (#10), CIRCA 1968

In late 1967 I was transferred from Firestone station to Malibu station. What a culture shock for a cop to go from the fastest station in the county, "Hookin' and Bookin" every night, to what was referred to by others on the department as "To Protect and To Surf." Malibu station was located right on Pacific Coast Highway between Malibu Canyon and Topanga Canyon, in the older section of Malibu.

My partner "Mace" was a seasoned veteran and I really enjoyed working with him. I had known him when I was in a senior in high school. He lived next door to one of my best friends whom I subsequently enlisted in the U.S. Navy with.

Mace at that time was a professional fisherman and he knew that I loved boats and the ocean. I remembered his sons he called Butch and Tiger. They were cute kids, always laughing and playing. My buddy and I would toss the football around with them at times.

So, when I reported in to Malibu, you can imagine my surprise when I looked across the briefing table and saw Mace. Both of us said, almost at the same time, "When did you come on the department?" Then to learn that he was going to be my training officer (basically just to help me get acquainted with the area) I was really happy. This was going to be enjoyable. I was pretty familiar with the overall area, having spent countless weekends and then almost every day in the summertime, from my high school years and even when I was in the U.S. Navy and then a civilian again, at Malibu Beach and of course, countless beach parties.

Mace was my first of three partners in three months; one month each on days (7 AM to 3 PM), PMs (3 PM to 11 PM) and EMs (11 AM to 7 AM). I had been working a relief shift covering summer vacations for guys and finally got a regular partner after about five months at Malibu.

We were working the "canyon car" (Malibu 103) on the PM shift. This particular beat covered the entire stretch of Topanga Canyon from Pacific Coast Highway, through the Santa Monica mountains, through the San Fernando valley and up into the foothills that lead into Ventura County. It is one of the most beautiful drives in southern California.

The one main area in the canyon during the 60s was a little community called Topanga. Naturally! What else? A quaint little area: beautiful scenery, trees, nice little creek, old buildings, a park, and even a post office. Of course, this setting was ideal for the hippie era. Flower-decorated VWs, people walking around in paisley print shirts and tops, faded denim trousers, sandals, many of them carrying a guitar. If you saw long blond hair from the back, you had a fifty-fifty chance of seeing a heavy beard on the front. Same thing in reverse: if you saw short hair from the back you had a fifty-fifty chance of seeing a set of boobs in the front. I used to remark that for folks who wanted to express themselves as individuals they had a unique way of looking just like the person next to them. So much for individuality, I guess.

This was a primary and key area in the Topanga/Hollywood pipeline, where many runaway juveniles would be hidden from the law if they did not want to be found. It was a word-of-mouth thing and in those days everyone hated the "pigs." Runaways would come to Los Angeles/Hollywood to get their "big break." Whenever the law started closing in, they would be "whisked away to Topanga" within a couple of hours. (The popular 60s singing group The Mamas and The Papas, had a song on one of their albums that was specifically about Topanga Canyon.)

The term "pigs" surfaced just shortly after the Watts Riots in 1965 and became a household word to the criminal element. Marijuana was rampant, along with the usual drugs of choice, in that era.

Over the months I had developed a small group of "snitches." It was easy at that time, as back then you could bust people for possession if they only had one joint on their person, or drug paraphernalia. In some cases, even a roach. Ah, yes . . . drugs used to be a crime where you could go to jail, even for a small amount, vis-à-vis today's method of giving them a ticket.

On this particular sunny, warm, light smoggy day as we were driving around, one of my snitches flagged me down. I pulled over and parked my patrol unit and he started walking toward our radio car. It was not an uncommon sight to see a patrol unit parked and people milling around it.

"Hi, Deputy Penny," he said as he got within a few feet of the patrol car. It was evident that he had forgone showering for quite a few days. His body odor arrived way ahead of him.

I said hello and asked him how it was going . . . the usual start of a conversation. I knew he wouldn't be stupid enough to be holding, especially since I had just busted him a couple of months earlier.

"I got somethin' you are gonna want. It's big, man. Real big," he said. This was not his first time in providing me with information and he was starting to get nervous and excited while he was talking.

"Man," he continued, "this is the choicest bit. You should get a medal or somethin' for pullin' this off," he said as he looked around. "A bunch of dope is comin' into the 'Canyon' later today."

The conversation continued with several topic changes. I almost had to drag the main point out of him. He told me that sometime around sunset there would be a car with two people—a guy and a girl—and they were supposed to have suitcases full of marijuana. He gave me the name of the road and a description of "just that white house that sits back from the road." I was familiar with the area. Then, just as suddenly as he appeared, he disappeared.

I looked at my partner, who gave an ever-so-light shrug of his shoulders, looked at his notebook to make sure he had written down all of the information—he was the "bookman" that day—and said "Why not? We've got nothing going right now." He then retrieved his *Thomas Guide* map and looked up the street. The map was a necessity in the Malibu area. We had RD—reporting district—maps but the *Thomas Guide* was much easier to use. The Santa Monica mountains were full of small dirt roads and trails intermingled with paved or blacktop streets. I put the car in gear and off we went.

We found the particular street and turned onto it and began winding around and up into the hills. Several houses were scattered sparsely throughout the area, most of them set back from the road with dirt driveways leading up to them. If you were to see a photograph, you would think it was a typical country scene found in many rural areas throughout the United States. Yet only three miles to the south and you were at the beginning of a twenty-seven-mile stretch of beach called Malibu.

We had gone up the road for about a mile and did not see any white houses and we were running out of houses quickly. I was looking for a place to turn the car around when my partner said, "There's a white house back in there," and pointed to it. It was just barely visible from our position on the road. I drove just a little farther and . . . lo and behold! Another white house. This one was on the opposite side of the road and was also barely visible.

"If I'm correct," my partner said, "there should be a pretty good spot just up ahead where we can park and scope out both houses."

I continued driving up the road and my partner pointed out a dirt road—more like a path—which was just wide enough for me to drive in without putting too many scratches on the side of the car. I pulled in, then had to back out, turn the car around and drive in backward for about seventy-five feet. Finally, there was a level area to park, which I did. We got out and, using our binoculars, we had a bird's-eye view of both houses and yet we were concealed enough where we could not be seen.

It was about 4:30 PM and we figured no action would happen until at least dusk. It was daylight savings time and sunset was somewhere around 7:30 PM so that gave us about three hours.

We got back in the car, pulled out, and continued back up the road to where it intersected with another road where we could get out of the area without going by the houses again. We would be able to come back in that way later and no one would be the wiser.

I drove back to the station to meet with the station Narco detectives. I explained what I had. I knew there was no way to even meet the criteria where they could get a search warrant based on this. The only way we could do it would be just to go to the door, ask to be admitted, and . . . ask if we could conduct a search. Sounds simple enough. But who in their right mind would agree to that? Especially if they were holding! Well, many of the residents and transients in the area were those who had jumped into the shallow end of the gene pool when the lifeguard was not looking. *Ah, heck . . . might as well give it a shot. Who knows? Maybe we would just get lucky.*

It was agreed that my partner and I would go back later and Code 5 (stake-out) the location and then advise, via radio, if the information would come to fruition.

Two hours later my partner and I drove back to the area, after filling up a few cups of coffee—always a necessity when doing a stake-out —and parked in the hidden observation area.

About thirty minutes later—time frame measured by how many cups of coffee had been drunk, which in this case was two each— we observed a car pull in to the driveway of the white house on the east side of the road. I quickly picked up my binoculars and focused in on the car: male driver, female passenger. Looks good so far. The car doors opened and the man and woman got out of the car and the man went around to the rear of the car and opened the trunk. *Hot damn! He's pulling out some suitcases! This is too good to be true!*

He closed the trunk and, carrying the suitcases, they both started walking to the house. My partner picked up the radio mike and asked dispatch to notify Malibu station "Narco" that the subjects had arrived at the location. We knew it would be about thirty minutes before the Narco detectives would arrive at our location. Just enough time to finish the other two cups of coffee before they got cold.

The two Narco detectives arrived in their undercover car: a 1961 VW that looked like it wouldn't get out of the way of a bicycle, much less run. Both of them were dressed like the average hippie: Long hair and the normal hippie attire. If you were to see them on the Sunset Strip you would want to shake them down just for no reason. I pointed out the house and car and we devised a plan of attack: My partner and I would casually drive down to the house, park the car, and then my partner would sneak around to the rear of the house. I would walk up to the front door with the two Narco detectives. Plain and simple. Piece of cake. Not!

Everything was going according to plan. I knocked on the door and yelled loudly, "Sheriff's Department" and then heard a voice from within . . . well, maybe it was coming from the rear, "Come In!" I put my boot to the door and it opened, spewing a shower of splinters and pieces of door-jamb into the room. Guns drawn, we burst into the room. (If we had had flash-bangs that would have been even better.)

"Everyone freeze!" said one of the Narco detectives in a voice that sounded like it was coming from a bullhorn but was just the timbre of his voice. Very commanding and very authoritative.

A quick scan of the room revealed fifteen or so males and females, all standing around with champagne glasses in their hands. All of them, with the exception of two older men and two older women, each with graying hair, were in their middle to late twenties, dressed nicely, clean-cut appearance, and . . . only the women had long hair. *What the . . . ? You sure don't fit the hippie image, folks!*

I went to the back door and let my partner in. On the way back into the living room I saw four suitcases lying on a bed in one of the bedrooms. *Aha! . . the plot thickens . . . there's the evidence . . .*

piece of cake. My partner stayed with the suitcases while I went and advised the Narco detectives.

We asked about the suitcases and received permission to search them. I brought the suitcases out to the living room and proceeded to open them up: wedding dress, slip, bra, white shoes, white clutch purse, and more accoutrements. The other suitcase had a black tuxedo complete with cummerbund, red bow tie, pleated white shirt, black shoes, black socks . . . *Uh-oh! This sure as hell is not looking good! Where's the dope? Maybe in the other two suitcases? Nope . . . ah, shit! Wedding presents, gift book, garter, corsages, . . . No wonder they agreed.*

Now it was time for "diplomacy 101." In my most profoundly sincere voice I explained to them what a tragic joke someone must have played on them. (If you think Michael Jackson was a pro at the moon-walk you should have seen me. I was doing a good version of

THAT'S 10–4 . . . I HAVE THE WARRANT, AND NOW MY TRAINEE IS KICKING IN THE DOOR TO APARTMENT 7!

the backward-ankle-express toward the door.) Apparently my charm and diplomacy—there was no such thing as sensitivity training at that time—worked. They were all laughing and enjoying the festivities, thinking it was just a carry-over of the jokes that were played on the groom at his bachelor party two nights before.

Just as we were about to depart a young teenage boy on a bicycle came riding up the driveway. "Are you officers looking for somebody?" he said, "'cause I just saw some guy and a girl throw some stuff outta their car over across the street and then take off when they saw your car."

Arrrrggggggghhhhhhh!

Ever so quickly, we left the newlyweds and their friends, still in good spirits—thank goodness for champagne—and went to the white house across the street. There were three old battered suitcases lying on the ground. The impact from hitting the ground had opened up two of them and bags of marijuana had spilled out. Of all the dumb luck . . . we had the right information . . . but just the wrong house.

Excerpt from *Murphy's Law of Law Enforcement: If you have cleared all the rooms and met no resistance, you and your entry team have kicked in the wrong door of the wrong house.*

Mr. Murphy had followed me from Firestone to Malibu.

ANOTHER REASON I DON'T LIKE RAINY AND INCLEMENT WEATHER

— Harry Penny —

LOS ANGELES COUNTY SHERIFF'S DEPARTMENT
MALIBU STATION (#10), CIRCA 1968

In late 1972, the song *It Never Rains in Southern California,* written by Albert Hammond, hit the top five in the charts. Obviously, he was not working a radio car on day watch out of Malibu station in 1968. I was.

I was never a big fan of working day watch in a radio car and especially not during rainy and inclement weather. Not only did it require me to get up very early in the morning—which is not one of my favorite things—but southern California drivers are not exactly the best when it comes to driving in the rain. Especially in the Los Angeles area.

I was working day watch out of Malibu station and my beat was in the western end of the San Fernando valley. Most of the populated areas were in the unincorporated area of Los Angeles County. Areas such as Westlake Village, Agoura, Lost Hills, and Malibu Lake were unincorporated communities and all were located adjacent to the Ventura freeway—Highway 101—and as such, required me to be on the freeway quite frequently. There were no main thoroughfares linking them, so I had to use the freeway quite often. Fortunately the California Highway Patrol (CHP) was responsible for enforcing traffic regulations on the freeways in the county area.

It was raining heavily and yet cars were traveling at faster-than-safe speeds on the freeway. CHP units were having their hands full today. Me? I just drove along in the far right lane and that seemed fairly effective. As soon as a car got near me and saw that my car was quite different—red lights on top, siren, and big yellow letters on the trunk that said "SHERIFF"—I could see them hit their brakes and the front end of their car would dip. They would pass me going just a little faster than I was, but not excessive. Of course, once they got out of my sight they would stomp on it again, but at least for a little while they drove safely.

I was westbound on the freeway and was approaching the Lake Lindero turnoff when I saw a group of cars hit their brakes and start swerving. *What the?* They were apparently trying to avoid something in one of the lanes.

I flipped on my red-lights and my emergency flashers to give warning to the cars that were approaching me from behind and slowed down. The rain was really coming down at this point and my windshield wipers were just barely able to keep up with it. Suddenly I saw what was causing the commotion. A 1954 Plymouth sedan was stopped in the right-hand lane just before the off-ramp, and had the right turn indicator on.

I pulled up behind the car and stopped. I could barely make out the lone occupant in the driver's seat. The individual was holding what appeared to be a road map and appeared to be looking at it. Well, talk about being one taco shy of a combination plate, this one was also missing the rice and beans.

I checked my rear-view mirrors and saw that the traffic was coming just a little too close to the driver's side of my car in this rain. Not good. So I decided to go out the passenger's side. Now this is a feat of contortion in itself. My radio car had the bench-type front seat, same as other four-door passenger cars, but the similarity stopped there. The radio console and microphone was mounted under the bottom of the dashboard, in the center, and rested on top of the raised portion of the floorboard that covered the transmission. Right next to that was the base-plate and rack that held the 12-gauge shot gun in an upright position. I take this time to mention that I am 6'2" and 185 pounds. In addition, I am wearing my uniform gun belt, holster, ammo cases, handcuff case, and baton holder ring. As if that's not enough, I am in a big yellow rubberized raincoat. You can imagine the visual on this. I looked like "Big Bird" trying to do a "Hip-Hop" step inside of a car.

I finally made it. I opened the door to step out on the shoulder of the freeway. One foot out. Yep, that's good so far. Here comes the other one. And now the situation takes on a whole new approach. The rain had washed away some of the road along the edge and there was a fairly large hole about six inches deep and full of water right where my right foot was making its descent to the ground. This is not going to bode well for me. If anyone were to score this I would have had a perfect "10." I was past the point of no return by this time, so I continued to get out of the car.

Slosh, clump, slosh, clump were the sounds I was making as I walked up to the Plymouth. I could see the driver, a little, gray-haired old lady in a black coat that was buttoned all the way up to her wrinkled little neck. She was holding up a street map and had a look of extreme confusion on her face. I tapped the passenger's side window with my flashlight as lightly as I could hoping I would not startle her. Nope! That didn't just startle her, it scared the hell out of her. The map flew out of her hands, her eyeglasses leaped off her face and she let out an ear-piercing scream that almost shattered the windows.

Ah, yes, Harry. This is going well.

I finally managed to get her to roll down the passenger's window.

"Are you all right, Ma'am?" I asked.

"Yes. I think so. You scared the bejesus out of me, young man. What are you doing out in this terrible rain?" Her voice was one of those that sounds like fingernails being scraped along a chalkboard.

"Ma'am, I'm a deputy sheriff. You are creating a terrible traffic hazard. Is something wrong with your car?"

"No, officer."

"What seems to be the reason for you to be stopped like this?"

"I'm trying to find out if this Lost Hills Road is the one on the map but I can't find it."

"Ma'am, this is the same road. You must move your car before an accident happens."

"Okay, young man. I will. Why isn't this road on the map?"

"Ma'am, I believe you were holding the map upside down."

"Oh. Well, thank you. I'll go now," she said as she rolled up the window, put the car in gear and started to drive forward.

She didn't get too far, but just far enough for her right rear tire to hit a large puddle which caused the water to splash out. Right into my left shoe! The dry one!

She stopped again, honked her horn, rolled down the window and said, "Officer, you should get out of this terrible rain before you get all wet and catch a cold."

PRECURSOR TO THE JERRY SPRINGER SHOW?

— Harry Penny —

LOS ANGELES COUNTY SHERIFF'S DEPARTMENT
MALIBU STATION (#10), CIRCA 1968

My partner and I had been working the EM shift (Early Morning 11 PM to 7 AM) watch for about two months. Both of us enjoyed this particular shift and had no problems swapping other shifts with the other deputies as not many of them liked the EM shift. For one thing, this shift only deployed two cars: one covered the coast and the other covered the west end of the San Fernando valley. We were working the valley car designated as Malibu 102 EMs.

The station was located at 23123 West Pacific Coast Highway (PCH) in Malibu, almost equidistant between Malibu canyon and Topanga canyon. They are named canyons because that is just what they are: very windy roads that in certain parts if you are driving over twenty-five miles-per-hour it is dangerous.

My regular partner was on vacation and I was partnered up with another deputy whom I had worked with before. Our shift and assignment was the same, still working 102 EM. We were on the fourth of our four days on, two days off rotation, and had spent the last couple of days in court during the day, then we went home, tried to get a little sleep, ate, and came back to work. This particular night neither one of us had eaten dinner and we were famished. There were only a couple of restaurants in our patrol area in the west end of the county and they were definitely not open during the EM shift. (The area would undergo a drastic buildup in the coming years). That left only one option: We would have to go into either Woodland Hills or Canoga Park, which just happens to be in the city of Los Angeles, covered by LAPD's West Valley division area. That was permissible as we had to drive through those areas to get to the northern end of our patrol area. However, that could be as sticky a situation as we had experienced the night before.

At about 1:30 AM we were returning from a prowler call up in the northern end of our area. We were in Canoga Park and spotted two burglars breaking in to a closed gas station. We radioed in to request an LAPD unit as it was their jurisdiction and then arrested the suspects. Unfortunately, no units were available from LAPD at that time and we were told to take them to West Valley station, which we did. We gave them the info on the suspects so they could make the report. (Our sergeant was not too excited that we had two felony arrests—the credit went to LAPD.) We finished that up and went back to patrol in our area. We didn't get two blocks from West Valley station and a drunk walked right out into the street and I had to do some defensive driving (and praying) to avoid running over him. Yep! You guessed it! We hooked him up, put him in the car, and went back to West Valley station. One misdemeanor arrest. Again, in the city. Our sergeant had calmed down, realizing that this was probably just a fluke. We again went 10-8 and this time we were back in the county area.

Tonight, this was going to be different.

We headed to the Woodlake Bowl; a bowling alley in Woodland Hills, on Ventura Boulevard just east of Valley Center Boulevard It was close, about four blocks, to the contract city of Hidden Hills, which was part of our patrol area. Our station was well aware of the limited places to eat in our jurisdiction and it was approved by the captain. We could make a quick run-through there, make a patrol, then go Code 7. We did not have the luxury of having portable radios with the microphone attachment to clip on our shirts. Not only was our radio attached to the car, it was wired into the ignition and we had to keep the engine running or the radio would shut off. Oh, well . . . this would not be a problem. We would just call in and advise we were Code 7 and give them the phone number. In this particular time frame we were working a straight eight-hour shift, so we had to grab a bite to eat whenever we could, but, we were to remain by a phone or the radio and handle any calls that might come in. Many times I had left a full meal sitting on the counter to handle a call. That may have been one of the reasons I was able to always stay at a nice desirable weight. Anyway, as I said, this presented no problem.

Oops. Did I say no problem? My mistake. What I thought would be no problem turned out to be one. A very large one, in fact. Bad timing to go into a bowling alley restaurant just as the night bowling league was finishing, bars closing, and . . .

We pulled in and parked the radio car in an area where we could see it. My fingers were crossed that some beer-filled-bowling-team-shirt-wearing individual would not accidentally run into it, thereby causing me to have to call LAPD to come and take an accident report, which would go through their chain of command and end up at my station. Oh, no . . . that was one situation I definitely did not want. Not after last night!

After making sure the shotgun was securely locked in its holder and all of the doors were locked—this was a very important check, especially after what I had done to an unlocked LAPD unit when I was working Firestone—we exited the car and started walking toward the entrance. I had to admit that my partner and I did give off an image. Both of us were over six feet tall, my partner weighing in at about 215 and me at 190. Both of us resplendent in our freshly pressed uniforms complete with badge, Sam Browne leather belt, gun, holster, handcuffs, and black leather gloves. As we made our way from the car, I noticed a male and a female sitting in one of the booths by the window. Normally their backs would be toward us.

They were, but their heads had both turned around and they had seen us. It wasn't but a few seconds when some of the other patrons, also sitting in several booths, looked around at us also. Word of mouth sure travels fast.

We got to the door and walked inside. The restaurant was connected to the bowling alley. There were two entrances—one from the east end of the parking lot, and one that came in from the bowling alley. The counter was in a semi-circle shape, with a split in the middle of the counter where the cash register was located. Waitresses would come out to the walk-way used for customers and normal foot traffic. This walkway separated the counter from the booths along the windows. The food was good and in those days it was a fairly decent place to eat. The customers could also get drinks served from the bar in the bowling alley.

This particular night happened to be a Friday. Again . . . bad choice. It was crowded. Oh, the joys of walking into a crowded restaurant full of alcohol-laden individuals who would immediately try to appear to be sober, hands automatically reaching for their coffee cups—it was like I could read their thoughts, *"I hope those cops don't see me leaving and getting into my car,"or "If I wait until they are seated then I can get in my car and leave without them seeing me . . . I can't afford a 502 . . ."* Well . . . you get the idea. We stood out like a pair of shower shoes on a tuxedo.

My partner and I had seated ourselves right at next to the cash register. There was a divide in the counter. This was normally where LAPD, CHP and of course, Malibu station deputies would sit. The phone was right there also. I used the phone, land-lined the station, and advised the sergeant of our location.

Now, most cops have an uncomfortable feeling sitting with their backs to the public—they usually find a booth where their backs are against the wall and they can see what is going on in front of them. For some inexplicable reason neither I, nor my partner, felt uncomfortable in this particular establishment.

The area behind us was a long, padded bench seat running the length of the window area, with tables and chairs. There were no separate booths. All of the tables were occupied. The one directly behind us had a man and a woman who gave the appearance of a "boss" enjoying a little time with his "secretary." The man, I estimated to be in his mid-to-late fifties, was dressed in a nice dark suit, crispy starched white shirt resplendent with glittering cufflinks, loud tie with a tie-tack that matched his cuff-links. He wore a large gold ring on his left hand (possibly a wedding ring) that was just as flashy as his tie-tack and cuff-links. His hair was neatly coiffed, highlighting the silver gray at the temples. The woman, much younger, estimated age of about twenty-five, was wearing a dress that was obviously not off-the-rack, which allowed an extreme view of her ample cleavage. She was seated very close to him. They appeared to be engaged in a very private conversation, (she was looking at him and he was looking at her, although not eye-to-eye), while at the same time just playing with their untouched breakfast. (Did I mention that she displayed a very ample cleavage? Cops are well trained in being observant of their surroundings.)

We gave the waitress our order. We had both decided that a Denver omelet, with hash browns, toast and coffee, would hit the spot. They were really known for their huge omelets. We "tuned out" the laughter, slurred speech conversations, and the like and each of us took a section of the newspaper and began to peruse the articles. My partner was big into the sports section. Me . . . ? I chose the comic section. Nothing like a good variety of reading material to improve my intellectual brain. (I had to think of some way to distract the vision of the ample cleavage.)

I was just folding the paper, so it wouldn't take up all my counter space, when I heard two voices behind me, one male and one female. I quickly glanced back and saw the couple standing behind me, just to my left. They were dressed nicely for the evening; suit and tie on him and a nice dress on her. I turned back to my comics. Within the next few seconds I heard the timbre change in their voices. I thought to myself, *Nah . . . nobody would be stupid enough to cause any problems with two cops sitting right in front of them.* Just then our food arrived. Oh, how delicious it looked and smelled. It probably would have tasted good . . . if the unthinkable hadn't happened.

My partner set down his sports section and was reaching for the ketchup bottle, as his normal custom was to put ketchup on everything . . . well maybe not his toast, but everything else that was on the plate. Just as his fingers were tightening on the ketchup bottle another hand quickly came from behind him and snatched the bottle. In the next second a voice yelled, "You dirty bitch! What do you think you are doing?" This was accompanied by the sound of the bottle hitting a solid object, quickly determined to be a human skull, breaking the bottle into pieces, the ketchup leaving the bottle and flying in all directions; especially in the direction of our uniforms. (*Murphy's Law* states that uniforms are a natural magnet to ketchup that happens to be in the nearby vicinity.)

"What the . . . ?" my partner and I both said simultaneously as we quickly turned around. In that short period of five to ten seconds, another couple had come in and now they were also standing behind us when it happened. Dave and I were out of our seats and right in the middle of this fiasco. There was no room for us to be anywhere else. What we saw was absolutely incredible.

Standing mere inches away from us were the four individuals; two men and two women. The second couple, like the first couple, were each nicely dressed for the evening. To our well-trained eyes and our keen powers of observation, it appeared that they had been out for the evening and were stopping in for a bite to eat. The only difference in this scenario was that one of the women had the remains of the ketchup bottle in one hand and a huge hunk of hair, a wig, in her other hand. The other woman had a large gash in her forehead with blood and ketchup surrounding the wound. The two men were standing in awe. However, that only lasted for another couple of seconds while the vision went from their eyes to their brains, along with the message that something was definitely wrong. Then they began pushing each other.

One of the men started yelling obscenities and then, not to be out-done, the other joined in. It was unclear as to who they were yelling at. One man pushed the other man into a table in the booth directly behind us. Yep, that's right! The man landed right on top of the table where the "boss" and his "secretary" were seated, and continued his falling motion, thereby sending coffee cups, water glasses, silverware, and plates with eggs, steak, hashbrowns, ketchup, and toast, right into their laps . . . along with him.

The woman who had been the recipient of the ketchup bottle reached out, grabbed the blouse of her attacker, causing the buttons to rip off, material to tear, exposing her attacker's bra, as they both started falling to the floor.

Many of the other patrons began yelling and screaming while attempting to push their chairs away from the tables and get out of the way. Of course, in their moment of panic, the plates of food, cups of coffee, drinks, and just about everything that wasn't nailed down, came into the field of play.

Now, my partner and I, being officers of the law, realized that it was our bound duty to take some course of action. Our first fleeting instinct, as anyone in this position would think, would be to go 10-8 and let LAPD handle it. Yeah, right! No such luck.

So, into the fracas we go. Jump right in . . . both feet!

I went for the man who was still standing and dropped him to the ground and handcuffed him in a very quick movement. Surprised myself on that one. Next, I went for the guy who had so rudely interrupted the other man and woman's conversation. He was still standing in a combative position after smacking the other man. I grabbed him, and of course, in doing so, I ended up adorning my uniform with more accoutrements to coordinate with the ketchup design. (*Murphy's Law* applies here.) I threw a hammer lock on him and took him to the ground. Again, another problem arose: I only had one set of handcuffs and they were on the first guy. So, being innovative, yeah . . . right . . . I un-cuffed one of the handcuffs on man number one and, hoping that they would not try to continue their combat, placed it on man number two. I sure could have used some of those plastic cuffs.

Dave had been close to the two women and he was trying to separate them. This is not as easy as one would think. Each time he

DO I LOOK LIKE JERRY SPRINGER?

would grab one, she would slip on the aforementioned ketchup, glass, and other foodstuffs, and fall back down on the other woman. The one who had the wig in her hand was refusing to let go of her piece of victory. Eventually, all three of them were on the floor.

After some doing we finally managed to get them separated and cuffed. Again . . . with each of us only having only one set of handcuffs . . . well, you get the idea. The main thing was to keep them from fighting. That was no easy task when some of the other patrons were yelling at them and trying to get out of the way.

We managed to actually drag them out of the aisle and into the area that separated the bowling alley from the restaurant and sat them on the floor. I went back to the phone and called the station. "Uh, Sarge? You're not going to believe this but we need you to call LAPD West Valley division and have them send a unit . . . " It took a few minutes for the situation to sink into the sergeant's mind. He finally relented when I told him we were 10-15 with one felony 245 and three 415/647-fs. Then another minute or so of getting my butt nicely chewed. This was the third arrest situation in the city in about two days. "Why don't you guys try to make an arrest in the county instead of the city?" was his ending statement.

I hung up the phone and went back to my partner and our suspects. Lucy and Ricky, Fred and Ethel this wasn't. Close though. It turned out that one couple had entered from the bowling alley and the other couple came in from the opposite end from the parking lot. No problem so far. At first, I thought they were arguing over the only vacant booth. No such luck. No, this was more complicated than that.

Long ago I heard a definition of a happily married couple . . . A husband out with some other man's wife. Well, this was in that situation. Couple number one: Mr. Brown was out with Mrs. White. Couple number two? Why of course . . . none other than Mr. White and Mrs. Brown. (I see the light bulb going off in your mind about now). Neither couple was aware of their spouse's extra-curricular activities. At least not until just a few minutes ago.

We finally managed to quiet them down a few decibels. I had gotten a wet towel for the injured lady and she was holding it to her head. It seemed like hours while we awaited LAPD, but they finally arrived. I began explaining the situation to the two officers. It was difficult to get through to them as they were laughing while I was talking. Finally, I got it out. Here arose another problem: They weren't going to take them!

"Oh no, you guys," remarked the more senior of the two officers. "There's no way in hell our watch commander is even going to believe us." They were going to just flat leave. *Uh, oh. This isn't looking good,* I thought. After compromising, and promising we wouldn't make any more arrests in their area, (they were the same two officers we had given the gas station burglars too), we finally managed to get them to take the two males and we would transport the two females to West Valley division, which we did. It took a while for us to convince the watch commander that they (LAPD) should handle the situation and that we would write a supplemental report.

A few weeks later we were talking with two LAPD officers who worked West Valley and they said that there was something at West

Valley division for us. So we decided to stop by. When we walked in we were met by one of the sergeants. He handed each of us a package. Just then, several officers appeared and we had an audience. We opened the packages and each one contained a custom made uniform shirt. One of the officers wives had taken an LAPD blue shirt (traffic type that had the LAPD shoulder patches) and one LASD shirt and split them in half. Then taking half of each shirt and sewing them together they had a new design. The objective: Whenever we were in LAPD territory we were to have the LAPD shirt side near the window. We all enjoyed a good laugh on that one; even our watch commander, who was in on it, got the chuckles. Now it was time to concentrate on making an arrest in the county.

A few nights later we were westbound on Ventura freeway and observed a vehicle with license plates that were on the "hot sheet." For those of you unfamiliar with the term "hot sheet" and probably didn't watch "Adam 12" or "Dragnet" I will briefly explain: the "hot sheet" contained the license numbers of stolen/wanted vehicles. It was prepared by LAPD on, I believe, a daily basis. Of course this was the latest thing at that time. These would be obtained from the nearest LAPD division and brought back to our stations throughout Patrol Division. They would be passed out at briefing and each car would take one and put it on the sun visor in the patrol unit. It was a normal procedure to check the "Hot Sheet" whenever you had a particular vehicle and wanted probable cause for a stop. Heck, there were a number of times when one would actually come across a plate from the sheet—more near misses than hits, unfortunately.

Now in this particular instance the only problem was that the "Hot Sheet" was a week old. So I picked up the mike and ran a "rolling 10-29." It is important to note that in this era we did not have computers in our cars, and everything was done in the radio room via teletype, which could take anywhere from ten minutes to an hour. In this case it was about twenty minutes. We were able to cover a good distance at sixty-five miles per hour.

We were following the vehicle when it passed Westlake Village and crossed into Ventura County. Again, I radioed to see if there were any results and was told to stand by as they were confirming with the R/O. About four miles into Ventura County, in the city of Thousand Oaks, the radio dispatcher advised us that the car had been stolen previously but had been recovered and the R/O had picked it up earlier today. We acknowledged the transmission and took the next turnoff to return back to our patrol area.

We went under the freeway and were approaching the on-ramp when we saw two individuals at the closed gas station at the bottom of the off-ramp, which we had to pass, pick up some bricks and throw them through the front window. Here we go again . . . a 459 right in front of us.

They didn't see us, and proceeded to break out the rest of the glass, enter into the building and start removing items from the shelves. Decision time: Do we kiss it off as it is in Ventura County? Nah . . . not us. Why should that make any difference? Our arrest powers were enforceable anywhere within the State of California. We were four-for-four on stupid crooks. One more situation wouldn't make any difference at this point.

So a quick pull into the parking lot, jump out of the car with guns drawn and, "Surprise! You've been busted!" A good felony arrest. Only one slight problem. We were about four miles inside the Ventura Count line and so we had to have our watch commander call Ventura County Sheriff's Department so we could give them the arrest.

"Look guys," said our watch commander over the phone when I called him. "When I said make an arrest in the county, dammit! I meant Los Angeles County!!!"

It is important to note that after we turned the suspects over to the Ventura Deputies we did make an arrest in Los Angeles County. A drunk who was hitchhiking and was standing just past the sign on the freeway entrance. You know . . . the sign saying . . . pedestrians and bicycles, etc. not allowed on the freeway.

THE
PLANE CRASH

— Harry Penny —

LOS ANGELES COUNTY SHERIFF'S DEPARTMENT
MALIBU STATION (#10), CIRCA 1968–1969

It was a nice summer and I was just finishing a two-month tour on day watch. I was really looking forward to going back to PM watch. The lieutenant thought I should do some rotation for a little while. Now most folks would say something like, *"Working Malibu in the summer on days, looking at all of those surfer-gals in bikinis? Who wouldn't like it?"* . . . and other things. Well, if you've never been to Malibu in the summer and had to maneuver in and out of traffic on Pacific Coast Highway (PCH or old Highway 101) with just two lanes in each direction, you might just think that. But I learned my lesson early.

It was mid-afternoon and I had just finished writing a traffic citation when the call came out: "Malibu 101 . . . a 903 on Malibu Beach . . . Malibu Colony, Malibu 101, your call is Code 3." *What the hell is a 903? It sounded familiar.* With it being a Code 3 call I immediately acknowledged the call and hit my lights and siren. I was at the intersection of Topanga Canyon and PCH. To get to the scene I had to take PCH. There are no other streets that go all the way through Malibu—through the populated area that was the original area of Malibu. Lots of apartments, cars, restaurants, stores that sold beachy-type stuff, and the worst part was that it became a narrow four-lane road with all of the cars parked in a not-so-orderly fashion. Malibu Colony was a gated community at the other end of old Malibu, right on the beach, near Malibu canyon and PCH (where Pepperdine University is located), and many famous people, movie stars, etc., had homes. I didn't have time to look in my code book to see what a 903 call was but I would figure it out when I got there.

Of course, *Murphy's Law* says: *"When a civilian sees your flashing light approaching at a high rate of speed, he will always pull into the lane you need to use."* Mr. Murphy made his presence known, more than once in this instance. I finally arrived at the location—along with a whole group of cars—(I felt like the Pied Piper of storybook fame, only instead of rats, I had cars, trucks, motorcycles, and, even bicycles) and observed a large group of people standing by the large wall at the east end of the colony, looking toward the beach. The security guard at the gate entrance was having a difficult time

Another saying from Murphy's Law: *Whenever you are not in proper uniform there is always a news photographer nearby.* Original photograph of Doug Andrews, *Evening Outlook,* circa 1968, giving to personally to the author.

Photo by Doug Andrews for the *Evening Outlook*.

keeping people out, but he was successful. (Still, no time to check my code book.) I killed the lights and siren and drove into the colony.

I picked up the mike and went 10-97 (arrived at scene) and saw a group of residents running over to the beach. Being astute, I followed them. I still didn't know what a 903 was. (It turned out to be "aircraft accident." I remembered handling another plane crash, fatal, when I was at Firestone.) This was, fortunately, a non-injury plane crash.

I made sure no one was injured and then went back to the radio car to put out the Code 4 (no further assistance needed) and gave the brief information of the situation. I then returned to the scene.

The pilot lost part of his prop when he was about 6,000 feet in the air and decided it would be safer to land on the nice white sandy beach than in the nice, ocean-blue water.

Smart choice. Of course, the traffic got very congested, and the crowd continued to grow and *Mr. Murphy* continued to muck up the situation. Here comes the press.

Another saying from *Murphy's Law: Whenever you are not in proper uniform there is always a news photographer nearby.*

You guessed it. I had my helmet off. (Department policy was whenever you were out of your radio car you must wear your helmet.) I had taken it off when I got back to the car to put out the radio broadcast.

I saw the photographer and his camera and I knew that this plane crash was going to make the newspaper. I immediately rushed over to him and said, "I'll give you five bucks if you will see that I get that picture you just took and take another one with my helmet on." Without hesitation he took my five bucks and I still have that picture. He took another picture and that was the one that appeared in the *Evening Outlook* newspaper.

Upon completion of the call, I was following the fire truck that had responded and was now returning back to their station on Carbon Canyon and PCH. Traffic was a bear. (Do you remember when I said we had drawn a crowd?) We were only doing about five miles per hour and it was stop and go. I was looking at the traffic and saw a group of bikini-clad, very tan, beach bunnies walking along the side of the road about ten feet from the side of my radio car. The firemen were looking as well, but then again, they weren't driving. I didn't quite see the *big, shiny red,* fire truck . . . stop.

Fortunately for me, the photographer had left earlier. *Well now, Mr. Murphy. It looks like I escaped your clutches this time!*

PROPER RADIO PROCEDURE? NOT EXACTLY!

— Harry Penny —

LOS ANGELES COUNTY SHERIFF'S DEPARTMENT
MALIBU STATION (#10), CIRCA 1968–1970

Proper use of the radio was a policy that was to be strictly adhered to on the LASD. This was drilled into us at the academy. We were given an official code book in class and tested on the numerous codes. Just about any situation had a radio code. After all we had to conform to the FCC (Federal Communications Commission) regulations. Then, after graduation, most of us went to the Jail Division or Corrections Division where we promptly forgot most of the codes other than the ones mostly used such as 10-8 (in service); 10-9 (repeat); 10-19 (return to station or desk as applicable); 10-7 (out of service); and of course, the one cops favor most Code 7 (out of service to eat).

After two years of working in the Hall of Justice jail, I finally got transferred to Patrol Division. That was the ultimate for me and for just about every deputy I worked with. Time to go out and ride around in a black-and-white and do "cop work."

What a happy day! I got my first choice: FIRESTONE STATION. (Actually all three of my choices were Firestone.)

I was assigned a training officer (T/O) and the first night in the car I realized just how much I had forgotten about radio codes.

OFFICIAL

CODE
BOOK

COUNTY OF LOS ANGELES

SHERIFF'S DEPARTMENT

Peter J. Pitchess — Sheriff

The Official Code Book, Los Angeles County Sheriff's Department, circa 1960s. Code Book image from the author's personal collection.

Firestone was reportedly the third busiest station in the U.S. with NYPD's Harlem Precinct at #1 and Chicago PD's south Chicago area at #2. The dispatcher at Firestone sometimes put out 100 radio calls during an eight-hour shift. My T/O gave me a green standard sheet of paper which was actually a copy of an official document explaining proper radio procedure. I was to tell my T/O what each call was no matter who the call was assigned to. My code book seemed like an extension of my hand. If I didn't follow correct procedure I would not only hear about it from my T/O, but I would have to answer to the watch deputy, the watch sergeant, up the chain of command, and, if it was really a serious violation, a memo to the radio room sergeant at the least. They, and the FCC, didn't take too kindly to improper procedure.

When I transferred to Malibu station in late 1967 it was quite a change. There would be times when I would not get a radio call during my whole shift, especially on EMs (Early Mornings, 11 PM to 7 AM). The only time we would use the radio would be if we initiated the call, such as license plate checks, checking for warrants on individuals, etc. There was one call however that was required.

The radio room, Station B, was the main radio dispatch center for the department and was located in the Sheriff's Department headquarters in the Hall of Justice in downtown Los Angeles.

There were six or seven frequencies for the overall area, and each area had only one dispatch frequency. There was more than one station on the frequency. Calls for service from citizens that were received at a sheriff's station would be taken by a complaint deputy who would write down all of the information on a call slip. The call slip would be given to the station dispatcher who would then pick up a phone that automatically rang in the radio room, which was staffed by four radio telephone operators (RTOs) and one sergeant.

The station dispatcher would give the exact call to the radio telephone operator (RTO) that was to be dispatched to that particular unit. The RTO would write it down on a specific form and then it would be broadcast. The broadcast from the radio room to the car/s could be monitored by all of the units and the stations that were on that particular frequency. However, the response from the car(s) could not be monitored by the other units. There was a special frequency (frequency 1) on the radios in the cars that was used for car-to-car.

August 1965
Jack Bennett - "Dispatcher"
Claude Anderson - "Watch Deputy"

Jack Bennett (left) and Claude Anderson (right), cartoonist, at work at Firestone station, August 1965. Photo courtesy of Jack Miller, LASD (Ret.)

The Radio Room, Station B, located in the Sheriff's Department
Headquarters located at the Los Angeles Hall of Justice. Photo
courtesy of Jack Miller, LASD (Ret.)

This was a valuable necessity to coordinate between multiple units
responding to a call and other "official uses."

To do this, a unit that wanted to talk with another unit would
have to go through the RTO, who would pass the information to the
other car using the radio call 10-31. A typical example would be:
"Firestone 11, 10-31, Firestone 12 . . . one-one." The RTO would
then broadcast "Firestone 12 . . . frequency one with Firestone 11."
Then by use of the toggle switch on the radios the cars would be
able to talk directly with each other. Now you may think this would
be a way to set up a meet at the local donut shop, which wasn't
unusual, but . . . the station also could hear that conversation. Too
many of those meets, however, could be an unwise choice. During
peak times there could be as many as 200 units in the field county-
wide and the radio room would send out as many as 5,000 radio
calls in twenty-four-hour period, or more than 400 transmissions an

hour. That's not including the incoming radio calls from the units themselves who might be requesting information such as warrant checks on suspects, etc.

There were twelve points in the Sheriff's training bulletin. Point #2: "Check your code book before going on the air. Use the standardized codes." Point #9: "Keep your voice emotionless regardless of the situation since emotion distorts the voice. Also avoid profanity, humor, or attempts at being a 'personality kid'." Proper radio procedure was a serious matter.

An Official Sheriff's Training Bulletin, vol. 1, no. 1, circa 1960s. Image courtesy of Jack Miller, LASD (Ret.).

The FCC license issued to the Los Angeles Sheriff's Department dispatch center was KMA-628. Mobile (hand-held radios that were about the size of a lunchbox) and radio car radios were assigned a separate license which was KA-4306. FCC regulations required that both licenses were to be verified over the air every thirty minutes, especially during the EM or graveyard shift. To do this, Station B would randomly select a patrol unit at one of the stations. Whichever unit, such as my unit (Malibu 101 or 102) would receive a radio call like this:

"Malibu 102, FCC"

Upon receiving this call my response would be:

"Malibu 102, King, Adam 4306 . . . one-oh-two." We used the phonetic alphabet when saying the letters.

Station B would respond, "KMA-628 . . . (and give the time), KMA-628 clear."

Now that I have given just the basics, I'll get into the story.

My partner "Mace" and I were working the EM shift when the call came out around three in the morning, "Malibu 101 . . . FCC"

Mace was a good cop and very conscientious. He was booking that night and as such, handled the radio. He calmly reached over and took the mike off of the clip, keyed the mike for transmission, and then . . . in his most melodious, rich, deep baritone voice, started his own version of the old song *Raggmopp*.

(For those of you who are not familiar with it, it was "R, I say RA . . . slight pause . . . RAG . . . RAGG . . . R-A-G-G-M-O-P-P, RAG-MOP . . . doodle eee ah . . . de . . . doodooo").

Mace's version however, was . . . "K . . . I say KA . . . KA four . . . KA four three . . . KA four three oh six . . . doodle eee ah de doodoo . . . one-oh-one," and then promptly returned the mike to its holder. Holy shit! I thought to myself. We are in deep kim-chi.

To my surprise and amazement the RTO came back on the air laughing, and we could hear the rest of the radio room, even the sergeant, laughing, as she said, "Ten-four, one-oh-one, oh-three hundred hours, KMA-628 Clear."

Nothing further was ever said.

Now, forty years later, in a conversation with a good friend of mine, "Skip" Ryzow (Sgt. LASD Ret.), who also contributed a story for this book, I would find out that Mace had done this when they were partners.

I was working with another partner, Ward, and we were working Malibu 101, Early Mornings. It was about 4:00 AM and we were parked in a parking lot of a church located in Malibu Canyon to grab a bite to eat. We had stopped in one of the local liquor stores just after coming on duty and picked up some sandwiches, chips, and sodas. There were no fast-food drive-thru's at that particular time in Malibu, and the only restaurants that were open past midnight had a bar in them and even then, they had to close at 2:00 AM.

The church was on a hill a couple of miles north of the Pepperdine University campus and afforded a beautiful view of the ocean. The moon was full and bright and reflected on the water and the view was breathtaking. The silence was almost deafening. Talk about serene.

Just as I had taken the first bite out of my sandwich the radio came to life.

"Malibu 101 . . . FCC" came the soft, warm voice of the RTO.

"I got it," said Ward as he reached over and grabbed the mike.

I really appreciated that as I would've sounded like a squirrel with his cheeks stuffed with food.

"Malibu 101 sitting high atop a hill in beautiful Malibu, on a warm, summer early morning, overlooking the big Pacific Ocean where the moon is full and shining brightly on the water. The surf is about one foot as the gentle waves make their journey to the shore. King Adam 4306. One-oh-one," and he calmly returned the mike to its holder.

Well, needless to say his response, definitely not being within the proper radio procedure, caused me not only alarm as I could just see how I was going to have to write this memo, it also was cause for the food in my mouth to look for an escape route back the way it had come in, and although the consistency had changed somewhat, it made a perfect mid-air collision with Ward's right sleeve.

Without hesitation, the RTO came back on the air and said "Ten-four, Malibu one-oh-one, sitting high atop a hill in beautiful Malibu, on a warm, summer early morning, overlooking the big Pacific Ocean where the moon is full and shining brightly on the water. The surf is about one foot as the gentle waves make their journey to the shore. Zero four hundred hours KMA six two eight, clear." She had repeated Ward's transmission word-for-word.

Of course, the soda in the soda can that I had just raised to my lips and taken a swig to stop from choking, also found a way to escape. This time the final destination was my clipboard and log sheet that was in my lap. Ward had moved his arm.

To my further amazement, there was not another transmission from the radio room, which I knew had to be forthcoming from the radio room sergeant. In fact, the next two times the radio room requested the FCC . . . guess what unit they called! Yep. Malibu 101.

Now you might think that these things happened frequently but no, they didn't. None of us were that dumb. But then again . . . to

TRAINING TIP #53: TRAINING OFFICERS SHOULD BE AWARE THAT NEW TRAINEES ON THE RADIO CAN BECOME "COCKY" AFTER THEY LEARN WHAT 10-36 MEANS!

TEN FOUR BIG MAMA. I READ YOU
FIVE BY SUGAR FIVE . . . YO!

quote the well-known radio personality Mr. Paul Harvey, when he says "And now . . . the REST of the story."

It was in the late summer of 1970, I believe. This time there were numerous units working out of Malibu station because of the enormous fire, supposedly the largest in California history, that started in Ojai (CA) and burned down through Santa Barbara County, Ventura County, into the western end of Los Angeles County, leaving widespread destruction in its wake. Miraculously it had spared the new community known as Westlake Village as it burned in and out of the canyons and worked its way almost to the Los Angeles city limits. Coming in from the north, it wound its way through the hills and canyons from the county line separating Ventura County and Los Angeles County, over the top of the Santa Susana Pass in the northwestern area of the San Fernando valley, down through the pass and into the canyon areas above Chatsworth, burning everything in its path. It even burned the Spahn Ranch—an old movie ranch—where Charles Manson and his followers were arrested for trespassing earlier that year.

(As irony would have it, old man Spahn was afraid that Manson and his group would come back and burn his ranch down in retaliation for him having them arrested, so when they went to court on the charge the next day, he refused to sign the complaint, and they had to be released.)

The section of fire that came in from the west, met up with the section from the north in the area where old Topanga Canyon and new Topanga Canyon meet in the Santa Monica mountains. The fire burned for several days and on one occasion the flames even burned all the way down to Pacific Coast Highway, where the flames jumped over and burned two houses sitting on Point Dume, a bluff overlooking the beach.

We were working twelve-hour shifts at a minimum, and many even longer, and as I said, we had deputies from other stations; detectives (who hadn't worn a uniform in a long time); California Highway Patrol (CHP), who was responsible for traffic on the highways in the unincorporated area; and even some LAPD units, as

I recall. We were evacuating people from all over the 188.94 square miles of our patrol area.

I had stopped at one of the fire command posts at old Topanga and new Topanga Canyons to get an update of information on what areas needed to be evacuated next. There was a compilation of fire trucks, ambulances, radio cars, other types of emergency vehicles as far as the eye could see, except you couldn't see much for the smoke. You could see the glow of the fires and the combination of the emergency lights from the vehicles and at night it was just like a scene out of a science fiction movie. Of course, I ran into many deputies I had worked with at Firestone and at the jail and hadn't seen in quite a while. Many of them had never worked at Malibu and were unfamiliar with the area—which caused some confusion and frustration at times. There were a few of us standing around a radio car and the radio had been switched over to the outside speaker.

"Attention any unit in the Malibu area. Any unit that can 10-13 (advise weather and road conditions) advise." Apparently it was change of watch at the radio room and they had not been watching the local TV or listening to the radio.

We all looked at each other in amazement. Finally, a deputy from another station reached in the car, picked up the mike and said, excitedly, "Things are really fucked up out here," and dropped the mike back on the seat. Well, that got the attention of the radio room sergeant in a big manner. The next voice was definitely a man's voice as he said, "Unit transmitting last message, 10-37 immediately!" He was wanting the person who transmitted that message to identify himself. Uh oh, The shit's going to really hit the fan, I thought to myself. But to my utter amazement, I couldn't believe what I was seeing. The deputy reached in the car, picked up the mike, but instead of saying, "Yes, Sir, Sergeant, Sir. I'm just going to go right back to the mike and pick it up and tell you my name and badge number and my assignment and all the information you need to take my nice shiny badge and stick it up my . . ." The deputy keyed the mike and said, in a calm, soothing manner, "We may be fucked up,

Station B, circa 1960s. Betty Sweets (left with glasses), Mary Burke (top), George Escobedo (center). The unidentified male is placing a request to the Records Section by using a vacuum tube. Photo courtesy of Betty Sweets, RTO, LASD (Ret.)

but we're not that fucked up!" then put the mike back in the car and returned to his cup of coffee.

I guess he didn't bring his copy of that green training bulletin.

Note: The RTOs were a radio car deputy's lifeline. They would constantly monitor their radio and often, when a radio-car had not been heard from in an unusual period of time, the RTO would come on the air and check to see if the situation was Code 4. All of us were grateful that they were there. I, myself, called them the "Angels of the Airwaves."

NEW MEANING FOR AN OLD TEXACO COMMERCIAL

— Dennis "Skip" Ryzow, Sgt. LASD (Ret.) —

LOS ANGELES COUNTY SHERIFF'S DEPARTMENT
MALIBU STATION (#10), CIRCA 1966

Malibu station was a unique type of station in its appearance when compared to the type of police/sheriff's stations you see on television. The station was located at 21323 West Pacific Coast Highway on that stretch of Pacific Coast Highway between Topanga Canyon and Malibu Canyon in what is now known as old Malibu. It is a long two-story brick building with a red Spanish-style stucco roof. The main entrance is in the middle of the building and once you enter, the sheriff's station is on your left. On your right is the Malibu Courthouse. On the west end of the building is a small parking area about one hundred feet long. In the middle of this parking area is a smaller building that looks like a gas station (which it is) with a covered gas pump island. This building was the locker room for the patrol deputies. And the gas pump was for filling up the patrol cars.

It was at the end of my shift and I had just pulled into the gas pump to fill up my radio car for the next shift. I got out of the car and filled the tank. When I finished I pulled the car into a parking space and began to unload my gear from the car when I saw a car pull into the lot and up to the pump island.

My keen powers of observation immediately detected that it was not one of our cars, so I began walking over to the car to advise the citizen of his mistake.

The driver opened the door and, with some difficulty (I shortly determined that he had been drinking . . . a lot), got out of the car and began walking, again, with some difficulty, toward me. My cop curiosity was highly piqued at this time. He had his car keys in his hand. When he got near me he handed me his car keys and told me to "fill her up" and started to walk away, toward the little building, mumbling something about the restroom.

Obviously this individual must have watched TV and been a Milton Berle fan. During this time you may recall the old Milton Berle TV Show that was sponsored by TEXACO and the commercial jingle "You can trust your car to the man who wears the star."

Needless to say, he didn't get his gas. He didn't complete his journey either.

A TRAINEE LEARNS TO ALWAYS AID
A MOTORIST WITH CAR TROUBLE.

HELLO, WEST HOLLYWOOD!

— Harry Penny —

LOS ANGELES COUNTY SHERIFF'S DEPARTMENT
WEST HOLLYWOOD STATION (#9), CIRCA 1970–1971

Located in between Hollywood and Beverly Hills is an area of unincorporated county territory approximately three square miles in size known as West Hollywood. Although the population is around 42,000, that figure does not reflect the number of people who frequent the well-known area called the "Sunset Strip." During the 1940s and 1950s, the glamour years of Hollywood, you would hear of famous restaurants and night clubs such as The Moulin Rouge, Ciro's, The Sunset Room, and of course . . . The Brown Derby, just to mention a few. You may recall in some movies where the gentlemen were dressed in black tuxedos, a red flower in their lapel, black bow tie on a starched white shirt, and sitting across from a lovely lady in a nice evening gown, at a candle-lit table for two, and couples, similarly dressed, out on the dance floor dancing to the music of a live band, which was also dressed alike. Yes, these were the days of the Hollywood glamour scene.

However, in the middle 1960s, this scene underwent a whole different take: Establishments with such names as the Whisky-A-Go-Go, The Pussy Cat Lounge, Pandora's Box, and stores selling clothing styles that reflected articles of clothing such as tie-dyed shirts, beads, head bands, sandals, jeans with patches, peace symbols, and various implements known as drug paraphernalia, and so on. The list was almost endless. Drugs, sex, and rock-and-roll was the mantra. Long hair, frayed jeans, tie-dyed shirts, sandals, and day-glo colors abounded. Each individual saying they were being individual. A whole new generation was surfacing.

Night clubs such as the Whiskey-A-Go-Go—well-known venue for the popular musical groups of that era such as The Rolling Stones, Earth Wind and Fire, Three Dog Night, The Fifth Dimension, Chicago, The Mamas and the Papas, and a myriad of others—songs like *Proud Mary, The Age of Aquarius,* and the list goes on and on, and of course the emergence of Go-Go dancers . . . again, the list is almost endless.

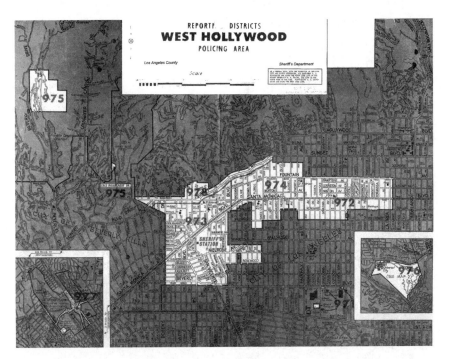

Reporting Districts for West Hollywood personnel, circa 1970. Map from personal file of the author.

The old West Hollywood station, 720 North San Vincente Blvd., West Hollywood, circa 1979.

At first, it was usually Friday and Saturday nights that crowds would form on the Strip, but that didn't last too long. Shortly it would be every night. It was estimated that in the length of one mile—the Sunset Strip—would be visiting crowds of anywhere from ten to twenty thousand people, hanging around in small to large groups. It was as if you would need a program to tell the difference between them as they were all dressed similarly.

Everything from pre-teenagers to folks in their thirties, each with the idea that they were pursuing their dream, to be an individual. This was a haven especially for runaway teens, along with those individuals who would come to the area to pursue their dreams of becoming an "actress."

Parking a car was a nightmare. Parking signs were erected along both sides of the Strip indicating "No Parking between 8:00 PM and 2:00 AM" The station decided to add one patrol unit on an evening shift, between the hours of 7:00 PM and 3:00 AM, dedicated primarily to towing cars that were illegally parked. Every night this unit, car 90-Adam, would start out at the east end of the Strip, followed by up to ten tow-trucks, and begin the sweep. Queuing down the strip with the yellow flashing lights looking like a giant dragon eager to swoop up the cars, this parade would go on nightly. Once the pedestrian crowd had seen it they would turn their heads and go back to what they were doing. No big thing. Those who were unfortunate enough to figure they could park and get away with it were in for a huge surprise. Expensive, too!

I worked West Hollywood station for about two years. In that time I managed to meet *Mr. Murphy* (Yes, he decided to follow me again) a few times, as you will see in the following stories. He also picked on other deputies . . . I wasn't the only one.

Welcome to West Hollywood!

WHAT'S GOING ON WITH THAT HOUSE?

— Harry Penny —

LOS ANGELES COUNTY SHERIFF'S DEPARTMENT
WEST HOLLYWOOD STATION (#9), CIRCA 1970–1971

My partner and I had just finished a month-long tour working the 90-Adam car and were eager to get back to working a regular—notice I do not use the word normal—patrol unit. We were working the PM shift (3 PM to 11 PM) and were about two hours into our shift when we received a man-with-a-gun call in our area. A man was seen running up a side street carrying either a rifle or a shotgun. Any cop will tell you that this is one of those adrenaline-rush types of call. My partner and I were no different.

We got to the location and located the informant who had called this in. I was getting the information when a young lad, about ten years old, came up to my partner and said he had just seen a man with a big gun go into an old house just down the street. The boy's description matched that of the one given by our informant. The house was in fairly bad shape compared to the others on the street. The paint on the house was coming off in large chunks, the front porch could have used a large bucket of nails, and there was trash strewn about the numerous tall weeds in the back yard. It had all the possibilities of a "shooting gallery"—a place commonly used by druggies. *Hmmmmmn,* I thought to myself, *maybe we can bag some accomplices or such.* Ah, yes . . . it's nice to dream.

Fortunately SEB, Special Enforcement Bureau, the predecessor to SWAT, had deployed some units to West Hollywood station to work for a few days. So we had ample units to be able to help as backup.

I put out the description of the suspect, his approximate location, and requested backup. We had arrived at the house and my partner went around to the rear of the house and I covered the front, thereby securing the house. My partner had yelled to me that he had seen movement inside the house and got a glimpse of the suspect, who was indeed armed. (We did not have those portable microphone radios that today's officers have on their shirts. No, we had to rely on hand and voice, sometimes downright yelling at each other, communication.) Within the next minute or so there were two regular West Hollywood units and two SEB units on scene and more were responding.

Our patrol sergeant arrived, and by now there were about ten or fifteen of us and the house was completely surrounded. I gave the sergeant the information. I then cautiously approached the house and took up a position in the bushes alongside one of the windows while other deputies took similar positions. This clown would have to be the invisible man to get out of the house and get past us.

After several failed attempts, using a bullhorn, to get the suspect to come out with his hands up, (standard textbook procedure, right?), somebody decided that it was time to put some teargas in the house. The Fire Department had arrived and was standing by. The next thing I saw was tear gas projectiles being shot into the house.

Windows breaking, tear gas coming out, and of course, this was one of those days when there was a slight wind. (*Murphy's Law: Tear gas will always blow back toward the good guys no matter what the wind direction.*) This is not going to bode well for me.

About thirty minutes have now passed since my partner and I first arrived at the location and the street has become crowded with on-lookers. (I take this time to mention that those yellow tapes you see on TV that have the black lettering indicating a crime scene and POLICE LINE DO NOT CROSS and so easily strewn about to cordon off an area have not made their introduction into the world yet— no, we are lucky if someone has a coil of rope.) More deputies are sent to the scene to control what could evolve into an ugly situation.

By now, it seems that there is not an unbroken window in the front of the house. Window curtains are flapping in the breeze, smoke and tear gas coming out. Ooops, did I say smoke? The old adage of where there is smoke there is fire is proving true in this case. Now I see fire hoses aimed at the house with water streaming out and this is causing more chaos with the crowd. And, yes . . . not only am I getting the effects of the tear gas and smoke, I am now getting wet! *Murphy's Law,* right?

Suddenly, I notice the bushes in front of me rustling and I feel something bump into my foot. Using my keen powers of observation —my sense of smell is somewhat preoccupied at this point—I look down and see the suspect. He had managed to crawl over to a window and slither out and down like a snake. His eyes were watering badly from the tear gas and he had inadvertently chosen the wrong direction, coming to a stop when he bumped into my foot. (As Gomer Pyle would say, "Surprise, surprise, surprise".) I said something a little different, as I pointed my gun at him.

I quickly handcuffed him and immediately yelled out that I had the suspect in custody. One bad guy, one nasty weapon off the street. Yep. That's not bad for a day's work. Good Guys: 1, Bad Guys with Guns: 0.

The fire seemed to be out and some other deputies entered the house to make sure there were no other persons inside. They ascertained that the house was clear of any other persons and emerged from the house with a recovered sawed-off shotgun. The house was not clear of broken glass, water, and lingering smoke and tear gas, however. They, too, got wet. Now it was time for the Fire Department to start mopping up. Literally.

My partner and I now were faced with one of those lots-of-people-to-interview reports. We headed back to the station. I would shortly learn that *Mr. Murphy* would again come and tap me on the shoulder and let me know he had one more surprise: *Can you spell possible lawsuit, Deputy Penny?*

During the incident an older, nicely dressed gentleman, in his late fifties, carrying a bag of groceries, emerged from the crowd. He was immediately approached by a deputy and told to stand back. His look of curiosity quickly turned into a look of horror; he dropped his bag of groceries, including a dozen eggs, pointed at the house and began yelling at the deputy.

"What's going on here?" he asked.

The deputy responded by telling the man that there was an emergency situation going on and it would be necessary for him, the man, to step back away.

"Dammit! I want to know what is going on."

This continued on until it became necessary for a sergeant to become involved.

Again, the man, his voice in that same loud volume, yelled at the sergeant, demanding to know what was going on. The citizen had almost yelled and talked his way to jail by demanding to know what was going on. He was irate, to say the least.

Just as the sergeant was removing his handcuffs from his belt and telling him that if he didn't step back beyond the line he could be arrested for interfering, the irate man said "But that's MY HOUSE!"

THE TWO CAPTAINS

— Dan Castrellon, LASD (Ret.) —

LOS ANGELES COUNTY SHERIFF'S DEPARTMENT
WEST HOLLYWOOD STATION (#9), CIRCA 1960S

This is a story about two captains of the LASD. One was the station commander of the West Hollywood station; the other held an administrative position in the department at the Hall of Justice. Over the many years both had worked together as deputies, sergeants, and lieutenants. They had become close friends. They enjoyed pulling "gotcha" pranks on each other every chance they could.

Even though they were captains they still enjoyed "doing the town," especially on the Hollywood/Sunset Strip. They both loved Mexican food, the hotter and spicier, the better. Unfortunately the food had a very gaseous effect on the station commander. His gaseous products were legendary. They could peel paint off a wall and corrode exposed metal. When they were really ripe, a gas mask was almost mandatory.

One night, after prowling the hangouts on the Sunset Strip, and gunning down many shooters and lots of Mexican food, they decided to make a pit stop at the West Hollywood station (WDH). After making a head call (a nautical term for making a bathroom visit), the station commander retreated to his office to make a few telephone calls. The other captain, who at one time had served as

WHD station commander, decided to wander about the station to see if he could find any old friends.

One of the perks of being a station commander was having a cozy and comfortable high-back chair from which to ride his desk. The station commander liked to place his feet up on a credenza behind the desk. While relaxing in this position, he was known for ripping off a few good ones, especially after a hearty meal of Mexican food.

The other captain, wandering around the station, chatting with old friends, was introduced to a brand new eighteen-year-old secretary. This was her first day at WHD station. She looked so young and so innocent. Immediately, a "gotcha" idea popped into the captain's mind.

Knowing that his friend was in his office, warmly tucked away in his chair, he decided to put a hasty plan into action.

After learning that the young secretary knew shorthand, the captain advised her that the station commander wanted to dictate a letter. Eager to oblige, she followed the captain to the station commander's office. The captain gently opened the door and told the young secretary to quietly enter the office and seat herself in the chair that was directly in front of the station commander's desk. She was to wait for him to finish his phone call.

The station commander, being comfortable in his chair, with the telephone to his ear, did not hear the secretary enter. After a minute or so, he let loose with a "long, slow rumbler." Taking a sniff, he knew he had ripped an especially ripe one.

The meal was working its gaseous effect on him and he had to relieve the buildup. One after another was let loose, each one more powerful than the last.

Suddenly he heard a weak whimper, like a newborn kitten crying for its mommy. He spun his chair around and his eyes opened to twice their normal size.

In front of his desk was a young girl with pale green skin, eyes filled with tears, holding her nose, while trying desperately not to breathe. The poor young thing was about to pass out.

HE JUST FINISHED DRIVING THOSE
TWO CAPTAINS AROUND WEST HOLLYWOOD.

Shocked to his senses, he leaped to his feet to get to the girl before she fainted. But as he did so, nature ran its course and another tremendous eruption propelled him around his desk, toward the girl.

That was it. It was too much for her. This crazy, foul-smelling man was now coming at her while erupting even more nasty gas. She had to get out. She leaped from the chair, burst from the office and ran down the hallway, gulping as much fresh air as possible.

He decided not to pursue the girl. Nothing could explain "this" away. He also knew that this had all the earmarks of one of his friend's "gotcha" gags. The captain who pulled off this prank was nowhere to be found.

Epilogue: I know this story to be true as it was told to me by both captains at separate times. During the Sunset Strip Riots of 1968 I was "volunteered" to act as a driver for both of these individuals. Although rolling around in a radio car in a riot situation with the windows down, is not safe, I had to because of the erupting gas from both of them.

THE NEARSIGHTED HOOKER

— Jack Withers, LASD (Ret.) —

LOS ANGELES COUNTY SHERIFF'S DEPARTMENT
WEST HOLLYWOOD STATION (#9), CIRCA 1963–1964

My partner and I were working the PM shift (3 PM to 11 PM) in car 92. We received a call to the Melody Room on Sunset Boulevard, between Clark Street and Larrabee Street The nature of the call was to assist a sergeant from Vice detail to transport a female prisoner to the station. This was a normal procedure.

NICE HAIR, SARGE. (SHE MUST HAVE LEFT
HER GLASSED IN HER OTHER PURSE.)

Upon arrival at the location, we contacted the sergeant (who was bald-headed) and he advised us that he had arrested a hooker for prostitution. We transported her to the station, turned her over to the jailer, and went back out and resumed patrol.

Approximately two hours later we received another call to assist the Vice sergeant again at the Melody Room. Upon our arrival we noticed that the sergeant was now wearing a toupee. Again, he had arrested a hooker for prostitution. It was the same hooker whom he had arrested earlier and had us transport to the station.

She would have been a great commercial for any optometrist! Need glasses?

LAST RITES?

— Harry Penny —

LOS ANGELES COUNTY SHERIFF'S DEPARTMENT
TRANSPORTATION BUREAU, TECH. SERVICES DIVISION, CIRCA 1971

I had just transferred from West Hollywood station, Patrol Division, to the Transportation Bureau, of the Technical Services Division. I was getting a little burned out pushing a black-and-white, working all the rotating shifts, and . . . having a sergeant with whom I did not get along didn't help matters. Besides, I was looking forward to working Monday through Friday with weekends off. Ah well . . . each of us has a story about those situations.

This particular day I was working at the Long Beach Courthouse, filling in for one of the deputies who was off for whatever reason. The lock-up area came under the Sheriff's Department and the court bailiff detail was part of the Marshal's office. My assignment was to do the paperwork for the prisoners whom we had brought for their court appearance and for any individuals who appeared in court and were remanded to Sheriff's custody. The transportation bus would come and pick them and me up at the end of the day.

Shortly after morning court had convened, I was at the desk when two deputy marshals brought in two teenage prisoners. The prisoners were still under the influence of alcohol to the extent that they were unable to be arraigned that morning. It was decided that they would be placed in a holding cell and maybe they would sober up before the end of the court day.

I opened up the cell and assisted the marshals in getting the prisoners inside. That was an ordeal in itself: "Hey, maaaannnn . . . whachoo doin' wit us?" one of them asked in a very slurred voice. These guys smelled like they had taken a bath in Jack Daniels whiskey and rinsed off with Red Mountain wine. Their clothes were covered with a mixture of dirt and cigarette ashes watered down by alcohol and urine. Their walking abilities were a sight to behold, to say the least. They were placed inside the cell and both of them decided to curl up, spoon fashion, on the metal bench as if they were romantically involved and within seconds of doing so, they were snoring quite loudly. The echo in the cell didn't help matters much.

I returned to the desk and one of the deputy marshals, Tim, remained. Tim was an old-timer as evidenced by the numerous hash marks on his sleeve. He had been working this particular court almost his entire career. I finished my morning paperwork as lunchtime approached. I asked Tim if he would watch the desk while I went down to the snack shop to get a sandwich.

"Sure," he replied. "Say, while you're down there would you mind picking me up some Alka-Seltzer?"

"No problem," I said and headed toward the elevator.

I returned a short time later with my sandwich and chips and his Alka-Seltzer. "I was only able to get this small packet," I said; "it was all they had."

"Those'll do fine," he replied. "It only takes two for what I use them for."

I sat down at the desk and began to eat my lunch.

Tim removed his gun belt, his badge, and his uniform tie and locked these items in his desk. He then went over to the sink, grabbed some paper towels, and returned to the desk and sat down. He was getting comfortable for lunch and didn't want to take a chance on spilling anything on his tie. *Murphy's Law* for cops: *New uniforms and ties will always attract gravy or catsup stains, espe-*

cially when you have a court appearance. I thought about this and, having had numerous experiences wherein *Mr. Murphy* and his laws would be involved, I removed my tie also.

I noticed that he had removed his gun belt, his badge, and his tie, and had put on a blue sport-coat over his uniform shirt. Maybe he was going to go out for lunch or something. But what aroused my curiosity was that he had taken a paper towel, folded it, and had placed it around the collar of his shirt. Now my curiosity was really getting pumped up. Most people tuck it into the collar of their shirt.

"You look as if you're doing double duty as a priest or something," I said, jokingly.

"Yeah . . . something like that. I do this every once in awhile just for some laughs."

I'd been a cop for nine years and I thought I'd seen some strange stuff, but this was taking on a whole different approach. I watched as he picked up a small metal wastebasket, went to the sink, and starting putting water in the wastebasket. By now my curiosity has really been activated.

After adding the water, the deputy started walking back to the cells while carrying the wastebasket with the water in it. Naturally, I decided to follow after him. I hadn't worked this particular court and had no idea of what he was intending to do. Maybe this was how they give the inmates water to go with the bologna sandwiches, or maybe he was going to disinfect the holding tank. Who was I to question this?

We walked back to the cell where the two drunks were still cuddled up and snoring. The deputy unlocked the cell door and walked inside. Well, being a normal cop, I remained there to back him up just in case. The deputy walked over to the two sleeping beauties and finally, after a few tries, managed to get them semi-awake and in a sitting position. He set the wastebasket right between their feet and began talking.

In a somber, soothing voice, he said, "Gentlemen, I am the prison minister and I am here to give you your last rites."

Sleeping Beauty number one was a little more aware of his situation than Sleeping Beauty number two. He lifted his head, shook it, and then said, "Whachoo mean last rites? Who the fuck'er you?" Now the bravado has started to surface, causing Sleeping Beauty number two to try and open his eyes and focus.

"I said, I am the minister who has been assigned to give you your last rites since you are in the gas chamber."

"GAS CHAMBER?" number one yelled. "WHACHOO MEAN THE GAS CHAMBER?"

Hearing the loud voice and the words gas chamber come from number one, number two became instantly awake. "Whazzz goin' on? Why you yellin' at this priest? What the fuck is a priest doin' here?" he asked.

"He says we's in the gas chamber an' he's givin' us our las' rites"

"Whadya mean las rites, man? We got our rights . . . ." number two slurred.

"Yeah, man," number one said. Whadya mean about our rights?"

By this time I am doing everything I can to keep from laughing hysterically and am having to lean against the cell door just to keep from doubling over.

The deputy marshal continued to stand in front of them with his arms and hands folded as if in prayer. Softly he said, "You two were convicted of murder, mayhem, and grand moprey, and were given the gas chamber. I am here so you can say your last words to your maker before the gas pellets are dropped."

"Wha' the fuck? We didn' kill no one. Didn't do that other thing or moprey or whatever the fuck you said," number one said as he looked at number two. "Did choo kill somebody?"

"WHADDYA MEAN . . . KILL SOMEBODY?" number two yelled as he lost his balance and fell off the bench and onto the wastebasket. "I didn' kill . . . what . . . I didn' even . . . I don' 'member any shit like that."

"I see," replied the deputy. "They all say that when the time comes for the pills to drop."

"Wha' pills?" asked number two as he struggled to pull himself back up on the bench.

"This pill," the deputy said as he showed them the two Alka-Seltzer tablets he held in his hand.

"What're those?" asked number one as he tried to focus his eyes on the tablets in the deputy's hand.

"These are the Cyanide pills that cause the poisonous gas in the gas chamber," came the still, calm, soothing voice of the deputy.

"SHEE . . . IT, MAN! screamed number two. "I didn' commit no fuckin' mur . . . mur . . . FUCK!" It musta' been some other asshole. Maybe even you," he said as he looked at number one.

"Whaddya mean me? . . . Asshole!" number one said as he grabbed number two by the shirt.

"Okay, fellas . . . You have had your chances and your last rites. Now, when these pellets drop in the water you will hear a fizzing noise. The gas is invisible so you will only be able to hear it . . . "

Number two, in a squeaky, trembling voice, interrupted the deputy. "Whachoo mean invisis . . . invisi . . . whatever the fuck you said?"

"He means we can't see the fuckin' gas, asshole!" said number one in his continuing attempt at bravado.

"GAS? WHAT GAS?" Oh, shit, man . . . wha' the fuck is goin' on?" cried number two. "We don' even have a car. We don' need gas . . ."

". . . when the bubbles start making the noise," continued the deputy, as if he didn't hear a word they said, "most people try to hold their breath so they don't breathe in the gas, but that won't work. The gas lasts longer than you can hold your breath. The pellets will be dropped in the water on the count of three. One . . . two . . . three," he said very slowly and then, as he started backing away from them, he dropped the two Alka-Seltzer tablets in the waste basket.

"Dominic . . . go frisk'em," he said as he made the sign of the cross and turned and walked back to where I was standing.

Then, with a loud bang, the cell door closed.

"Hey, man . . . tha' shit is makin' some bubbles and noise," said number two.

"Hole yer fuckin' breath, asshole! We's gonna las' longer and call our lawyer," said number one.

"Man, I didn' kill no . . . it's all your fault . . . ," cried number two. "Whad'ya have to call that priest a asshole for?"

They both tried holding their breath and then it dawned on them that they were still breathing. They both lay back down and curled up spoon-fashion and passed out.

They were arraigned about three hours later. Neither one of them said a word about their experience in the "gas chamber."

ANOTHER WAY TO STOP THE BLEEDING

— John Vogel, Lt. LASD (Ret.) —

Los Angeles County Sheriff's Department
East Los Angeles Station (#2), Circa 1961

During my training in the academy, after completion of five weeks, the class would be assigned to ride on weekends with patrol deputies at various stations. This would provide us with the first-hand experience of what it was like to be out "on the streets" in a radio car with a regular patrol deputy. This particular weekend I was assigned to the East Los Angeles (ELA) station.

During the shift a radio call came out regarding a 902-R (rescue) and the unit in the next area got the call. We were almost on top of the location of the call and we rolled on it.

It was sad. A young man was quite disturbed and had attempted to slash his throat with a razor. He had made two incisions, one over each jugular vein. He actually clipped a jugular vein on one side and there was a lot of blood.

The ambulance rolled in and I was assigned to ride with the victim and assist the ambulance attendant as needed.

The sirens are blaring, the lights are flashing, and I am sitting at the side of the gurney holding the victim's hands so he can't

227

interfere with the ambulance attendant who was holding the gauze bandages over the wound to try and control the bleeding.

I felt the victim attempt to move his hands and I leaned forward just in time to hear the victim say to the ambulance attendant, who was trying to save his life, "Careful, you're choking me."

THE NUTS, BOLTS AND WASHERS CAPER

— Russ Sletmoen, LASD (Ret.) —

LOS ANGELES COUNTY SHERIFF'S DEPARTMENT
EAST LOS ANGELES STATION (#2), CIRCA 1960S

I worked East Los Angeles (ELA) in the 60s and was assigned to work Bell Gardens, a contract city, for most of that time. My partner and I experienced a most unusual FIRE RESCUE backup call one evening in that city. It is the norm on these types of calls that when you arrive someone is crying, someone is shouting, and most people are standing around looking.

Well, this time the lady of the house was standing in the doorway laughing and waving us inside the house. The other people from the neighborhood were standing by, looking bewildered and saying nothing. We entered and followed the lady to the rear of the residence. She gestured toward the bathroom door and said, "It's my husband; he's in there," then stepped back so we could enter. There we observed a grown male submerged to his shoulders in the bathtub. He immediately said, "It is not funny," then stood up so we could see him completely in the nude.

He pointed to his penis and advised that he had placed a washer over it, then got an erection and could not get it off nor would the erection go away. About that time the Fire Department arrived with three or four big husky men all dressed in turnout coats, fire axes and bolt cutters. The bathroom became too crowded for all to partake in the decision-making process, but the firemen offered to hack the washer off with their bolt cutters. That seemed too risky to the victim and he declined.

After the fire crew captain considered other choices, such as soap, ice cubes, Vaseline etc., he suggested that we, the Sheriff's Department., call for an ambulance to transport him to the assigned medical emergency facility. The ambulance did arrive in record time with sirens blaring and red lights flashing. Two paramedics wheeled in a gurney and promptly inspected the victim. He was prepared for the trip to the medical emergency room and promptly hauled out into the street where his neighbors, not knowing what the medical problem was, wished him well and a speedy recovery.

At the emergency room, the staff of young nurses working the late shift was all briefed of the serious nature of the victim's condition. I believe every nurse in the hospital was called upon to aid in the removal process. The word for assistance seemed to spread rapidly. My partner and I issued the EAP slip and returned to our area where we prepared the handwritten incident report—person Injured, transported to and treated at the emergency room. LACO FD captain was at the location and secured the area.

When my partner and I came off shift at 8:00 AM that morning the report had reached the secretaries' pool and they were all gathered around the desk of the clerk assigned to prepare the final typewritten document. For several months the clerical staff kidded us about making up the story we called, the Nuts, Bolts, and Washer Caper.

THE GREAT AVOCADO CAPER

— Larry Brademeyer, LASD (Ret.) —

LOS ANGELES COUNTY SHERIFF'S DEPARTMENT
LAKEWOOD STATION (#13), CIRCA 1959

Some folks are of the mindset that all cops have to do is ride around and hassle the decent folk. When not doing that, they are sponging coffee and doughnuts from the coffee shops. Well let me tell you, when it came to my partner and me . . . our thing was avocados.

While working day shift in adjoining cars one day in October, we acquainted ourselves with most of the avocado ranchers in the east Whittier area. They liked to see our patrol cars around to discourage theft. It is such a big concern that a California law was passed making it a felony to steal a mere $50 worth. The avocado people told us that we could have all the avocados we wanted when they ripened the following month.

That was music to our ears for we were scheduled to work as partners on the graveyard shift in November. Just the thought of a ripe avocado with a good sandwich made the old mouth salivate . . . and how about some avocado dip at the next party?

We were busy for the first two weeks of November but we finally caught a slow shift. My partner, Jim, always came prepared and

231

TRAINING TIP #17: WHEN MAKING A DONUT RUN
ALWAYS BE AWARE OF YOUR SURROUNDINGS.

carried two or three extra paper bags in his briefcase. On this night we were ready.

We began driving up this long winding road that was full of avocados on either side of the street. The night was as black as a coalmine but we had the perfect idea. I would let Jim out of the car with his bags and flashlight and then drive slowly on up the hill and return for him after a few minutes. We would each have a bag full and we would be on our way, no harm, no foul. So far everything was going according to plan . . . but as I began to drive away I observed a pair of headlights coming up the hill toward us. I called to Jim, "There is a car coming," and added that I would go ahead as planned and give the appearance of really looking for avocado thieves. After the car had passed I would whip a u-turn and come back to pick him up. I told him to signal me with his flashlight.

I drove my patrol car on up the hill while Jim kept on picking avocados. I had to admire that partner of mine; he was a cool guy under pressure.

Now you all have heard of *Murphy's Law* . . . well, that's what happened. I kept on watching those headlights in my rear-view mirror, but as they reached the spot where I had left Jim off . . . they stopped. I just could not believe this was happening. The night was so dark . . . how could anyone see that we were in the avocado grove? I figured the guy for a private guard hired by the ranchers and that somehow he had spotted us. The only thing to do was to go back and tell the guy the truth . . . after all we were not really stealing . . . we were told to help ourselves.

I turned the car around and started back down the hill as the sweat began to ooze from under my collar. As I neared the place where I had let Jim out, the other car started up the hill toward me at a high rate of speed.

I found my partner and we took off after this mysterious driver, thinking now we really had a thief on our hands! I threw on the reds and tapped the siren and the guy pulled over. I could see right away that he was more rattled than we were so we took our time checking him out. We learned that he was a local rancher who had been out drinking beer and had stopped to relieve himself before driving home. He was very appreciative of our alert patrol efforts and could not thank us enough. After a stern lecture about driving under the influence we sent him on his way.

We didn't get any avocados that night. Suddenly we had lost an appetite for them . . . and besides . . . we lost the place where Jim had left the two full bags.

As we drove on Jim said to me, "Do you know what I was going to say if he had found me there in the trees? I was going to tell him that I had the EVIDENCE but the suspect got away!"

IN PURSUIT
OF HOMER

— Larry Brademeyer, LASD (Ret.) —

LOS ANGELES COUNTY SHERIFF'S DEPARTMENT
LAKEWOOD STATION (#13), CIRCA 1960

Homer was a man of steel . . . at least he had been. In all his seventy-two years he never held a job that wasn't working with steel. His face mirrored the grim etching of a steel worker and his gnarled hands reflected those many years of manly toil. When he retired six years earlier, he had moved from his home in Pittsburgh, PA to southern California. His daughter and son-in-law wanted him to live closer to them. His wife had passed away several years before so there was nothing to keep him in Pennsylvania. But Homer never adjusted to life in California. He missed the steaming smoke stacks of the old steel mills and longed to be back there again.

He began drinking heavily for want of something to do and one day noticed a swelling in his left leg. He ignored it as long as he could but finally informed his daughter of his problem. She insisted upon taking him to the doctor where he was diagnosed as having an advanced case of diabetes. They advised him that his left leg would have to be operated on to remove some of the diseased tissue or he could face amputation.

As the result of this operation Homer was left a semi-invalid and unable to walk any distance without the aid of crutches. In time, his

234

condition deteriorated to the point that he was incapacitated and in need of daily nursing care.

This was the situation in which Homer found himself one spring morning . . . wheelchair-bound, in a nursing home, and hating every minute of it. He had been there thirteen months and the visits from his daughter and grandchildren were becoming more infrequent. Homer decided that there was only one way to get their attention. He would escape these dreadful conditions in the only way he knew how. When the nurses and assistants were busy after dinner he would just wheel his way out of there to freedom.

He had become friends with one patient named Jacob, another "guest" who was also confined to a wheelchair. They often engaged in "wheelchair races" in the courtyard adjacent to the rear of the hospital. He had mischievously confided to Jake his intentions for his flight to freedom. He had jokingly told Jake, "I will be home before they miss me." (Little did he know that his home had already been sold to help pay for his hospitalization.)

Jake never gave it much thought either, other than to give Homer a wink and a nod of encouragement. So the evening that Homer did not show up for their usual game of checkers . . . Jake realized what had happened and sounded the alarm.

My partner and I had just seated ourselves at a patio table of the A&W on the corner of Ashworth and Bellflower enjoying an orange slurpie. We were killing a little time while waiting for the rush-hour traffic to dissipate. Our radio was tuned to the outdoor speaker so as to monitor it for urgent calls. Around six-thirty we heard the radio dispatcher bark, "Car-132Adam come in . . ." I walked over to the car and picked up the mike and responded, "Car 132-Adam, go ahead."

"Car 132-Adam we have a report of an elderly man leaving the Artesia Convalescent hospital and was last seen northbound on Clark street . . . (chuckle) . . . in a wheel chair!"

I replied "10-4 . . . are you sure I am reading correctly . . . did you say an elderly man in a wheelchair?"

"Yes, that's 10-4 . . . 132-Adam, handle at once!" followed by more snickers. "That's 10-4," I responded.

I motioned to my partner and we dumped our remaining slurpies in the trash. In police work you never know what to expect on your next assignment, but this was unusual, to say the least.

The traffic was still quite heavy, so I used the assistance of the red lights and siren to negotiate through the traffic along Bellflower Boulevard. We drove westbound on Artesia Boulevard and as we approached the corner of Clark Street, we caught sight of our quarry hurriedly rolling his wheel chair through the intersection and heading for the on-ramp to the ninety-one freeway. Sure enough, as we reached the intersection of Clark and Artesia, there went our escapee, wheeling that chair up the on-ramp with all the dexterity of an Olympic athlete. I leaned on the siren to get the intersection cleared as I nudged the patrol car through dense traffic and swung in behind the fleeing wheelchair.

Our task was made more difficult because of the many amused onlookers who were attracted to the sound of our siren and were beginning to honk their horns and point in amazement at the escaping suspect. I positioned the patrol car directly behind his wheelchair as he pushed forward with Herculean strength. Meanwhile, my partner, who was still a rookie, had his hand on the door handle and was ready to jump out at the first opportunity. He jokingly shouted to me, "Should I fire a warning shot?" I looked back at him with a look of displeasure. My partner had been raised on a ranch in Wyoming and was an expert horseman and cowboy. I thought to myself, "If only he had his rope now he could lasso him . . . hmmm," but somehow I couldn't see the humor in these circumstances.

The freeway traffic had all but halted now on both sides of the median. I could also hear the screech of tires and a few fenders being buckled and bent as we continued to give chase. But our quarry was proving to be elusive and was wheeling the chair along on the curbside of the roadway. Each time we drew near him he would speed up and each time he slowed down and Doug attempted to jump from our car and give foot chase . . . then he would speed up again. The westbound traffic had now all but halted and some of the motorists were beginning to clap and shout encouragement to the escapee. The eastbound traffic was creeping along behind us like a gigantic funeral procession and I could hear more shouts of support.

So far all our attempts to apprehend the subject had been futile, so we devised another plan of attack. I told my partner that I would drive up close behind our fleeing man and he could alight from our vehicle and then I would drive past him and stop. If it worked we could stop his flight and between the two of us we should be able to grab hold of him. However the cagey old steelworker had other ideas.

By the time I stopped my car in front of him he had already veered his wheelchair to the left and whizzed by me with the speed of a thoroughbred racehorse. Now we were losing patience as well-being totally embarrassed. "Instead of firing a warning shot . . . I wish you had shot the son of a bitch!" I shouted to my partner as I pulled the patrol car in behind him again. Then, thinking of how gung-ho my partner was, I added, "I was only kidding . . . but we have to do something!"

Our culprit was now nearing the Bellflower Boulevard off-ramp and I began to fear for his safety. If he took the off-ramp, the incline was so steep, he would not be able to control his speed and stop when he reached the boulevard light. The thought of him rolling out into the oncoming traffic was chilling, to say the least. We agreed that the only way to stop him was to just cut him off with the patrol car. I proceeded to drive abreast of him and gradually inch closer and closer. Suddenly he made a sharp turn to the right and went flying down the ivy-covered embankment, his wheelchair rolling over and sending him sliding face first through the ice plant.

Before I had the patrol car stopped my partner was out of the door and running after our disabled patient, but he too found himself slipping and sliding down the foliage. To my surprise however, my partner recovered and grabbed onto our suspect and after a brief struggle had him handcuffed before I got down to their location. Covered in green stain and dirt we slowly assisted our subject to the patrol car and then struggled to retrieve his wheelchair. After col-

WHEN A DEPUTY WINS THE "DEPUTY
OF THE MONTH" AWARD, HIS OR HER TRAINING
OFFICER ALSO RECEIVES A CERTIFICATE.

lapsing his wheelchair we placed it in the trunk of the car and then
got back inside and sat down with a huge sigh of relief.

The traffic began to move again and as we drove away we could
hear the catcalls and wisecracks, "Don't you guys have anything
better to do? Did you have to treat him so rough? He could be someone's father, you know!"

Upon returning to our station we assisted Homer out of the car,
placed him back in his wheelchair, wheeled him into the station and
pushed him into the booking cage . . . chair and all. The wheelchair
had sustained little damage and appeared to be as functional as
before. No sooner had we closed the door to the booking cage than

we heard a PA announcement. "Car 132A report to the watch commander's office at once!"

"Now what the hell is wrong?" I thought as we hurried to the
lieutenant's office. His face was red and I could see the anger
seething from under his collar . . . he didn't hesitate, but exploded
immediately.

"What the hell were you guys thinking of, bringing that guy in
here? Do you see all those people from the press out there in the
lobby? You get him out of that booking cage now and call someone
to come get him . . . and do it yesterday!!!!!!" he fumed. "Geez,"
I said to myself, "and here I thought we had done a good job."

Well the upshot of it all was that we located his daughter by
phone and she came down and picked him up and offered us nothing but praise for rescuing him. In a hastily called news conference
she made her feelings known to the lieutenant, who later issued my
partner and me a written letter of commendation, which I suspect
was his way of apologizing.

A few weeks after this incident, we returned to the nursing home
and found that the notoriety was just what Homer had needed. The
press coverage had made him a hero of sorts to all the other patients.
We found him out in the courtyard playing checkers with Jake and
quite happy with his celebrity status. Many years have passed since
that evening on the freeway and my thoughts have often drifted back
to Homer and his great escape. It would be my guess that he is
upstairs right now . . . just having a ball retelling his story about how
he wheeled his way to freedom . . . to any angel who will listen.

THE REAL MCCOY. . .
A COP'S STORY

— Larry Brademeyer, LASD (Ret.) —

LOS ANGELES COUNTY SHERIFF'S DEPARTMENT
NORWALK STATION (#4), CIRCA 1958

Have you ever known a guy that just stands out in a crowd? Sure . . . we all have. Carl McCoy was one of those rare kinds of guys. He had a commanding presence that could be a bit intimidating. He was the spit-and-polish type too. His shoes were always shined and his Sam-Browne and leather gear glistened . . . even the bill of his cap gleamed, and his badge . . . it was as bright as a real star. When he walked into the room no one could doubt that here was the "real" McCoy. You see, our station had two McCoys . . . Carl and Billy. Though they were unrelated, no one would ever confuse the two . . . in fact, when Billy wasn't around, we always referred to Carl as the "real" McCoy. On this night, as I arrived for graveyard watch briefing, I was pleased to learn that I had been assigned as Carl's partner.

I was what they called a "boot," fresh from doing two years jail duty; I had finally been transferred to Patrol Division. For the first few weeks I had been filling in for almost anyone who had been on sick leave or on vacation. I had drawn a different partner on nearly every shift. Now I hoped to make a good impression on the "real" McCoy. I

240

had been told that he had all sorts of connections . . . that he was even part owner of a successful restaurant in the nearby city of Bell-flower. He was also a veteran of five years in patrol and knew his way around the block . . . I wanted to get to know him better.

As the new guy, I was the "book" man . . . meaning my partner would drive and I had to write all reports and keep the log current. The lead officer always acted as the backup and supervisor. This was a Tuesday morning and the radio was not very active so I kept trying to make small talk with the "real" McCoy. However, he wasn't in the mood for talking. He yawned a lot and complained of being tired from working all afternoon at his café.

About 3:00 AM in the morning the radio had died down and McCoy drove into a new housing development. After exchanging pleasantries with a watchman at the guard shack we drove on into the construction area. The homes were in various stages of comple-tion; some had only rough framing, while further on we found others almost ready for occupancy. McCoy pulled up in front of a nearly fin-ished home and proceeded to back our patrol car into the driveway and told me to open the garage door. I thought this was a little pecu-liar but I didn't want to offend my experienced partner, so I did as I was told. Next he backed the patrol car into the garage and cut the motor off, and turning to me said, "I'm going in the hole (cops' lingo for sleep) to catch a few zee's. Close the overhead door and listen for the radio and wake me if we have to roll." To my amazement, he took off his Sam Browne belt, neatly folded it, placed it on the front seat and within minutes he was on the back seat snoring away.

Well, I was devastated . . . the man I thought was my hero was breaking every rule in the book. I didn't even want to think of the consequences if we got caught. Here I was, a new transfer from the Jail Division where I had already ridden a beef for falling asleep on duty, and had been formally reprimanded. Another incident report and I would probably be terminated.

I wanted to tell old McCoy to wake up and get the hell out of there . . . but I demurred. After all he was the supervising officer and

what would the guys at the station think of me if I beefed the "real"
McCoy for sleeping on duty? They would be snickering behind my
back from now on! So I just sat there listening to the radio and working on my log by flashlight. I thought of what a waste we were to the
taxpayers . . . !

I was startled to hear voices outside and I thought I was dream-
ing. Then more talking and sound of lumber being moved about.
Good God Almighty . . . I had fallen asleep and my watch said 7:35
AM . . . we were due in the station at 7:30! I reached back and shook
the "real" McCoy awake but he seemed to take forever getting up
and putting his gear back on. Then the radio barked, "Car 43-Adam,
how soon ten-seven?" I grabbed the mike and said, "In about fifteen
minutes, 10-4?" The dispatcher responded, "OK, 10-4." I was now
sweating bullets but that damn McCoy kept taking his sweet time.

Finally he was dressed and satisfied with what he perceived to
be proper attire. He signaled for me to hoist open the garage door
and then got behind the wheel and settled back as if he were some
kind of god-damned royalty. I raised the overhead door and sheep-
ishly slid into the front passenger's seat as he started the engine and
began to drive out. There were several workmen already on the job
but McCoy appeared unconcerned. "Just wave to everybody and
they will think we have been on stakeout all night," he said. He
rolled down his window and made a point of waving to one and all.
He even had the guts to honk the horn. I avoided looking at anyone
and only hoped no one would be able to identify me. That's not the
end of the story . . . there's more.

I tried to sleep when I got home but I tossed and turned all day.
I dreaded my next shift. I just knew I was in for a major disciplinary
action or maybe even a suspension. Perhaps I would be fired!

In our locker room at the station was a mailbox for each officer
that we would check for messages when arriving for duty. At that
time our department used a yellow inter-office memo pad for instructions and/or whatever. When I entered the locker room I immediately looked at my box . . . yep! There it was . . . I just knew it . . .

a nasty little yellow memo sticking out of my mail slot. I yanked it out of there post-haste and sure enough it was from the day watch commander . . . !

To my surprise it wasn't at all what I had been expecting. The watch commander wanted to inform McCoy and me that the construction foreman had phoned the station thanking us for our excellent stakeout efforts and theft prevention. He went on to say that a commendation for excellent police work would be incorporated into and made part of our personnel files. For a moment I thought again about wasted taxpayer money . . . but believe me . . . it was only for a moment. I felt as if I had just won the lottery!!!

I never worked again with the "real" McCoy, but he still lives in my memory. Billy McCoy died about three years after that from a heart attack. It has occurred to me that perhaps his heart condition was brought on by stressful situations similar to what Carl McCoy put me through that night.

The "real" McCoy resigned from the department after about ten years on the job. He just walked in one day and threw his shiny badge on the sergeant's desk and said, "adios." I never saw the "real" McCoy again. Last I heard he had married for the second or third time and was plying a fishing boat out of Anchorage. But, if like so many of my old friends, he has passed on . . . it wouldn't surprise me if he's upstairs trying to talk the Man into letting him get up a pool for Super-Bowl Sunday!

LA CANTINA
DE LAS TRES
HERMANAS OR THE
THREE SISTERS CAFE

— Larry Brademeyer, LASD (Ret.) —

LOS ANGELES COUNTY SHERIFF'S DEPARTMENT
NORWALK STATION (#4), CIRCA 1958

In 1958, La Cantina de las Tres Hermanas (Three Sisters Café) and the El Siglo 20 (the 20th Century) were the only bars in the Norwalk/Artesia area that catered to Latino field hands. By and large there were hardly ever any police problems. Trouble usually occurred after a drunk left the bar and got into some kind of mischief. The three Mexican sisters ran a fairly decent place as far as beer bars go, and seldom were we called.

Their cantina was an old church that had been converted into a café after WW II and was quite successful due to being located near lettuce and strawberry fields. The front door looked out over a large porch that had three wide concrete steps leading up to it. When I worked night patrol I enjoyed hearing the strains of mariachi guitars emanating from within.

On this Monday morning I was working day watch patrol out of Norwalk Sheriff's station. Because it had rained heavily the night before, I wasn't expecting any unusual calls other than perhaps a routine burglary or theft report that might have occurred over the weekend. The last call I expected to hear was that of a disturbing drunk. At 9:00 AM most bars were not even open yet . . . but those sisters also served breakfast along with a little red-eye, if you were so inclined.

The radio shook me out of my doldrums . . . "Car 45 handle, 45-Adam and 45-Boston, assist a 415-D (fighting drunk) at the Three Sisters Café, Norwalk Boulevard south of Alondra." This was definitely not the kind of call I wanted to hear. When a 415-D call goes out, you don't even want to acknowledge it, let alone make a quick response. More often than not (if you took enough time) the fight would be over before you arrived. I was taking my time in getting to the Sisters and keeping my eye peeled for the other two radio cars that were to back me up.

As I neared the location I could see only one vehicle parked in front and one parked in the rear. I knew the one in the rear belonged to the sisters. I stopped my patrol car near the front entrance, all the while scanning up and down the street for my backup. About this time I heard a man's voice from within using one profanity after another. He was loud enough to be heard from the street. Then came a crashing sound like someone breaking furniture. I had planned to wait for my backup but now I wasn't so sure that was the thing to do. I took a deep breath and started up those three wide steps to the front door. Just before I made my entry I observed a former partner (Carl) in car 45-Adam coming west on Alondra Boulevard about to turn south toward my location. He was a welcome sight, I can assure you . . . it spiked my confidence as I opened those swinging doors.

When I stepped inside the café the three sisters were peering out from the kitchen doorway and pointing with their fingers towards a white male of approximately forty-five years old standing at the south end of the bar. He was a big fellow and appeared to be in some kind of stupor. His face was ashen and he kept mumbling to himself. I saw several tables overturned and broken glass strewn on the floor. The sisters pointed their fingers at him and then back to their own heads in a circular motion which I took to mean that this guy was nuts.

"Sir," I called down to him, "could I have a word with you outside?" With this the big man appeared to pull himself together.

"Why sure, Sonny," he replied and began staggering toward me as I leaned against the swinging doors to open them. We were now outside on the porch and both of my backup units had arrived and were getting out of their radio cars. "Sir, I am placing you under arrest for disturbing the peace," I advised him.

"Sonny . . . you mean you gonna arresh me?" he asked in a slurred Dutch accent.

"That's right," I told him and took out my handcuffs and reached for his arm while my assistance was bounding up the steps. I looked away for one second and . . . POW . . . I was seeing tangled stars as he hit me on the side of the jaw knocking me clear off the steps. I landed on the graveled driveway skidding backward so hard that the keepers on my Sam Browne belt—the name for the big leather gun belt worn by law enforcement officers—broke loose dragging my gun, holster, and baton down around my knees. I tried vainly to get up and my jaw was aching from a chipped molar. When I finally struggled to my feet, I had my nightstick in hand and was ready to administer some curbstone justice . . . but Carl waved me away. I am sure I gave more the appearance of a mud wrestler attempting to hold my Sam Browne and gun belt up with one hand and baton in the other. The suspect dropped his head, put his hands behind his back and said in his thick accent, "I gots von of youse guys, . . . ya, I go mitt you now." Somehow I wished that Carl wasn't such a straight arrow . . . he should have let me get in a few good licks.

I was a sight, mud and grime all the way down my back to my heels. All of my polished leather gear, including my cap, was caked in mud. Carl agreed to book the guy for me so that I could go home and change uniforms and clean up. At the time I lived only about three blocks from Norwalk station.

We determined that our drunk was an old Dutch dairy farmer from Artesia who had had a fight with his wife and then had gone out on a drinking spree. He had not slept for two days. His rap sheet indicated no prior arrests, so when I returned to the station, I just let him sleep it off.

He subsequently made restitution to the Sisters Café, paid a fine to the court and later wrote me a letter of apology. In those days assaulting a peace officer was considered only a misdemeanor and more or less an occupational hazard. It is seldom that I have thought of him since . . . only when I have had a dental appointment!

Epilogue: A psychotic named Carl Eckstrom in Midway City, California murdered Detective Sergeant Carl Wilson and his partner Detective Donald Schneider on January 3, 1973. Eckstrom had shot three people, killing two at a Cerritos (CA) mall. Wilson and Schneider were conducting the follow-up investigation. This killer is now doing a life sentence, yet he he comes up for parole every few years. He also made news after it was learned that for a number of years he had collected Social Security benefits while in prison. I think of Carl and Don often . . . over 200 police vehicles formed their funeral procession. They were both buried with honors and laid to rest in Forest Lawn Cemetery in Whittier, California.

INFORMANT: ANNIE MOUSE

— Ron Weber, LASD (Ret.) —

LOS ANGELES COUNTY SHERIFF'S DEPARTMENT
NORWALK STATION (#4), CIRCA 1966

I was working car 45-Adam out of Norwalk station. These were those "good old days" when patrol vehicles exclusively used "live" dispatchers for all communications. Normally a call originates when a phone call is received at the station. The person making the call is designated as the "informant." The complaint deputy is a deputy assigned to the desk and he takes the incoming calls. If the informant does not wish to be contacted, the code is 911-N. This advises the responding unit not to contact the informant. However, it does happen on occasion where the informant needs to be contacted, at which time the responding unit will request the informant's information. The call is written down and processed. It is relayed to the main radio room at the Hall of Justice in downtown Los Angeles. The radio telephone operator (RTO) then broadcasts the call to the assigned unit. This all happens in a very short period, depending on the nature of the call.

I was on patrol when I heard a radio call to one of our other units, regarding disturbing juveniles (415-Js) and the dispatcher gave the location.

The call went like this:

Dispatcher: "Norwalk, 45-Adam, 415-Js at 12345 Hayford Street, 911-N, 45-Adam?"

"45-Adam, 10-4."

About ten minutes later car 45-Adam came back on the air, apparently needing additional information for whatever reason.

"45-Adam, request informant last call, 45-Adam."

Dispatcher: "45-Adam, informant, Annie Mouse, 45-Adam?"

"45-Adam, 10-9?" (Repeat)

The request for the informant's name is repeated three more times with the same response being given of "informant, Annie Mouse" by the dispatcher. With each request by 45-Adam, the dispatcher sounds more upset in having to repeat the message to 45-Adam. Finally, on the fourth time of asking for the informant, the exchange was:

"45-Adam, request again informant's name on last call.

Dispatcher: "45-Adam the informant last call was ANNIE MOUSE!" (The dispatcher was literally screaming the name of the informant.)

Just then I heard the voice of a dispatch supervisor say:

"45-Adam, informant last call, ANONYMOUS!"

THE WRONG DRIVEWAY

— Ron Wisberger, LASD (Ret.) —

LOS ANGELES COUNTY SHERIFF'S DEPARTMENT
NORWALK STATION (#4), CIRCA 1967–1968

My partner and I were working the EM shift (Early Morning 11 PM to 7 AM) out of Norwalk station. We were working car 48—West Whittier county car—adjacent to the city of Pico Rivera, which would later have its own station.

I was driving and we were traveling east on Whittier Boulevard about 2:00 AM on a very slow night. We had just driven past a closed pizza parlor and were about twenty-five yards away when we heard the audible burglar alarm on the pizza parlor go off and start ringing. This was not unusual at this location—what made it unusual however was that we heard it activate.

I immediately blacked out the patrol car—turning off the headlights—and made a u-turn and entered the parking lot of the pizza parlor. I grabbed the radio mike and requested a backup unit to respond. I dropped my partner off with the shotgun, advising him that I would cover the rear until the backup unit arrived. (Keep in mind that this particular location was devoid of any artificial lighting of any kind and the area was completely dark.)

After dropping my partner off at the front of the location I floored the gas pedal and headed for the driveway in front of me

250

that led to the rear of the pizza parlor. While rapidly accelerating, I turned into, and entered, the driveway at which time there was a loud crash and I came to a sudden stop. I was thrown against the steering wheel and dashboard, and I was aware of a loud engine screaming at a very high rpm. I was in a daze and completely confused. I face was bleeding and could not figure out where I was or what had happened.

My partner then ran up to me. I could not understand why he was laughing hysterically or why he asked, "What the fuck did you do that for?" Again, keep in mind that it was totally dark and I was in a daze.

My partner, after realizing I had been hurt, reached in and turned off the ignition (as the engine was still screaming) and helped me out of the car. He was still laughing and still holding the shotgun.

After getting out of the car I finally realized why my partner was laughing and I, in fact, joined him in the laughter. It turned out that the driveway I attempted to enter was not a driveway—rather it was and eight-foot-high, cinder-block wall separating the pizza parlor

WHO PUT THAT BUILDING
IN THE DRIVEWAY?

from an adjacent business. It was painted a charcoal gray. In the darkness, and with the adrenaline following, my perception was that it was a driveway extending to the rear rather than a wall.

The patrol car was totaled—the engine had been pushed back against the firewall which separated the engine compartment from the car interior. This had caused the screaming noise on impact. The sad thing was that at this time the department was using 1967 Chevrolets which were notoriously unreliable. My car was a 1965 Ford which we had just received from the Gorman resident deputy and it had hardly any mileage on it so it was prized as a patrol car over the Chevys. Anyway, immediately after realizing what I had done, I attempted to cancel the backup unit, without success. Everyone at the station, if not the entire department, was well aware of my mishap long before my arrival back at the station.

I wrote up my accident report, just as this story is written, knowing that I was going to receive "time-off." To my amazement, the accident was deemed non-preventable, and I received no "time-off." It turned out that the accident-review board, upon reviewing my report, decided that it was so preposterous that it had to be TRUE.

LET'S DO LUNCH!

— Ron Wisberger, LASD (Ret.) —

LOS ANGELES COUNTY SHERIFF'S DEPARTMENT
CITY OF INDUSTRY STATION (#14), NARCOTICS, CIRCA 1974–1975

While I was assigned to the Industry station Narcotics crew, we (myself and one of my partners) were hanging around the Narcotics office, in no particular hurry to go home, when I received a phone call from an informant. The informant advised me that a local heroin dealer was about to depart his home in La Puente, and deliver a couple ounces of heroin to one of his clients in Irwindale.

We immediately set up a surveillance of the "suspect's" home and after approximately one-half hour, we observed him leave his residence in a vehicle. We followed the suspect in his vehicle on the northbound 605 freeway to close to the 210 freeway, at which time, because it was in close proximity to Irwindale, we initiated a traffic stop on the freeway.

Upon stopping the suspect, and searching him and his vehicle, we discovered a package containing two ounces of heroin, and arrested the suspect for possession of heroin for sale, and transported him to Industry station for booking.

At Industry station, we initiated the booking process in our Narcotics office. I sat the suspect down and was processing the booking slip at my desk while my partner processed the evidence. He placed the evidence into an evidence envelope and eventually put it into our evidence locker, all while I was processing the suspect on the booking slip.

My partner placed the evidence into the evidence locker (a closet at one corner of the Narcotics office), closed the closet door, and left the key to the closet hanging on the door handle. After doing so, he left the office, in order to go to the secretaries area in order to get a booking number for the suspect for the booking slip that I was initiating.

Shortly after my partner left the office, the suspect suddenly stood up. I nonchalantly, without thinking anything was suspicious, told the suspect to sit down. He ignored me and bolted toward the evidence closet. (I did not realize had the key hanging on the door handle.) Upon reaching the closet door, the suspect opened it, removed the key from the door handle, and entered the closet with the key. He then slammed the door behind him and locked himself inside the evidence locker. All of this took less than five seconds to occur.

I immediately realized what the suspect was attempting to do. I yelled out for help and immediately the station night detectives who were in the adjacent office came in to help me. Even with their help I was unable to do anything productive about the suspect who was locked inside of the evidence locker. Leaning against the wall outside of the evidence locker was a heavy weighted battering ram, which we in the Narcotics crew utilized to make entry into residences and buildings when we served our court-ordered search warrants. I picked up the battering ram and began battering it against the door of the evidence locker.

I have to now describe that the door to the evidence locker (closet), opened outward into the office itself. The closet was approximately six feet deep and seven or eight feet wide, with shelving from approximately three feet above the floor to the ceiling which wrapped around the three walls of the closet.

After several rams into the closet door with the battering ram, the door gave way and entered into the closet. It immediately stopped because the door itself was wedged onto the edges of the shelving, stopping the door from completely entering the closet. At this time I could plainly see the suspect tearing apart evidence envelopes in his attempt to locate his evidence envelope.

I continued to batter the door of the closet without success and continued to pound into the shelving, which did not give. At this time my partner arrived at my side, and he immediately yelled at me, "Why don't you just use the key?" I looked into his face, and yelled back, "You dumb fuck, you left the key in the door and he has it inside." He then grabbed the ram from my hands and started ramming the door himself.

We eventually splintered the door and gained access into the closet, at which time we extricated the suspect from the closet and administered first aid to his body. This was necessitated by our physical force rather than anything else. Long story short was that the suspect had torn open nine separate evidence envelopes and eaten the contents of two of them, in an attempt to dispose of the evidence contained in his envelope. It turns out that when he locked himself in the closet, it was totally dark and he could see absolutely nothing. Hence, he could only go by feel. He picked a shelf that contained only evidence from previously adjudicated evidence that was all "diversionary evidence" waiting to be delivered to the downtown evidence locker. The "new" evidence shelf was untouched; hence, his evidence was untouched. The two pieces of "diversion" evidence that he ate were both small amounts of marijuana that were rolled up into small balls, similar as to how his heroin was packaged. In other words—no loss.

I eventually notified the Detective bureau desk about the events that had unfolded at Industry station, and requested that the duty detective notify and advise the Narcotics captain, which he did. He called me back and told me that our captain specifically asked, "Great, now what the fuck do they want me to do?" Needless to say, we had no answer to that. We wrote our memo as to the damage to the station, the loss of evidence and "force used" against the suspect.

The worst thing about the whole caper is that several months later, the suspect pled "not guilty" and I had to testify to the whole event at a jury trial, which was embarrassing to say the least. He was found guilty, however, and received ten years in prison, as he had been on parole for narcotics sales when we arrested him. The suspect even took the stand and attempted to sway the jury into thinking that I had forced him into the evidence locker and locked him inside. However, upon cross-examination, he couldn't come up with an answer as to why he had the key with him inside.

We later learned—from our ramming the door and striking against the edges of the shelving inside of the closet—that the force against the shelving caused the hallway wall on the exterior of the closet to bend outward. To this day, the hallway wall which leads from the entryway to the Detective bureau area of the station is bent into the hallway, and those of us who were involved that night know why.

THE DUAL
MEANING OF DUSK

— Ron Wisberger, LASD (Ret.) —

LOS ANGELES COUNTY SHERIFF'S DEPARTMENT
HOMICIDE BUREAU, CIRCA 1994

We all have stories of events dealing with the unsophisticated individuals that we dealt with, e.g., testimony of the black defendant telling the judge that he understands what the allegations are, but he just wants to know who the alligator is!

Well, during my assignment to the Homicide bureau, I handled a murder in the city of Paramount. You guessed it—the murder involved a white trash suspect as well as a white trash victim, who was beaten to death with a baseball bat, a choice of weapon by many white trash suspects. Early on in the investigation we determined who the likely suspect was by the process of elimination.

Anyway, we finally reached a point in the investigation wherein we decided to interview the suspect in hopes of possibly obtaining a confession. We had already discovered inconsistencies in details he had given to us earlier at the beginning of the investigation.

We picked him up at his home and brought him to Lakewood substation where we advised him of his rights and ultimately interrogated him at length.

Like most interrogations of suspects, the first half hour or so did not elicit much from the suspect other than denials. We finally looked him squarely in the eyes and told him why we thought he had killed his friend, and I asked him flatly, "Where were you on the day of the murder around dusk?" He looked somewhat confused at us, then looked upwards toward the ceiling of the interview room, rolled his eyes as if he were still confused, and finally looked at us and asked, "Are you talking about evening dusk or morning dusk?"

Finding it very difficult to keep from laughing out loud, I turned away from the suspect for a couple moments. I then turned back, facing him and said very seriously, while holding my hand in front of my mouth, "We'll assume that you were sleeping at morning dusk, so why don't you just tell us where you were at night dusk." He then answered, "That's what I was afraid you were talking about, 'cause you're right. I was asleep at morning dusk, and I can't remember where I was at evening dusk that night. Maybe I was playing baseball."

I will make this story short now by saying that the interview continued from there, and the suspect eventually admitted to killing his best friend because he was "making fun of me, but I didn't mean to kill him, I just wanted to hurt him, cause he hurt my feelings." The suspect was subsequently convicted of second-degree murder and received twenty-five years in prison because of his past record.

And I found out that the term "dusk" has a dual meaning . . . yep, we learn something new every day!

HOMICIDE TRAINING

— Harold W. White, Capt. LASD (Ret.) —

LOS ANGELES COUNTY SHERIFF'S DEPARTMENT
HOMICIDE BUREAU

It was common practice for our captain, lieutenant, and anyone else who happened to be around, to sit and listen to an investigator tell about his case—what he has done and plans to do. Most of the time, while telling his story, he comes up with his own solution. Those brainstorming sessions really paid off on many occasions. That is why our Homicide Bureau had one of the highest clearance rates of any law enforcement agencies anywhere.

Our method caught the attention of Dr. "X." He was an M.D. as well as an attorney licensed to practice law in California. Dr. "X" wanted to produce a training film using the Los Angeles County Homicide Bureau as an example. The idea was to show our method of solving homicides and to make the film available to other law enforcement agencies.

Art Stoyanoff was the captain and I was a lieutenant in charge of the investigating crew. Casey Sturm and Jim Scrivens were the investigators assigned.

The murder was supposed to have happened in a motel room on the west side of Los Angeles. The victim had been found by a motel maid when she went to clean the room the next morning.

259

TRAINEE, I THINK HOMICIDE HAS A MUCH
BETTER IDEA FOR THEIR NEW TRAINING FILM.

Dr. "X" had rented the motel room, provided the live model who was to pose as the victim, and brought in his team of photographers, grips, and a script girl. In other words, a full crew was necessary to film the murder story. Everyone was in their place and ready to roll the cameras.

The "victim" was a nude, well-built blonde who was supposed to have been stabbed several times in the chest. Make-believe blood was all over the place, including on the victim. When Casey Sturm saw the nude actress with her big boobs lying there he whispered to Scrivens, "I sure would like to kiss one of them nice big titties."

Scrivens whispered back, "Give you five bucks if you will."

Dr. "X" overheard this exchange, unknown to Sturm, and he told the cameraman, "No matter what happens, keep the camera rolling until I say cut."

Sturm took his notebook out, scribbled something in it, got down on his knees to get a better look, bobbed his head down and kissed on one of the large, brown, nipples with a big smack. He then turned to Scrivens, held out his hand, and said, "Gimme my five bucks." The model screamed, sat up and joined the rest of us in a good laugh.

Dr. "X" and his crew completed their on-scene shooting, then came to our office where he filmed our usual brainstorming, round-table discussions.

Our department made copies of that film available to any police department that asked for it. It turned out quite well and was representative of other good works done by Dr. "X."

NEW WARNING
SIREN?

— Jack Wise, LASD —

LOS ANGELES COUNTY SHERIFF'S DEPARTMENT
CITY OF INDUSTRY STATION (#14), CIRCA 1990

I had been a civilian volunteer for the Sheriff's Department for over ten years and was assigned to the station Detective Bureau (DB). One day we had a couple of young "pups" (juvenile suspects) climb on an automobile hauler and break mirrors and the usual vandalism stuff.

A citizen grabbed one of them, literally, and held him for the black-and-white. The lad was brought back to the station and placed in an interview room. This was all done unbeknownst to the guys in DB, who reside just across the hall from the interview rooms.

Eventually, we heard a high-pitched sound, like a bearing going dry. The guys were looking at the heating/air conditioning vents and trying to figure out where the high-pitched sound was coming from. The volume of the sound continued to increase and we were wondering what the hell was going on with the equipment. All of a sudden the high-pitched sound stopped, and then we heard crying and sobbing.

We all cracked up when we realized that it was the detainee in the interview room across the hall, who was just winding up for a good cry.

A TRAFFIC STOP TO REMEMBER

— Roy Beyer, Sgt. LASD (Ret.) —

LOS ANGELES COUNTY SHERIFF'S DEPARTMENT
SAN DIMAS STATION (#8), CIRCA 1986

In 1986 I was working San Dimas station and stopped a woman for a traffic violation. After writing the cite, which was the last one in my book, I was standing with the woman by the hood of my patrol car explaining the ticket and court date. When I handed my pen to the woman to sign the cite, a big blob of bird shit suddenly splashed across the middle of the ticket. We both looked up to see a large crow flying above. Since it was the last ticket in my book, I gave her a warning and went back to the station to have the watch commander void the cite as I did not feel it was appropriate to submit a ticket covered with bird shit to the court.

THE CRITTER

— Dan McCarty, Capt. LASD (Ret.) —

LOS ANGELES COUNTY SHERIFF'S DEPARTMENT
SANTA CLARITA STATION, CIRCA 1979

One night, while I was working Santa Clarita station with my partner, we got a call to assist a man at his home in a trailer park. It was in regards to some type of critter in his home.

When we arrived at the residence we were met outside by the informant. He was an old man in his eighties and very visibly shaken. He told us that there was some kind of critter inside his trailer-home and I asked him what it looked like. He said he did not see it, but it would let out a loud screech that sent chills down his spine. He also added that he had searched the trailer for the critter but could not find where it was hiding.

We entered the home and observed that all of the furniture had been turned over, and all the drawers and doors in the house were open. After we checked the location from top to bottom, not a critter inside, we went back outside where the old man was waiting for us. I told him that we could not find any critter in his home and that it must have escaped out the open window.

Just then there came a loud screech from within his home and the old man said, "There it is again. Did you hear that?"

I told him that I had heard it also and he said, "Thank God. when you couldn't find it, I thought I might be crazy."

I started to laugh and the old man asked, "What is so funny?"

I told him to follow me back inside the trailer and I would show him the critter.

Inside the trailer and I removed the "critter" for the old man. It was the old nine-volt battery in his smoke detector that was sounding an alarm every few minutes to warn that the battery was getting low.

THE CAT KILLER

— Floyd A Feese, Det. SDCS (Ret.) —

SAN DIEGO COUNTY SHERIFF'S DEPARTMENT
CITY OF LEUCADIA

Katherine was not especially attractive. A white female adult, mid-thirties, 5' 6" tall, 130 pounds, size six with short blonde hair. She had a Cheshire cat grin, no pun intended, with gray blue eyes that could take in a whole room and really not see anything. She was not unattractive but was just there waiting and watching to see what happened next.

The location was a small coastal community north of San Diego. A type of community that had million-dollar houses overlooking the ocean and million-dollar houses owned by the migrant workers who had lived in the area for generations. Leucadia was a quiet, peaceful community where everybody did their own thing and didn't get too upset when you did your thing.

My partner, John M and I were area detectives working for the local Sheriff's Department. We specialized in crimes of violence and politically sensitive crimes. Which meant that we handled whatever our boss would give to us. John was a seasoned detective with many years in the department. He was a man's man who liked to lift weights and chew. He also didn't have a neck. He was just muscle and then a head. John's only fault was that he liked to bang his fist on the table during an interview. This was his way of giving a suspect their rights. He always liked to play the bad cop.

It was a warm February morning. We had already received our four inches of rain for the year and were not expecting any more when we received the call to return to the station and interview a suspect who was in custody. Now you have to understand that this is not like the movies. We weren't told who was in custody, or for what, or what the charges were, or where they were. Just return to the station and interview a suspect. OK. We could do this. This was normal. However, I have to be honest; we did stop and look for Valentine's gifts for our wives before we went to the station. This actually took only about fifteen minutes.

The Detective Bureau was your typical detective office with desks, tables, interview rooms and lots of action. After a few minutes of searching we found Katherine sitting in interview room #B. She was sitting upright, in a hardback chair, with her hands cuffed behind her back. This was due to a small altercation she had with the female arresting officer. The room itself was an eight-by-ten with no windows, one door with a two-way mirror, one desk, three chairs and hidden wires, used for recording interviews, hanging from the ceiling.

Our boss met us at the door and with his thumb pointed into the room and stated "She is a Cat Killer. Go for it." and then he left the room.

Since it was my turn up I took the first position across from Katherine. John took the position next to the door, which was left open due to the heat. I placed my tape recorder on the table and started.

Det. Feese: We are here to ask you a few questions.

Katherine: Really? Wait until I slap handcuffs on you too, Mister.

Det. Feese: Well, you've got handcuffs on because you're not free to go.

Katherine: So you're not free either.

Det. Feese:	You're under arrest. You're under arrest for killing a cat, okay?
Det. M:	You're recalcitrant.
Det. Feese:	Yeah. She's a what?
Katherine:	For killing a what?
Det. Feese:	For killing a cat.
Katherine:	Really? Wait till I shackle you down, man.
Det. Feese:	All right. Before I ask you any questions I would like to give you your Miranda Rights. You have the right to remain silent.
Katherine:	And watch you—
Det. Feese:	Do you understand the right that I just gave you? You have the right to remain silent?
Katherine:	I don't want to
Det. Feese:	You don't want to remain silent?
Katherine:	No.
Det. Feese:	Okay.
Katherine:	I don't give a fuck if you write me for public fucking slander and give me life and 99 years in fucking CIW, motherfucker.
Det. Feese:	If you give up the right to remain silent, anything you do say can and will be used in a court against you; do you understand that right?
Katherine:	So? Who's your groovy judge?
Det. Feese:	Do you understand that right?
Katherine:	That dead fucker?
Det. Feese:	No. Do you understand that right? Let me read it to you again. If you give up the right to remain silent, anything you do say can and will be used in court against you; do you understand that?
Katherine:	Who's the judge this time?
Det. Feese:	I don't know.
Katherine:	For doing what? For killing a cat! My ass buddy!
Det. Feese:	Can you read?
Katherine:	Uh-huh.

Det. Feese: Okay. Can you read this here? It says here in small print, "if you give up the right to remain silent, anything you do say can and will be used in a court against you."

Katherine: Uh-huh.

Det. Feese: Do you understand that?

Katherine: Uh-huh.

Det. Feese: Okay. I assume "uh-huh" means yes. You have the right to speak with an attorney of your choice before questioning and to have an attorney –

Katherine: You dumb fuck, I am an attorney also.

Det. Feese: —present during questioning. Good. The California Bar?

Katherine: Yes.

Det. Feese: You sound like it. Okay. You have a right to speak with an attorney of your choice before questioning and to have an attorney present during questioning; do you understand that right?

Katherine: What are you, a new attorney? I am an attorney. I don't need an attorney.

Det. Feese: Being an attorney, you should understand that right. Do you understand that right?

Katherine: Do you want to hear your rights?

Det. Feese: Yeah. Go ahead.

Katherine: You have the right to suck men.

Det. Feese: I do.

Katherine: You also have been accused of handcuffing a police officer when she has asked you to please remove them and you have not. You are also under arrest for saying that I am committed to CIW forever for committed murder, public manslaughter on somebody's stupid fuckface kid now. And furthermore, you have also said the stupid fucking bitch also just walked in and said she's a paid informer now, and she didn't kill the stupid fuckface kid, the stupid bitch did that you are letting wear a fucking stupid white uniform. Furthermore, you also then said that you are also a net bag Satanic murderer of a new dead bitch's kid if she don't shut her fuckface mouth now and shut her ass up before I kill this pig. See?

Det. Feese: Okay.

Katherine: The one that just sit down.

Det. Feese: You have a right –

Katherine: And you don't say nothing now, dipshit, 'cause in a minute I'm going to walk up to you and shoot you in your fucking punk face, zitface scarred up head because you stupid son of a bitching little Satan slut, you are the one that killed those fucking kids, didn't you, shithead? And you told them don't say nothing fuckface, but I'm testing her for her fear of what? For the fear of saying nothing wrong. But let me tell you something else, motherfucker. What the fuck do you think of that now?

Det. Feese: You have the right to speak with an attorney of your choice.

Katherine: And then said you have the right to just sit there and tell me the whole fucking everything I said, and then you said furthermore, I'm also arrested for public fucking bullshit, ain't you?

Det. Feese: No, you're under arrest for killing a cat.

Katherine: Why?

Det. Feese: I don't know. You have the right to speak with an attorney of your choice before questioning and to have —

Katherine: How are you going to prove I killed the cat?

Det. Feese: —an attorney present—

Katherine: What cat?

Det. Feese: I don't know.

Det. M: Probably the dead cat.

Det. Feese: I'm just trying to find out if you understand the right you have to talk with an attorney.

Katherine: Well, where is the dead cat, and where's the weapon I used to kill it, and where are my fingerprints?

Det. Feese: I don't know.

Katherine: Then what the fuck is your evidence that I killed the Goddamned cat?

Det. Feese: All I'm trying to do is give you your rights. You have the right to speak with an attorney of your choice before questioning and to have an attorney present—

Katherine: I don't the fuck need one. I am one.

Det. Feese: All right. You don't need one. Okay. If you cannot afford an attorney, one will be appointed for you by the Court prior to any questioning—

Katherine: I don't want your fucking dipshit attorneys—

Det. Feese: All right.

Katherine: —to even call me idiot.

Det. Feese: Can I ask you a question?

Katherine: What?

Det. Feese: Would you get your fucking foot off of my desk?

Katherine: Oh, you fucking make me. Ouch! OK.

Det. Feese: Thank you.

Katherine: Did you build it?

Det. Feese: Okay. Now, can I ask you another question?

Katherine: What?

Det. Feese: Are you on any kind of medication or any kind of drugs or you do not understand the questions I'm asking you?

Katherine: I understand everything you said perfectly well, Mister. And furthermore, you are the one on drugs because you sit there and ask me if I am, and I've just told you that I am the FBI asshole.

Det. Feese: Okay. Are you into killing cats under—

Katherine: No.

Det. Feese: The FBI rule of killing cats. Rule Number 3.

Katherine: What's that mean?

Det. Feese: That means the FBI rule of killing cats. Obviously you killed a cat; you mutilated this poor, defenseless little animal by butchering it and taking its jaw out and leaving it in your sink. Did you do that?

Katherine: No.

Det. Feese: Were you there when it happened?

Katherine: No.

Det. Feese: Why did you do that?

Katherine: I didn't.

Det. Feese: Who did?

Katherine: I don't know. I left it in the bathroom and went to the Laundromat and prayed.

Det. Feese: You left it in the bathroom with its little, poor body mutilated with blood everywhere and its jaw ripped out; you left it like that?

Katherine: Its jaw was not ripped out by me.

Det. Feese: Who ripped its jaw out?

Katherine: I don't know.

Det. Feese: Why did you mutilate this poor little defenseless cat and rip its body apart and tear its jaw out and leave it in the bathroom?

Katherine: I didn't tear its jaw out.

Det. Feese: Well, how did its jaw get taken out?

Katherine: What does its jaw look like now?

Det. Feese: Well, it looks like a cat jaw. I don't know. I've never seen a cat jaw. Have you ever seen a cat jaw?

Katherine: No. Would you have liked to meet its pissed-off mother?

Det. Feese: Pissed—the cat has a pissed-off mother?

Katherine: Uh-huh.

Det. Feese: Where's the pissed-off mother cat?

Katherine: At home in my living room.

Det. Feese: What's it doing in the living room?

Katherine: It lives in my living room.

Det. Feese: Is it alive or dead?

Katherine: It's alive.

Det. Feese: Where is the dead one at?

Katherine:	Probably in your stomach in a minute fuckface
Det. M:	Can I ask you a question?
Katherine:	Huh?
Det. M:	Isn't the mutilation and removal of a jaw Satanic? Is this for some kind of ritual?
Katherine:	I don't know.
Det. M:	You don't know?
Katherine:	It's my cat. My cats are not satanic.
Det. M:	No, with the removing of the jaw and the hip and other parts of the animal, those parts are used in a satanic ritual, aren't they?
Katherine:	Now, people do that.
Det. M:	I know people do that. Did you do that?
Katherine:	They do that so that their big fucking coming boyfriend right there can say that I killed the cat. Dick.
Det. M:	Are you into that?
Katherine:	No. Wait till I kill this cat.
Det. M:	Did your boyfriend do that?
Katherine:	No.
Det. Feese:	Who did?
Katherine:	But when I find your kitty, motherfucker, I'm going to take its tongue out, and I'm going to fucking pull it out. And I'm going to go like this, and I'm going to make it fucking . . .
Det. Feese:	Sit down.
Katherine:	— tickle your nose, honey.
Det. Feese:	Quit running around and sit in the chair. Thank you.
Katherine:	Now what you going to do, boyfriend? Want me to sit in your chair and lay on your bed, I'm saying you killed the cat, didn't you? You're under arrest for what you have done? Then what are you going to do when you're sitting here handcuffed, huh?
Det. Feese:	Did you kill the cat?
Katherine:	No!
Det. Feese:	Who killed the cat?

Katherine: You most likely did, dumb-dumb.

Det. Feese: I didn't kill the cat.

Katherine: So? Why are you sitting here saying I killed the fucking cat?

Det. Feese: I was sitting here the whole time —

Katherine: Go call animal protection or national field—or wildlife, dummy.

Det. Feese: Have you ever killed a cat before?

Katherine: No.

Det. Feese: Why? You look like a cat killer.

Katherine: Really? You're going to eat a cat killer pussy in a minute, motherfucker —

Det. Feese: Yeah?

Katherine: And also a baby killer wearing the badge and the fucking outfit's cunt, motherfucker, and you pussy you are going to find penises too.

Det. Feese: You have the eyes of a cat killer.

Katherine: Really?

Det. Feese: Yep.

Katherine: You know what, motherfucker? I have cat fever over you.

Det. Feese: Cat fever? Is that why you killed the cat, because you got cat fever?

Katherine: No, but you know what?

Det. Feese: What?

Katherine: I am also related to the kitten. Hate that kitten, punk. See my eyes?

Det. Feese: Yes.

Katherine: That (unintelligible) is one of my families.

Det. Feese: Are you cursing me now with your eyes?

Katherine: No. Do you see my eyes? Don't they look like cat—?

Det. Feese: Are you Satanic cursing me with your eyes?

Katherine: No, but you're going to wake up and meet Satanic cursing of your own eyeballs—

Det. Feese: Are you a satanic sacrifice—

Katherine: Nasty asshole.

Det. Feese: Do you sacrifice cats to Satan?

Katherine: No. You do.

Det. Feese: How about dogs?

Katherine: No.

Det. Feese: Are you into chickens too?

Katherine: No.

Det. Feese: Have you mutilated any other type of animals besides this cat?

Katherine: No.

Det. Feese: Why did you mutilate the cat?

Katherine: I didn't.

Det. Feese: Why did you kill the cat?

Katherine: I didn't.

Det. Feese: Did the cat do anything to you?

Katherine: No.

Det. Feese: Did it attack you this morning?

Katherine: No.

Det. Feese: Why did you take the jaw of the cat out?

Katherine: I didn't.

Det. Feese: Who did?

Katherine: You, most likely.

Det. Feese: Was it someone else besides you?

Katherine: No.

Det. Feese: What do you have to say for yourself?

Katherine: You're going to meet the cat's fucking boyfriend, dude.

Det. Feese: Cat's got a boyfriend?

Katherine: Yeah. You want to meet my dog?

Det. Feese: Yeah, I'd like to meet your dog.

Katherine: All right.

Det. Feese: Where's your dog?

Katherine: Wait till you find out where it's going to be found.

Det. Feese: What type of dog do you have?

Katherine: I'm not telling you.

Det. Feese: Why don't you like cats?

Katherine:	Huh?
Det. Feese:	Why don't you like cats?
Katherine:	You're the one that don't like cats. I do like cats.
Det. Feese:	No, I don't like cats either myself. They all deserve to get squished.
Katherine:	Uh-huh. Why is that?
Det. Feese:	Why did you squish this cat?
Katherine:	I didn't squish the cat.
Det. Feese:	Why did you take the cat's tongue out?
Katherine:	I didn't take the cat's tongue out.
Det. Feese:	Why did you tear it apart?
Katherine:	Motherfucker, would you like to meet the cat's mother and have her rip your eyeballs out?
Det. Feese:	You don't like me, do you?
Katherine:	No, I don't, punk.
Det. Feese:	Why?
Katherine:	Because you're a fucking nut bag murderer.
Det. Feese:	What have I ever done to you?
Katherine:	You have sat here and said I've done this and that to a cat, and I'm this and that and a witch. If you want me to, I will start practicing, Mister, and then we'll see who the witch is.
Det. M:	Who?
Katherine:	Because I can test you now.
Det. Feese:	Do that, please.
Katherine:	In the name of the Lord Jesus Christ I do admit to what I've done to your self. Tell me everything you've done today and the truth, the whole truth, and nothing but the truth, so help you God, in the name of Jesus Christ yourself.
Det. Feese:	Why did you kill the cat?
Katherine:	(laughing hysterically) And all he can say is "Why did you kill the cat?" (laughing) Oh, shit. What cat?
Det. Feese:	The dead cat, the cat that's in your sink.
Katherine:	What sink?

Det. Feese:	The sink at your place.
Katherine:	What place?
Det. Feese:	Why did you kill the cat? You got something against cats?
Katherine:	What cat?
Det. Feese:	Do you have anything else you'd like to say?
Katherine:	Do you?
Det. Feese:	Yeah, I'd like to know why you killed the cat.
Katherine:	What cat?
Det. Feese:	Your cat.
Katherine:	I don't have a cat.
Det. Feese:	I thought you said you had a cat in your front room.
Katherine:	I have a cat in my living room at home where—back in Texas.
Det. Feese:	Texas?
Katherine:	Uh-huh. What do you want? You gonna go there and kill it?
Det. Feese:	Did you kill that cat too?
Katherine:	No, but it's going to kill you, bigot.
Det. Feese:	You ever been committed to a mental hospital?
Katherine:	Uh-huh.
Det. Feese:	Which one?
Katherine:	Every fucking one I've ever even heard of.
Det. Feese:	When did you get out?
Katherine:	I always get out; I just walk right out. They always release me.
Det. Feese:	Well—by the way, what is your name anyway?
Katherine:	Why do you ask? You want to meet my fucking dad or something?
Det. Feese:	No, I'd just like to know who I'm talking to.
Katherine:	Don't ask. It's none of your fucking business if you don't know.
Det. Feese:	No, I don't know your name.
Katherine:	What is your name?
Det. Feese:	My name is Floyd.

Katherine:	Floyd? Floyd what?
Det. Feese:	Floyd "M."
Katherine:	Oh, where?
Det. Feese:	From here.
Katherine:	Your name is not Floyd M or whatever you said. Your name—
Det. Feese:	Well, what is my name?
Katherine:	Is also.
Det. Feese:	Also?
Katherine:	Do you remember me, Mister?
Det. Feese:	Nope.
Katherine:	Yes, you do, don't you? I believe you do know who I am, so tell me nothing else, Mister.
Det. Feese:	I would like to show you some pictures, see if you recognize this animal here. What I'm holding in my hand is a picture of a bathroom sink, white bowl with an obviously mutilated cat, Siamese type, inside the bowl. Do you recognize this picture? Have you ever seen that cat before?
Katherine:	Uh-huh.
Det. Feese:	Whose cat's that?
Katherine:	(unintelligible)
Det. Feese:	You did that.
Katherine:	I did? (unintelligible)
Det. Feese:	Yes, you did. You did it in a fit of rage.
Katherine:	When was that?
Det. Feese:	That was this morning. Here's another picture of this mutilated cat with its jaw ripped out sitting in the sink. Do you recognize that picture there?
Katherine:	Uh-huh.
Det. Feese:	Whose cat's that?
Katherine:	I don't know. I didn't kill it. (unintelligible)
Det. Feese:	Did you ever see that cat before?
Katherine:	No.
Det. Feese:	Why did you kill that cat?

Katherine: I didn't kill it either.

Det. Feese: Okay. Who killed that cat? Here's another picture of the same—

Katherine: You did probably, boyfriend.

Det. Feese: —same thing showing a mutilated cat sitting a bathroom sink with his jaw missing. What did you do with the jaw?

Katherine: Oh, fuck.

Det. Feese: That's your cat, isn't it?

Det. Sgt: (standing by the door) Oh, by the way, Floyd?

Det. Feese: Yes sir.

Det. Sgt: ARO is here. They say the cat was killed in the bathroom. The Blood was still oozing out of the capillaries and everything else. So it's a fresh kill when she was there.

Det. Feese: Here's another picture of this mutilated cat with its jaw ripped out. Is that your cat? Why did you kill the cat? Does that cat deserve to die? Is that it? Did that cat do something? Why did you kill the cat?

Katherine: Why don't you ask the dead cat?

Det. Feese: I can't because you killed it. What did it do wrong? That was your cat that you killed. Why?

Katherine: Huh?

Det. Feese: Why?

Katherine: That ain't my cat, and I didn't kill it, sir.

Det. Feese: Had you ever seen that cat before?

Katherine: No.

Det. Feese: Where was that cat before you killed it? Did you find it? Was it a stray cat?

Katherine: I didn't kill that cat.

Det. Feese: Did you steal that cat?

Katherine: Huh-uh.

Det. Feese: Why did you kill the cat?

Katherine: You know what? I've never even killed a cat before in my life, Mister.

Det. M:	Who else was with you today?
Katherine:	Those cops that work with you, groovy boyfriend.
Det. M:	Just the cops?
Katherine:	Uh-huh.
Det. M:	You were alone except for the cops today?
Katherine:	Uh-huh.
Det. M:	And the cat was killed today?
Katherine:	That cat?
Det. M:	That cat.
Katherine:	No, I didn't kill those cats.
Det. M:	Well, if you were alone, who did?
Katherine:	Ummmmm (unintelligible).
Det. M:	I don't know, either.
Katherine:	So what bitch found my cat that I put in the bathroom sink, okay?
Det. M:	Did the cat—
Det. Feese:	Okay. Okay. Who found—who found the cat that was put in the bathroom sink, what bitch; what bitch are we talking about?
Katherine:	The groovy blonde one, dipshit.
Det. Feese:	That groovy blonde deputy bitch, the one standing out there, she was the one that found the cat that you put in the sink? Why? Is she some kind of a jerk? You don't like her?
Katherine:	No. But you know what? The cat that she found is not dead, is it?
Det. Feese:	No, the cat that she found wasn't dead. The cat that you put in the sink wasn't dead, so you didn't kill it, did you?
Katherine:	No. I don't kill cats. (unintelligible)
Det. Feese:	Why—okay. So that bitch walked in here, that blonde bitch, she didn't like you, you didn't like her, and that's what this is all about, isn't it?
Katherine:	Yeah, because I don't like handcuffs slapped on me.

Det. Feese: Okay. What was wrong with the cat when you put it in the sink; was it sick?

Katherine: Uh-huh. I found it while I was on the road. I picked it up and carried it, man—

Det. Feese: Okay.

Katherine: All the way there.

Det. Feese: All the way there?

Katherine: I walked around for a while trying to figure out where I was going to put it.

Det. Feese: Well, what kind of sick was it; was it—

Katherine: I picked up some shit on the street then, defecation—

Det. Feese: Was it throwing up, that kind of sick? Did it have cat worms, something like that?

Katherine: No.

Det. Feese: What was wrong with it?

Katherine: What was wrong with it?

Det. Feese: Yeah. What was wrong with it?

Katherine: Not much, but its eyeballs started coming out of its head.

Det. Feese: Eyeballs coming out of its head?

Katherine: Uh-huh.

Det. Feese: Okay. Like this picture right here showing the eyeball coming out of its head?

Katherine: No.

Det. Feese: No? Well, that's a picture of a cat in a sink with its eyeball coming out of its head.

Katherine: But this one is a little bit different.

Det. Feese: This one's different?

Katherine: Yeah, because nobody pulled it out, okay?

Det. Feese: Nobody pulled it out?

Katherine: No.

Det. Feese: Oh, okay. Well—

Katherine: I found it like that.

Det. Feese: You found it like that? Where did you find it?

Katherine:	Where do you think?
Det. Feese:	I don't know.
Katherine:	You want me to walk you there with handcuffs this tight—
Det. Feese:	Well, we might—
Katherine:	On you, Mister?
Det. Feese:	We might want you to show us where you found this cat that obviously is mutilated beyond description here.
Katherine:	I didn't find those cats.
Det. Feese:	Oh, you didn't find this cat?
Katherine:	I'm not—I never even seen those cats before, okay?
Det. Feese:	Okay. You never saw this cat before. Okay. Where did the—the cat that you put in the sink that had its eyeball coming out, where did you find that one at?
Katherine:	Okay. Do you know where—fuck? Okay. I remember I was way down – there's a few places where I've been. It's an old place where I've walked, the same damn spot where everybody always finds cats, lying in the middle of the street, okay?
Det. Feese:	Okay. What city was that in?
Katherine:	It was Leucadia, somewhere up there.
Det. Feese:	Leucadia? Do you know what street you live on?
Katherine:	I don't live up there.
Det. Feese:	Okay. Do you know where this cat was found?
Katherine:	Uh-huh.
Det. Feese:	—the residence you were in? Where was that at?
Katherine:	I didn't find any of those cats.
Det. Feese:	Okay. You were contacted by a deputy this morning—
Katherine:	But I seen them—
Det. Feese:	Okay. And you were contacted—
Katherine:	—and I know who killed them.
Det. Feese:	Who?
Katherine:	You and a few other people, okay?
Det. Feese:	So the cat that you put in the sink was sick that you

	found out on the street. What street was this? This was in Leucadia?
Katherine:	What?
Det. Feese:	You said you found a sick cat, and you put the cat in the sink. What city was this in; was this in Leucadia?
Katherine:	Uh-huh.
Det. Feese:	Do you remember what street it was on?
Katherine:	It's kind of hard to remember because it was real early in the morning.
Det. Feese:	Do you know what the address is?
Katherine:	Huh?
Det. Feese:	Do you know the address the street is on, the house that—
Katherine:	Last thing I remember I was in the white groovy dip-shit Mexican's front seat, man. And in the back—
Det. Feese:	What were you doing in there?
Katherine:	Motherfucker wanted to have sex with me and shit.
Det. Feese:	Did you have sex with him?
Katherine:	No, I got away with a good one this time.
Det. Feese:	How'd you get away with that?
Katherine:	I told him that I was going to the bathroom. I took my shit and then fucking told him period: I told him that I don't like guys like you because I have found out that I've been in this car before, and I did not easily get in back seats of people's cars, and furthermore, I do not like it, and its rubber upholstery in there, and I've got somewhere to take a piss. And furthermore, Mister, every time I see this car, stupid girls in it are always men. You don't know this motherfucker, but I used to be your wife, dig it. And furthermore, idiot, don't you ever fucking try me like this lady used to do to me. Remember that bitch you used to always run with, with all those other ones? Where are they now, idiot, huh?
Det. Feese:	Why did you kill the cat?

Katherine:	And then I told him I bet you can't fucking kill me with all them tools in the fucking back of your car, dig it. I said what you going to do now, beat the fuck to death with them because I'm telling you this right now, Mister, I dare you to start your shit again, and you (unintelligible.)
Det. Feese:	Why'd you kill the cat?
Katherine:	I didn't kill any cat.
Det. Feese:	What did you do with the sick cat that you found out in the street that you put in the sink?
Katherine:	That one?
Det. Feese:	Uh-huh, that one.
Katherine:	What did I do with it?
Det. Feese:	What did you do with it?
Katherine:	I—it's still alive.
Det. Feese:	It's still alive? Where is it at?
Katherine:	I don't know. Somebody took it.
Det. Feese:	Is it still in the sink? It's alive but still in the sink?
Katherine:	No, I think that cop took it. I don't mean it's still alive in the sink or if she took it and put it in the trunk or—
Det. Feese:	Did you put this alive cat that was in the sink—
Katherine:	It may be alive in the sink.
Det. Feese:	Could it still be in the sink alive? Maybe it needs some help. Maybe we should send somebody to help it?
Katherine:	Who?
Det. Feese:	The cat. Maybe it needs some first aid.
Katherine:	Yeah.
Det. Feese:	Okay. Where is the house at so we can send somebody to help this cat?
Katherine:	Back at the gas station where your groupie cop picked me up at probably.
Det. Feese:	At the gas station?
Katherine:	Uh-huh.
Det. Feese:	Why—were you going to wash the cat in the sink?

Katherine: Unless she put it in a plastic bag and put it in her car or something. Maybe she manhandled it worse than—

Det. Feese: No, we're talking about the cat that's alive that's in the sink in the gas station that you put there.

Katherine: What about it?

Det. Feese: Why did you put the cat in the sink?

Katherine: Why? To wait there.

Det. Feese: Why?

Katherine: Until I could figure out how to get some money to bankroll some medical attention. Why do you think, stupid?

Det. Feese: Did—when you were helping this cat that was sick, did you enjoy this? Did you get a high out of this, a little bit of a rush, make you feel like, you know, you're doing a good deed?

Katherine: To what, kill it?

Det. Feese: Yeah.

Katherine: I didn't kill it.

Det. Feese: No, to help it.

Katherine: Did I do it to get high?

Det. Feese: Yeah.

Katherine: Off of what?

Det. Feese: I don't know. To help this cat get better. You put it in the sink, and you were trying—

Katherine: Motherfucker, why don't you go get high after you eat it?

Det. Feese: Were you going to eat the cat?

Katherine: No, but you're going to.

Det. Feese: Is this the cat that you found that was sick on the street that you put in the sink? Take a look at this picture. Have you ever seen this cat before? Where have you seen this cat at?

Katherine: By the beach.

Det. Feese: By the beach? Is that where you found the cat that was sick, by the beach, and you took it to the gas station to put it in the sink for it to get better?

Katherine: That's not the one.

Det. Feese: Okay. Where did you find this cat at?

Katherine: Let me tell you something. I watched the whole hit, dig?

Det. Feese: The hit on the cat?

Katherine: I don't say—say that I killed them.

Det. Feese: Who killed the cat?

Katherine: The fucker that I was with was also at the people who did do it, and then he started killing them himself also. And then they started killing the babies, stupid.

Det. M: What babies?

Katherine: Babies.

Det. M: What babies?

Katherine: That I saw him kill.

Det. M: Where?

Katherine: I don't know where it was. There were (unintelligible) motherfucker. I don't give a fuck because I don't even have to tell you.

Det. Feese: What's this person's name?

Katherine: Because you ain't fucking going to win my groovy new fucking problem, are you? You think you can sit there and ask me this and that and this and that with hand-cuffs on me saying that I done something wrong? Fuck you, punk, because it's my fucking job to tell you this: I have already fucking taken care of the whole mess, okay, and you can't ask me this and that so that you can possibly say well, now I have just proved the mur-der myself. See this? I have wroten it all down, and I'm sorry, but I'm the one who seen it. And I'm sorry.

Det. M: Seen what?

Katherine: You ought to say Mister because you are not supposed to ask a fellow employee of the same type of people you

	work for what did this, what did that, what did this, what did this. Who did this, who's the killer of this and that—
Det. Feese:	Is this the cat that—
Katherine:	—because, motherfucker, you're also a mayhem murderer cop yourself.
Det. Feese:	Was this the cat you found at the beach? Is that the cat you found at the—
Katherine:	Most likely.
Det. Feese:	Is that the cat that you found at the beach that was sick that you took to the bathroom?
Katherine:	No.
Det. Feese:	No? Is that a different cat that you found at the beach?
Katherine:	Motherfucker, you're the one that killed it, dig? I saw you do it.
Det. Feese:	Can you do me a favor?
Katherine:	What?
Det. Feese:	Get your fucking foot off of my table.
Katherine:	Make me. Ouch. Oh, thank you.
Det. Feese:	You're welcome.
Katherine:	(unintelligible) thinks he's (unintelligible) kung fu.
Det. Feese:	Is this the cat that you killed?
Katherine:	No.
Det. Feese:	Is this the cat that your friend killed in the bathroom?
Katherine:	I've seen them all be killed, idiot.
Det. Feese:	Who's your friend?
Katherine:	They aren't my friends—
Det. Feese:	How many cats have you killed?
Katherine:	—they're yours! Quit saying they're my friends.
Deputy B:	Detective Feese, one quick question. Can you do me a favor?
Det. Feese:	Sure.
Deputy B:	Can you put it on the envelope—
Det. M:	An ARO (Animal Regulation Officer) wants to come over here—

Katherine: Can someone please call my boss?

Deputy B: Where she got the cat or where it came from.

Det. Feese: It came from the beach on Leucadia, that she took it to the bathroom because it was sick.

Katherine: And I left it there, and I also tried to give it some water and tried to see if there was any one thing I could do to help it.

Det. Feese: Okay. Have you killed other cats before?

Katherine: I didn't kill any cats.

Det. Feese: Well, how many cats have you helped?

Katherine: Lots.

Det. Feese: Lots? How do you help them?

Katherine: Most of the time I have a way of taking their money—

Det. Feese: You take—

Katherine: —but this time Smokey Bears, he wouldn't let me come with me own police vehicles because they know that mine are better than theirs and they just buy them from the department, and I build my own police vehicles. And the fuckers are so jealous that I sit here with handcuffs on me, and they all say I killed cats, Mister. Now what?

Det. Feese: Why did you kill this cat?

Katherine: You killed it, fuckface.

Det. Feese: Sit down.

Det. M: Have a seat.

Det. Feese: Sit down. Thank you. Your name, sir?

Mr. Trump: Steven Trump. (coming into the room).

Det. Feese: I'm Detective Feese and this is Detective "M."

Katherine: Will you tell this (unintelligible) from saying why I killed the cat when I didn't kill a cat. I'm sick of this nut.

Det. Feese: Basically the situation is this. What we believe to have taken place was that this young lady here found this cat somewhere on one of the beaches in Leucadia, took it to a bathroom—

Katherine: And none of those are any of the cats that I found.

Det. Feese: —took it to a bathroom—

Katherine: The cats that I found are still alive. Now what you're telling me, eat his picture and shut his mouth.

Det. Feese: —in a gas station and mutilated the cat. Here are the pictures of her escapades. The—you recognize this cat, don't you?

Katherine: Where's my picture?

Det. Feese: I don't have your picture here.

Katherine: Then how can you say I killed them if you don't have any evidence. Tell me. Is that my hand there, right there? See that left hand? Is that my hand?

Det. Feese: Do you recognize the cat?

Katherine: It looks more like—let me see you all's hands, man. Let's see whose hand it really is.

Det. Feese: Sit down.

Katherine: See my hand? See my hand? My hand don't look like it, does it?

Det. M: Have a seat.

Det. Feese: Have a seat, please. Thank you. Appreciate your cooperation.

Katherine: Maybe means investigate it.

Det. Feese: Basically she took the cat into the bathroom to—it was sick, and she decided to make it well, and at this point we have not figured out how she's made it well. But— how did you make the sick cat that you took into the gas station bathroom and put in the sink, well?

Katherine: I gave it some water, and it drank it. I washed off his blood, and I also investigated his eye and looked at the other eye and washed it out, and it was clean. I prayed for it, and I cried. I tried to wash it off. I looked at all of its feet, and there were fingernails.

Det. Feese: Why did you want the cat dead?

Katherine: What cat dead?

Det. Feese: That cat dead.

Katherine: I don't want any of those cats dead. I never did. And I'm not the one who killed them.

Det. Feese: Who did?

Katherine: I don't know.

Det. Feese: You said that your friend killed them—

Katherine: No.

Det. Feese: —that was in the bathroom with you.

Katherine: I didn't say that. You said that, and you said that I said that again, Mister, you are also under arrest again for that one, dig it?

Det. Feese: Uh-huh.

Katherine: I mean you can't sit there and say things I didn't say thinking that I'm some dummy who's going to sit here and say oh, (unintelligible) I'm sorry, I'm sorry, I killed that cat. Not this time, fuck-face. Go look in the fucking —back there and sit here and say wait a minute, you work here, don't you, lady, and then can I slap the cuffs on you and fuck with your head like this. Mister, do you know who you are talking to, huh? Are you crazy? Tell me something else. What have you done today yourself, huh? Where have you been today all day long? Have you been inside that bathroom at all because those hands look like your hands. See that hand right there in that picture? It looks like your hand, Mister. Where have you been today? I seen you in that bathroom also. I have seen you around that area.

Det. Feese: I was in the bathroom with the cat with you? You saw me there?

Katherine: Yes, I've seen you.

Det. Feese: Well, was I with that cat right there that you saw me—

Katherine: I watched you murder it, Mister—

Det. Feese: —you watched me murder the cat?

Katherine: —and now what you gonna do about it?

Det. Feese: How did I murder it?

Katherine: How?

Det. Feese: Yeah.

Katherine: Motherfucker, we were all standing there watching you like we were (unintelligible)

Det. Feese: Well, I had—I had my eyes closed. You tell me how I murdered the cat.

Katherine: Why don't you just kill all the cats and the kids too? Like you said, you were going to, and then you all made bets and placed bets and said we going to, we going to, we hate cats, we hate cats, because (unintelligible) this Satanic sick facers, killing babies and shit, and they say this and that, and they also stab people and run around laughing and crying, you know, don't they, officer, now no, we won't, and nobody won't loosen my handcuffs, and you're going to lose your jobs, dig it, because you know how tight they are?

Det. Feese: How did I kill the cat?

Katherine: They are one cylinder off. You (unintelligible)

Det. Feese: Detective M doesn't like you.

Katherine: I don't care. Detective M.

Det. Feese: I can tell by looking—

Katherine: —had better fork over my badge and my uniform—

Det. Feese: I can tell by his appearance that he doesn't like you.

Katherine: Why?

Det. Feese: I don't know. How did I kill the cat? You saw me do it; how did I do it?

Katherine: (screeching) You put my fucking wrist (unintelligible) you fucking did that to my (unintelligible) take the truck (unintelligible) and you better mind me, murderer.

Det. Feese: How did they kill the cat? You said you saw me do it.

Katherine: It was your friend.

Det. Feese: I was with my friends, and they did it? How'd they do it?

Katherine: I don't know. Go ask the other fuck-faces that fucking

watched you do it. Why don't you sit them here—
down here in their own fucking plain clothes? Why'd
you sit here with my fucking uniform and my badges
on and look at them and fuck do the same fuck-face
bullshit you've done to me, you—

Det. Feese: Have you had an opportunity to talk to the officers that
were on the scene?

Katherine: And what're you going to do when my badge is hard
and—(unintelligible)

Katherine: —and everybody's in this whole (unintelligible)

ARO: The witness saw her go into the head.

Det. Feese: With the cat?

ARO: Went in there with a bag. When he went into the head,
she had the cat in the sink.

Katherine: Would you like to see gross—

ARO: —and the cat was dead from the—

Katherine: —or would you like to see blood (unintelligible) San
Diego (unintelligible)

ARO: —smashed, eyes protruding out, and there's no puncture hole or puncture marks.

Katherine: —a tan right there. Would you like the back of my
white black shoulder too.

ARO: —incisions, or anything else, so I would say it was
dead from a, you know, trauma to the head. There's a
fair amount of blood that's there—

Katherine: —buddy? It's sunshine underneath it with the rising
sun. And on my right—

ARO: —and cat had a lot of blood on it, so --

Katherine: —and on my right pupil, it's sunny—

ARO: You know, he said he saw her go in there about eight
o'clock or so or a little bit after—

Katherine: —rose (unintelligible) and on the left part—

ARO: —and like I was saying, you know, without going
through an autopsy this afternoon.

Katherine: Now tell me this—

Det. Feese: So it's possible that it was in the bag when she went into the bathroom.

ARO: Could have done that. Also in her bag they found a large can of aerosol spray that's got blood on it.

Katherine: —a little messed up—

Det. Feese: So maybe she smashed—

ARO: —smacked with that, yeah.

Katherine: And I've asked you nicely please (unintelligible)—

Det. Feese: Well, she's admitted to taking the cat and to finding the cat—

Katherine: Shut the fuck up.

Det. Feese: —and she's admitted to everything other than actually killing it.

ARO: Uh-huh.

Det. Feese: We're not going to get any more out of her.

ARO: So there was—she did find it in Leucadia in the beach area?

Det. Feese: That's what she said. Well, she said she found a cat on the beach in Leucadia and that it was a sick cat and that she took that cat into the bathroom at the gas station but this cat here is not the cat that she took into the bathroom, according to her—

Katherine: People warned you guys not to do this. (unintelligible)

Det. Feese: Of course, it's more obvious that this is the cat that she's talking about, but she's not admitting to that specific cat—

Katherine: (unintelligible)

Det. Feese: —and the fact that she wants to kill all cats. How many cats have you killed before?

Katherine: I've never killed any cats before in my life. I killed humans.

Det. Feese: Humans? Okay.

Katherine: Yes.

294   BEHIND THE BADGE

Det. Feese:	How many humans have you killed before?
Katherine:	I don't know.
Det. Feese:	Okay. What did this cat do to you? Did the cat bite you or something to make you mad, the one that you killed in the bathroom?
Katherine:	I didn't kill the cat.
Det. Feese:	Well, that one somebody killed in the bathroom. Did this cat make you mad?
Katherine:	No. People kill them because they say they're sick of the little scum there running around, making those ass—they're sitting around and work these fucking, dumb-fuck punks who fucking ass go around making love to our women, and then when you have to raise their kids and put up with their fucking pretty kitty Spanish shit and feed them with our money work so hard for. Doing what? Murdering people—
Det. Feese:	Well, based upon what she's said there's probably enough to go ahead and draw up a felony charge.
Katherine:	—is that your dog, murdering kids, and locking up people that work here. And these dummies fucking do it too with you. Then they wind up with you on the firing shot dead—
Det. Feese:	She a little unstable—
Katherine:	—and I get to shoot them, man, because this is against the law, and they know it too—
Det. Feese:	—a psychiatric evaluation will need to be conducted.
Katherine:	Now take me to the highest head honcho of the FBI—
Det. Feese:	—well, we will charge her with a felony of animal abuse, for the time being.
Katherine:	—department in this building now, sweetheart.
Det. Feese:	—and that's probably the best thing. Is there anything you want to ask her?
Katherine:	And you will find my badge there, all right?
ARO:	All right. The primary thing was the location of the cat, the reason why—

Katherine: And then you are fired. It's like you're fired, you.

ARO: —like I say, it's not—

Katherine: Because I've asked you to—

Det. Feese: —she's giving out bits and pieces of information, but it's not the whole story.

Katherine: —and you said no, you scum fuckface zitfaced slut, I don't have to. And furthermore, I don't like you and I don't—

Det. Feese: You have to pick up a piece here and pick up a piece there. You'd have to sit and listen to these prior conversations again, which are basically fragmented.

Katherine: —know, and you have never worked here, have you, darling? And furthermore, when I take the cuffs off, I will be standing here telling that head honcho—

Det. Feese: But every now and then she lands on the earth and we get a glimpse at what happened.

Katherine: —one I said what am I supposed to do now? And she said well, wait a minute because, bitch, you have to suck my dick before you get there.

Det. Feese: So then she—she killed the cat.

Katherine: That's what you said, Mister.

Det. Feese: I'm Detective Feese, F-e-e-s-e.

Katherine: You go home to your jail cell and masturbate—

Det. Feese: Okay.

Katherine: —over that one.

Det. Feese: We will have a Deputy transport her to the San Diego Jail and book her on a felony. I will see if I can get a rush on an autopsy. Since I'm stuck with this one, John gets to go home early. O'K, darling it's time to go for a little ride.

Katherine: Bite me, asshole.

It was the next day around 10:00 AM while I was sitting at my desk when I got the phone call. I had thirty workable cases and about fifty non-workable cases scattered over my desk and I was

THE WORST CASE OF CAT
SUICIDE I'VE EVER SEEN.

pawing through them (no pun intended) trying to make heads or tails out of them. Couple of rapes, some robberies, the normal stuff.

The ARO started the conversation by telling me that they had been up all night working on the cat killing case. (Some people have no life.) They had to bring in a specialist and he wanted to know who to send the bill to. I told him that this was a formal investigation, so bill the county. After pausing for a few seconds he finally stated that it was the formal opinion of the specialist that "the cat was killed by a small dog or coyote." There was no blunt trauma.

Det. Feese: Well, I'll be damned! Oh, well.

NICE DOGGIE

— John A. Davis, El Centro PD (Ret.) —

EL CENTRO POLICE DEPARTMENT
EL CENTRO, CA, CIRCA 1976

While serving as patrol officer with the Brawley (CA) Police Department, I was the first K-9 patrol officer for the department. The police chief was apprehensive of the program, but, with the urging of the patrol commander, agreed to a provisional K-9 program.

After graduating from Fon Johnson's Police and Sheriff's K-9 Training program in Pacific Beach, California, Kelso, a trained utility police K-9, and I were partners in the field. The chief, the city councilman, and the city manager were anxious to see how effective the K-9 program would be, so they monitored our first field call.

The 900 block of Main Street was a bar area where most of the agriculture workers would go for a Saturday night outing. The bar patrons were Hispanic and Filipino farm workers who were quite handy with "lettuce knives." Apparently a lettuce worker was not happy with the music the band was playing, and he went up on the stage and threatened the band members with a twelve-inch blade until they played the music he wanted to hear. The bartender called the police, telling the dispatcher that there was a, "Man with a knife threatening to cut up the band."

297

SO, YOUR NEW PARTNER IS A GORILLA
UNTIL KELSO GETS HIS 'SNIFFER' READJUSTED.

My patrol sergeant and I responded and I took point, walking into the bar. There was a band member standing with his back to the wall, and a short, drunk fellow holding a knife pointed at the other man's throat.

The patrons were standing back. There were women screaming and men telling the drunk to put the knife down. There was bar music playing as I walked up to the bar with Kelso, who was barking and growling as we approached the stage.

The chief, city manager and the city councilman were standing behind us watching how we were handling the call. There was a woman sitting on a chair at a table to my left as we walked toward the "man with a knife." Kelso, who had a sensitive nose and could sniff out a burglar a block away, darted to my left toward the sitting woman. She was wearing a dress and her legs were spread apart. Kelso went right up to her and buried his snout between her open legs!

Using my commanding, army-trained voice, I kept yelling at him loudly, "NO-OUT, NO-OUT," and pulling on his head to bring him out from under the woman's dress. I finally got him out and dragged him away from the screaming woman. All the while the city executives were behind us. The chief was looking down at the floor, the city manager was standing with his hands on his hips, and the city councilman was laughing up a storm. (He was a retired World War II paratrooper first sergeant.)

What the Fon Johnson training program forgot to tell me was that male Dobermans do not work well around females who are on their menstrual cycle. Kelso was no exception.

We finally got up to the stage and Kelso smiled his big pearls at the drunk. The drunk thought he was a "nice doggie" until Kelso bit his hand when he tried to pet him. The drunk was taken into custody and when I walked out of the bar the woman was still hysterical about the slobber Kelso had left between her thighs.

So much for our first K-9 operation!

DETECTIVE HUMOR

— Jerry Timms, Gardena PD, LA School Police (Ret.) —

GARDENA POLICE DEPARTMENT
CITY OF GARDENA, CA, CIRCA 1974

I was working as a day shift detective. There were two detectives continually feuding over smoking. Obviously, one of them smoked and the other one didn't. In those days smoking was allowed inside the police station and the smell of smoke filled the air. This was one of the problems between the two detectives.

Over a period of time the two detectives would pull little pranks on one another. The smoker, I'll call him Detective Smokey, found out that the non-smoker, I'll call him Detective Airwick, could not stand raw eggs, to the extent that just the sight of a raw egg would make him extremely nauseous.

Detective Airwick had the assignment of "filing detective" and as such, would arrive at the station early every morning. This gave him the opportunity to hide all of the ash trays, causing Detective Smokey to play hide and seek, or use something else in place of an ash tray.

One morning Detective Smokey arrived at the station very early, even earlier than Detective Airwick. Detective Smokey had brought in a dozen fresh eggs just for this occasion. The Detective Division offices all looked basically the same: nondescript gray metal desks and chairs, push-button phones with the buttons and lights along the bottom for multiple lines, coffee cups, paper clips, and miscellaneous personal items on each desk. Detective Smokey broke open each egg and carefully arranged them on Detective Airwick's desk, being especially careful as to not disturb any of the items on the desk top. To make it even more disgusting, he reached into a paper sack and removed twelve cigarette butts and artistically placed one but in the center of each egg.

When Detective Airwick arrived for work all eyes were on him. To everyone's surprise, Detective Airwick left the creative arrangement on his desk top so that it could be seen by others. He went about his daily routine and when he returned from court he took a lot of ribbing from his fellow detectives, of course. (They couldn't pass up this opportunity.) But surprisingly, he didn't act upset. He just cleaned his desk as if it was a part of his normal procedure.

Everything was calm for about three days. On the fourth day I, along with Detective Airwick and another detective, planned to go out to lunch. Being the junior detective I went and checked out a detective car and waited in the rear parking area of the station. The other detective came out of the station, laughing hysterically as he got inside the car. When I asked him what was so funny he said "I'll tell you later," and continued laughing.

Detective Airwick came out a few minutes later and he too was laughing. I asked him what was so funny to which he replied, "I'll fix Smokey. I put black powder in the bottom of his ash tray."

The other detective, who was a close friend of Detective Airwick, got a shocked look on his face and said, "I hope you didn't because I . . . put black powder inside the ash tray."

Detective Airwick said he thought the black powder was brought for him to use, not both of them. They estimated that probably over one-half ounce of black powder had been placed in the ash tray. Both detectives again began laughing uncontrollably. I started up the car and we drove out of the station lot and headed for lunch.

Being typical detectives on Code 7, we had left the car radio off—we didn't want to be bothered by radio calls . . . why disrupt a perfectly good lunch?

We finished eating, returned to the car, and proceeded back to the station. As we approached the station it looked like bedlam. There were two fire engines, three plainclothes, unmarked vehicles (later determined to be FBI vehicles), and several of our day shift patrol cars all with their red lights on. We had no idea what the situation was as our radio was still in the off position. I made my way around the emergency vehicles and pulled into the rear parking lot where I observed an ambulance parked by the rear entrance. What the . . . ?

I parked the car and we all entered the station through the rear entrance. Inside there was a large commotion near the burglary detectives office . . . right where Detective Smokey's desk was located. Upon entering I saw Detective Smokey's desk chair turned over on the floor, several feet away from his desk, and the phone lying on the floor next to the chair. The phone had been unceremoniously

LET ME GUESS . . . YOU WERE
TALKING TO JERRY TIMMS AGAIN.

pulled out from the wall. Several firemen were standing around Detective Smokey, who had a bandage on one of his forearms.

Detective Smokey was telling them what had happened . . . He was sitting at his desk, talking to an FBI agent from the Redondo Beach office, and smoking his cigarette. He went to put his cigarette out in his ash tray when suddenly there was some type of explosion in his ash tray. He instinctively jumped out of his chair and in doing so knocked the chair over while at the same time he pulled the telephone out of the wall.

The FBI agent whom he was talking to heard him scream and then the phone line went dead. The agent tried to call back but only got a busy signal. The agent then attempted to call the main number for the police station and again, only got a busy signal. (It would later be determined that when Detective Smokey yanked the phone from the wall the action caused a disruption to the entire phone system.) The agent, fearing something drastic had occurred, put out a notification which caused the fire and police units and the ambulance to respond.

Luckily, Detective Smokey lost only the hair on his forearm from his hand to his elbow.

In addition to a major ass-chewing from the chief of police, plus other ramifications, the hide-and-seek-egg battle came to an abrupt halt. From that day forward, however, Detective Smokey had a new nickname: FLASH.

MY CAR IS STUCK

— Lupe Avalos, California Highway Patrol (Ret.) —

CITY OF RIVERSIDE POLICE DEPARTMENT
RIVERSIDE, CA, CIRCA 1961

What a night to fight crime . . . a warm, spring night on the dogwatch. As a plus, they gave us a nice car with all the gas we needed to catch criminals.

Old "Giff," six months from retirement, was working as dispatcher. He was still fighting past demons and was awfully moody from being on the wagon. The watch sergeant briefed us and spent another ten minutes chewing out the shift for picking on our "voice of the night." It seems that someone had keyed the mike when the local freight train passed through town on its 3:00 AM run. It took the watch commander fifteen minutes to coax old Giff off the file cabinets. But that's another story.

The dynamic threesome had the west end of town. Gerry in Casablanca, George in Arlington, and I had Magnolia Center. For some reason, the powers-that-be switched Gerry and me. Thank You! It could sure get boring patrolling a residential/agricultural area surrounded by nothing. It was a blue-collar neighborhood that rolled up the sidewalks at midnight during the week. As a result, you spent a lot of time in the boonies looking for "stolens" to stay awake. *Now, maybe I could catch me a burglar and Gerry can bat-tle the sleep-demons.*

The first half of the shift was uneventful . . . a very quiet night. Even the 3:00 AM limited didn't show up.

"R-4 to R-3," came Gerry's voice over the radio. I wondered what Gerry wants? I picked up my microphone . . . "R-3 in Mag Center."

"R-3, meet me in White Gates."

Ah . . . Gerry found him a stolen car, parts, or maybe he needs help with the form 180. "R-3 enroute," I replied and started heading his way. I could tell by his voice that it wasn't an emergency situation, so I didn't have to hurry. I wondered why he didn't call the "S" unit (sergeant). I knew it would take about ten minutes to get to his location. I hoped he would position himself so I could see him because there are a lot of arroyos, washes and areas where one can get lost!!!

When I arrived at the location he was nowhere to be found. I picked up the mike.

"R-3 to R-4, 10-97, where are you?"

"R-3, turn left at second drive and the look for the light," he replied.

This particular area was an arroyo that would be called a sand dune if it were in the desert. I was saying to myself as I was driving toward him . . . *My damn luck! Clean uniform, shoes shined, and the dust really shows up on this blue uniform. Ash . . . there's the light, but what is he doing on the top of the hill? And why isn't he using his spotlight? Big Dummy . . . he could be spotted much quicker if he used it. Sure hope they don't steal me blind back in civilization!*

"Holy Shit! What happened to you?" I was looking at a ghostly apparition. "Are you hurt?"

"Nah, I'm all right . . . just had a little run of bad luck," he replied hesitantly.

"Man . . . you've got seventeen coats of dust on you. What happened? And . . . where is the patrol car?"

"Down there," he said as he was pointing down into the arroyo.

Automatically, the 5-Ws—the standard who, what, where, when, why—the basics of report writing—came to mind. I knew paper was going to have to be written on this one.

"Lupe, you're not going to believe it."

"Is the patrol car damaged?" I asked.

"No . . . it's just hung up on a boulder," he said, as if it were a regular every-day occurrence . . . to get a car hung up on a boulder. Yeah, right.

"How'd it get there?" I asked as my mind was trying to vision the situation. I couldn't yet see the car.

"Lupe . . . I'm a city boy. I'm not used to these washes and arroyos, and all the soft dirt. I got stuck in the one behind you."

"You mean the one I just came through?"

"Yeah, but I wandered a little to the left of the road and got stuck."

"OK, then what?"

"Well, I tried everything they teach you at the academy: dug away some dirt, put boulders under the wheels, finally forward and back wheels. Nothing worked. It just spun. As a last resort I got this bright idea."

"Wait a minute. Before you go any further, why didn't you call me before? Both of us could have gotten it out."

"Well," Gerry replied. "I wanted to try everything first, so I grabbed some small boulders, dug around the wheels some more, put the boulders in the tracks and got ready to shove her out."

I could see where this was going and so I asked him, "Dummy, how were you going to accelerate out by yourself?"

"Hey, I got this brainstorm. I got another boulder, started the engine, and then put the boulder on the gas pedal . . . then I ran to the rear of the car and pushed. Oh, yeah . . . I put it in drive before I pushed it."

By this time, Gerry was getting animated and began talking in a more excited manner that increased with each sentence.

"Well," he said, "the sucker came out like a shot. Then it took off up the side of the arroyo and down over and into the next one.

I chased it but the wheels were spinning and throwing out dirt so bad that I couldn't see. For a minute I thought I was back home in the middle of a tornado. Lupe, thank God the boulder rolled off of the gas pedal or I'd still be chasing it." He took another deep breath and continued. "With both of us, it should just come off that boulder."

Seeing him in his disheveled and completely dust-covered uniform, it didn't take me but a snap second to reply, "Oh, No! We're getting a tow. I'm not going to get all dirty like you."

I grabbed an 11-44 cover blanket from the trunk of my car and wrapped it around him. He looked like a mummy. I opened the right front passenger door and helped him get into the front seat, trying to stay at arm's length so I wouldn't get dirty. I would have put him in the trunk of the car if it weren't full of equipment.

I got in the car and we drove over to my favorite towing service company. I had to get Ted, the owner of the tow service, out of bed and then re-tell the story. Big mistake! It took another thirty minutes before Ted could compose himself enough to drive. After Ted successfully removed the patrol car from its "unusual" parking place, Gerry and I headed over to my house, where we spent the rest of the shift cleaning his patrol car.

It was a good thing I stocked plenty of rubbing compound because it sure came in handy.

The "secret" came out at the next "choir practice." I sure benefited from that because the more beers guys bought for me . . . the better the story got.

THE UNLUCKY ROBBER

— Harry Penny —

BURBANK POLICE DEPARTMENT
BURBANK, CA, CIRCA 1963

While I was working the Hall of Justice Jail I was attending college at night. In one of my police science—now known as criminal justice—classes. All of the students were law enforcement officers and we all developed a good relationship with each other. After class, a group of us, including the instructor, an LAPD robbery/homicide sergeant, would sometimes go to a close-by "cop bar," a local Italian restaurant near the college, for a couple of "toddies" and to tell cop stories ("choir practice").

On one occasion one of the students, a Burbank police officer, told us of a robbery gone awry.

It was a Friday and he was working an afternoon watch patrol car when he received a call of an attempted bank robbery in progress. He started responding Code 3. As he was headed to the call, he received another call from dispatch: the bank robbery suspect had gone across the street to try to rob the market. Other units were also rolling to the location.

Upon his arrival he observed a male suspect fitting the description he had been given over the radio. He arrested the suspect without incident. In gathering the information he contacted the bank manager and the market manager, who gave him their separate versions of what the suspect had done.

The suspect had entered the bank. Since it was a Friday, and the bank was open until 6:00 PM, (banks weren't open on weekends then) it was always crowded. There were long lines of people waiting to take care of their banking transactions and the robber apparently didn't want to wait. So he went to one of the teller windows where there was no line. The teller, a young female, was counting her receipts for the day.

The suspect approached her and in a quiet voice, told her that he had a gun and wanted her to take her money and put it in the paper sack he had in his hand. The teller looked up from what she was doing and said, "I'm sorry, sir. This window is closed. Just take your stuff and go over to one of those lines and wait your turn."

The suspect, taken by surprise at her remark, said, "Lady, you don't understand. This is a stick-up. I've got a gun."

The teller responded in a stern manner, "Look, I don't care. This window is closed. Now go get in line." With that she took her "closed" sign, slammed it on the counter and walked away.

The suspect grabbed his paper sack and quickly left the bank— without any money!

While the bank manager was calling the police to report what had happened, the young teller looked out the window and saw the suspect go across the street and into the market.

In the market it was the same scene . . . a lot of people shopping for groceries for the weekend and the checkout lines were long.

The suspect walked up to one of the check stands, where the clerk was taking the items saying something like, "two for forty-nine," and then punching the keys on the register and so forth. The suspect threw his paper sack on the counter, laid his gun on the counter (no reason was given for this dumb move), and said, "This is a stick-up. Take the money from the drawer and put it in the bag!"

The teller put down the item she had in her hand, reached over, picked up the suspect's gun and handed it back to him saying, "Look. There are a lot of people ahead of you so just take your stuff and go to the end of the line."

"Hey, lady! I said I want the money. Now!" as he took the gun from her.

"I don't care what you want!" the clerk replied. "Now take your stuff and go back in the line before I have to call the manager." With that said, she then turned to the customer she had been waiting on and picked up another item and began ringing it up.

The suspect then turned around and fled. He was just coming out of the market when the police arrived.

The funny part of the story was when the suspect told the arresting officer that this had been his first attempt at robbery and about the two ladies who didn't care and weren't scared of his gun.

He did not know that the bank teller's ex-husband was a cop and she was used to guns and stories about crooks. The market check-out clerk was married to a cop and also knew about crooks and guns.

What made it even funnier was the fact that this particular officer was the bank teller's ex-husband and he was now married to the market check-out clerk!

The suspect pleaded guilty . . . probably by reason of insanity!

CHIPS AND DIPS TECHNOLOGY OR PARTY TIME AT THE STATE LINE

— Harry Penny —

SAN DIEGO, CALIFORNIA, CIRCA 1990

This is one of those "choir practice" stories between two cops. It was a beautiful, summer day in San Diego and we were sitting on the back deck of my boat in the slip in post-card-gorgeous Mission Bay. We were just visiting and having a "boat drink," the kind of drink that is a pink-colored concoction, has a neat little umbrellas, and is served in a tall, frosty glass. My wife was preparing her special recipe of tasty, mouth-watering shrimp on the barbeque on the stern rail of the boat.

Dave Gabrieilli was a chief hospital corpsman in the U.S Naval Reserve and was doing his two weeks active duty by training in San Diego. He was attending a class to become certified as an instructor for his Naval Reserve unit. I was the certifying instructor for the class in combat casualty medical regulating.

I knew his full-time job was serving as an Arizona Highway Patrolman with the Department of Public Safety (DPS). We had both been chief petty officers in the U.S. Navy. Because of this, and with my law enforcement background, an automatic friendship quickly evolved. Naturally the funny stories started coming out about the military and law enforcement. This is one of the stories I'll never forget.

311

Dave was working day watch and was sitting in his highway patrol car near the California/Arizona state line on Interstate 40. This particular location was also a good spot to meet with officers from the California Highway Patrol (CHP) and exchange information or just to shoot the breeze.

Traffic was busy and many of the vehicles were large commercial trucks, you know, the eighteen-wheeler variety, with the big radio antennas mounted on the side rear-view mirrors indicating they had CB radios. CB radios were the professional truck driver's version of entertainment and also came in very handy when a driver would see any vehicle resembling a police, sheriff, or highway patrol car. If a trucker saw one of these vehicles, it was an automatic reaction to get on the radio and advise any other drivers of the location. (We all know that truckers obey the speed limit and just want to let their fellow drivers know, just in case of an emergency or such. Yeah. Right!)

Well, cops are highly trained and enjoy the many technological wonders of radar guns and such. Gone are the days when the motorcycle cops would hide behind those billboard advertising signs that dot the highways of the nation. They also like CB radios and many of them have them in their patrol units. Dave was no exception.

Dave had spotted a CHP unit parked off the side of the road so he pulled off the road and parked next to the other patrol car. Good police work. Stay visible and traffic will see you and slow down. Right? Not always, but it's worth a try.

Dave was monitoring his CB radio and so was the CHP unit. They would laugh at some of the conversations and remark how the voices would all sound alike: twangy, "red-neck" deep south accents, and other versions of cultured-English. And of course the topics were all very intellectual and deep conversations. Yeah, right! "Hey, driver . . . did ya see the blonde in that there convertible? She's a wearing a mini-skirt and she's got legs up to her ear-lobes, by golly!" And always, the response was like "uh yuh, uh yuh, ya'll got that right, driver."

It only took about five minutes after Dave parked his DPS unit next to the CHP unit when the CB radio speaker blasted out.

"Breaker, Breaker, nineteen," one voice called out.

"Go ahead, Breaker," came another voice.

"Thank ya, driver. All you eighteen wheelers on this here forty, looks like a party goin' on. I just saw that you got CHIPS and DIPS at the state line."

The chuckles abounded over the speaker.

Officer David Gabrielli, EOW, August 31, 1990. Photo from the Arizona Department of Safety website.

Epilogue: Shortly after this visit, Sadam Hussein invaded Kuwait. I was sent to Kuwait with a marine unit on August 12, 1990 for the beginning of Operation Desert Shield/Desert Storm. I got a letter from Dave on September 13, 1990. He was getting ready to be recalled to active duty to come over and we agreed to try to link up. On August 31, 1990, Dave was on duty in Arizona, investigating a traffic accident when he was hit and killed by a drunk driver. My wife held off telling me until I returned home from the Gulf. I'm thankful she did.

AFTERWORD

A large majority of our American public has no idea that humor sometimes presents itself in the field of law enforcement. Most people have never faced someone armed with a knife or a gun; felt the razor-sharp blade as it slices through their skin; felt the searing heat and pain as a bullet enters their body, or seen the look in the eyes of that individual who is trying to kill them. The following article was written by *Los Angeles Times* Staff Writer Boris Yaro when I was working patrol at West Hollywood station.

MISFIRES—LUCK REALLY IS CLICKING FOR DEPUTY

If you ask Harry Penny whether he would like to change occupations to something like chief volcano inspector or referee at a riot, he is likely to say, "No, I'm happy where I am."

Penny is a deputy sheriff assigned to West Hollywood station and according to him, he is contented. He also believes he might be lucky.

Three times during Penny's six-year career as a peace officer someone has pointed a loaded gun at him and pulled the trigger.

Hears Only Click

Each time Penny heard only a sharp click.

Wednesday, Penny and his partner, Bill Ross, were pursuing three auto theft suspects on a narrow side street just off the Sunset Strip.

"My partner went after two of the suspects and I was chasing the third one," Penny said. "I happened to glance out of the corner of my eye and saw the suspect step from behind a tree with a gun in his hand."

Hears That Click

"I just had time to start a dive when the suspect shouted 'Mother, you're dead' and then I heard the click."

By the time the deputy regained his balance and drew his service revolver, the suspect was disappearing down the street. A bystander crossed the deputy's line of fire, so he could not shoot at the fleeing man.

Meanwhile, other deputies arrived and were able to capture the other two suspects, both 16-year-old boys.

The first misfire occurred when Penny was a member of the Buena Park Police Department in December, 1962.

Walks Into Holdup

"I walked into a liquor store to buy a package of cigarettes," Penny said. "Unfortunately, I didn't know there was a robbery in progress."

The bandit whirled and pulled the trigger on his .45 caliber automatic.

"When I heard the click, I knew the gun had misfired, and I jumped the bandit," the deputy said. "I had to, there wasn't any place to hide."

By August 1968, Penny had joined the Sheriff's Department and was assigned to the Malibu station.

Traffic Call

"I had just pulled a traffic violator over and was approaching the car when the man leaned out of his window, aimed a .25 caliber automatic at me and pulled the trigger," Penny said. "The gun jammed and I arrested him."   *continued*

About a year later, a youthful sniper fired two rounds at Penny. Both bullets struck within inches of his feet, but luck held and the deputy wasn't hit.

Penny says the incidents, in retrospect, "are scary . . . you almost know you are going to be shot dead, but so far, I've been fortunate.

By Boris Yaro, *Los Angeles Times* Staff Writer, circa 1971

The humor is greatly overshadowed by the inherent dangers of the job which cops face on a daily basis. Cops have faced this terrifying experience, sometimes on more than one occasion. In some instances, they have given the ultimate sacrifice—their lives—protecting these citizens.

The first recorded police death was in 1792. Since then, 17,535 officers have given their lives in the line of duty. Between 1996 and 2006 there has been a yearly average of 56,292* assaults on officers, resulting in a yearly average of 16,138* injuries. During that ten-year period, 1,635* officers gave their lives. Averaging 165 deaths per year equates to one officer death every 53.5 hours.

So, to those of you who put on your badge and gun every day, I hope you will always have an opportunity to come home from the end of your watch, and be able to laugh. It is one way to keep you healthy. To those of you who rely on these brave heroes to keep you and your loved ones safe, I say again . . . The next time you have the opportunity to speak to a cop, a sincere THANK YOU and a smile will bring you both a moment of happiness.

—*Harry D. Penny, Jr.*

---

* National Law Enforcement Officers Memorial Fund, www.nleomf.com/TheMemorial/Facts/history.htm

BEHIND THE BADGE

THE FUNNY SIDE OF THE "THIN BLUE LINE"

and

Radiocartoons

the training Officer

Museums and tax-exempt
organizations may
order at a discount.

Please contact:

BOOKMASTERS

(800) 537-6727